Racial Attitudes in English-Canadian Fiction, 1905-1980

Terrence Craig

Racial Attitudes in English-Canadian Fiction is a critical overview of the appearances and consequences of racism in English-Canadian fiction published between 1905 and 1980.

Based on an analysis of traditional expressions in literature of group solidarity and resentment, the study screens English-Canadian novels for fictional representations of such feelings. Beginning with the English-Canadian reaction to the mass influx of immigrants into Western Canada before World War One, it examines the fiction of novelists such as Ralph Connor and Nellie McClung. The author then suggests that the cumulative effect of a number of individual voices, such as Grove and Salverson, constituted a counter-reaction to the English-Canadian attitude, a counter-reaction which has been made more positive by Laurence, Lysenko, Richler, and Clarke. The "debate" between these two sides, carried on in fictional and non-fictional writing, is seen to be in part resolved in synthesis after World War Two, as attitudes are forced by wartime alliances and intellectual pressures into a qualified liberalism. The author shows how single novels by Graham, Bodsworth, and Callaghan demonstrated a new concern for the exposure and eradication of racial discrimination, an attitude taken further by the works of Wiebe and Klein.

The book concentrates on single texts that best portray, deliberately or not, racist ideology or anti-racist arguments, and attempts to explain the arousal in Canada of such ideas.

Terrence Craig is Assistant Professor of English at Mount Allison University in Sackville, New Brunswick.

Racial Attitudes in English-Canadian Fiction, 1905-1980

RACIAL ATTITUDES IN ENGLISH-CANADIAN FICTION 1905~1980

Terrence Craig

Wilfrid Laurier University Press

Canadian Cataloguing in Publication Data

Craig, Terrence L., 1951-
    Racial attitudes in English-Canadian fiction,
1905-1980

Bibliography: p.
Includes index.
ISBN 0-88920-952-9

1. Canadian fiction (English) — 20th century —
History and criticism.*   2. Racism in literature.
I. Title.

PS8191.R33C73 1987   C813'.5'09355   C87-093825-8
PR9192.6.R33C73 1987

Copyright © 1987

WILFRID LAURIER UNIVERSITY PRESS
Waterloo, Ontario, Canada   N2L 3C5

87 88 89 90 4 3 2 1

Cover design by Polygon Design Limited

Printed in Canada

To
Orma and Ernie Bradley

Contents

Preface

This book was written to illustrate the racial attitudes that have been written into Canadian prose fiction in English in this century. I have not had any particular axe to grind, nor am I trying to make this topic out to be anything more than what it is—one of the many themes that constitute Canadian literature. I have tried to be comprehensive in my coverage of significant works that demonstrate racial concerns, and any failings in that respect I regret. Despite the recent increasing number of more sociological books appearing in Canada on the topic of race relations, there has been little attention paid to its appearance in literature. Although the focus of this book is somewhat specialized, I have tried to strike a balance between the necessity of some plot summary and the discussion of theme, a balance that I hope will attract the attention of readers with interdisciplinary interests.

There are a number of people who must be thanked for their contributions to this study, although, of course, its weaknesses and omissions are entirely my own responsibility. I owe much to the patience and discipline of Professor W. J. Keith of the University of Toronto, without whose advice and encouragement the work would be far less than what it is. In an earlier form this study benefited from the constructive criticism of Professors Frank Watt and Jack MacLeod of the University of Toronto, and Professor John Moss of the University of Ottawa. I thank Fred Bodsworth and Austin Clarke for their interviews on this and other subjects. So many people provided "tips" along the way that they cannot all be mentioned, but I would like to thank Professor Tom Tausky of the University of Western Ontario, Professor Russell Brown of the University of Toronto, Professor Jack Healey of Carleton University, and Dr. Henry Makow. I thank Beth Miller, Head of Special Collections at the D. B. Weldon Library at the University of Western Ontario, and Richard Bennett, Head of Archives and Special Collections of the University of Manitoba libraries, for their assistance in obtaining the unpublished Grove material. Finally, I am greatly indebted to Kenna Marshall of London, Ontario, whose speedy and careful proofreading was a great help at a difficult time.

Parts of this book have appeared in different forms in the *Journal of Canadian Studies*, *Studies in Canadian Literature*, and *The Native in Literature: Canadian and Comparative Perspectives*.

I am grateful to Mount Allison University for a grant in the summer of 1985 towards the preparation of the manuscript for publication.

This book has been published with the help of a grant from the Canadian Federation for the Humanities, using funds provided by the Social Sciences and Humanities Research Council of Canada.

Chapter One

Introduction

One of the primary objects of racism is to turn the victim against himself.

Racism and National Consciousness, by F. I. Case

I

The terms race and racism are used to define a social problem as serious in the present as it has ever been in the past. Hardly a day passes without the Canadian press reporting incidents of racial discrimination against one minority or another, and periodically opinion polls on the subject reveal widespread feelings of an intensity approaching and at times reaching racism. Traditionally, English-Canadians have considered themselves free of the most blatant forms of prejudice which have so obviously afflicted the histories of Central Europe and the Southern United States. If we disregard, for the purposes of this study, the tensions between the French and English groups in Canada, we are left with what might be termed the multicultural tensions of a multi-ethnic nation, and these tensions have at times, sporadically and often independently, achieved the level of racial prejudice. While the artistic intentions behind works of literature are as varied as they are difficult to determine, this study is predicated on the belief that, among its other purposes and effects, literature has a responsibility and an established function to draw attention to social problems and to provide the moral leadership to search for solutions. In exploring ethnic tensions in Canadian prose fiction in English in the twentieth century, I am restricting myself to a sociological view of literature, but as I am concerned with a sociological phenomenon which has the kind of ideological ramifications that humanists

1

have traditionally protected by means of literature, this approach seems not only necessary but legitimate.

In general the popular sense of the word "race" has several discrete meanings, and its appearance in literature is consequently often ambiguous and vague, particularly in situations where confusion with nationalism has arisen.[1] There is a popular sense of races being well-defined divisions of humanity, with recognizable boundaries which should be respected as fixed and unalterable. This approach leaves science behind as it merges with cultural and religious prejudices to approximate the equally loose term of "ethnic group." Thus anti-Semitism, which may be simply religious intolerance, takes on a racial aspect when Jews are perceived as a race, as they officially were in the first half of this century by Canadian immigration authorities. Used in such a manner, the concept of race provides a means of over-simplifying a complex and still controversial question, reducing a physically diversified community to a limited racial group. Within this study the broader, popular meaning of race is usually used in the same sense as it so often appears in literature, but with the important qualification that as such it is almost always mistaken and misleading. Much that has nothing to do with race, in the limited scientific sense that may justify its maintenance as a term, is popularly used in a practical sense that attempts to force a philosophy out of unfounded prejudices.

Nativism, the historiographical term applied so usefully to the United States by John Higham in *Strangers in the Land* (1963), and applied with equal success to Alberta by Howard Palmer in *Patterns of Prejudice* (1982), has not been used in this study, for I have concentrated on the ethnic component of nativism. Although some of the attitudes discussed below may seem more nativist than ethnic, it is their contributions to the effects of ethnocentrism (contributions which are often neither predictable nor logical, but rather emotional) that I am most interested in. In addition, nativism seems a very mild, almost euphemistic term for such a destructive ideology.

Modern theories of race owe much to Arthur Gobineau, whose notorious *Essai sur l'inegalité des races humaines* (1853-55) solidified in prose a topical aristocratic argument, derived in part from Boulainviller's distinction between the plebian Gauls and the Frankish nobility,[2] to found a comprehensive theory of racial determinism which was presented as *the* explanation for history. Gobineau's pessimistic racism is so closely linked to class or caste, and so concerned with the power and authority that his own (adopted) group, the royalist nobility, had lost in the French Revolution, that the

---

1 See John Higham, *Strangers in the Land* (New York: Atheneum, 1966), p. 11.

2 Michael D. Biddis, ed., *Gobineau: Selected Political Writings* (London: Jonathan Cape, 1970), pp. 18-19.

racial logic he presses into service seems an unnecessary varnish applied to a bitter class-conscious interpretation of French history. A separation of class- and race-oriented historiography took place in the nineteenth century, and Gobineau was chiefly responsible for providing a pseudoscientific and quasi-philosophical literary status for an ideology which could be used to counterbalance the atheistic, materialistic egalitarianism of Marx. Michael Biddis has summarized this dichotomy most succinctly:

> The major works of Marx and Gobineau, directing loyalty to Class on the one hand and Race on the other, are in essence responses to the same crisis—that of alienation from the social, economic, and cultural state of contemporary Europe.[3]

Darwin's theory of natural selection, applied to humanity by Herbert Spencer, provided an additional intellectual stimulus and support for Gobineau's basic tenets. The argument that only the stronger races survive and succeed supported rising racial pride among Northern Europeans who could thereby explain their apparent superiority over non-whites in their various empires. By the time Houston Chamberlain further idealized Social Darwinism and Gobineau's racism, the importation of the philosophy of race (as distinct from the omnipresent background noise of public prej- udice) into the New World had begun. Here the European line of argument was imported whole, and a new "American" racism arose to protect a new "American race." Repeating the established European race myths and falsehoods, American racists produced a spate of pretentiously erudite texts in an attempt to give their theories respectability.

Two books in particular stand out from the rest on account of their unabashedly racist tenor. Madison Grant, a curator at the New York Museum of Natural History and one of the founding members of the American Eugenics Society in 1905, was a well-known racist propagandist before 1916 when his book, *The Passing of the Great Race*, first appeared, to be followed by three more editions within seven years. Condemning the destructiveness of the melting pot theory, demanding an end to immigra- tion, justifying the continuation of slavery for the good of the uncivilized slaves, and denying the possibility of "inferior" peoples ever rising to the level of the New American Master Race, itself composed of the best Nordic strains from Europe, Grant brings together almost every racial argument possible. The personal bitterness, the sense of a heritage of privilege lost or endangered, which permeates Gobineau's gloomy writings, is detectable in Grant's prose as well. The new American Nordic aristocracy is presented as threatened by hordes of inferior immigrants. Essentially a desperate conser- vative attempt to have history halted and the current situation preserved by forbidding further immigration, the book represents a class attitude elabo-

3 Biddis, *Gobineau*, p. 21.

rately but weakly disguised as racial fact. Grant's elitism, threatened by egalitarian idealism, is repressed into racism. A member of the upper class, denied privileges he feels are his due, and with his elitism threatened politically and socially, he could not employ Marxist analysis without betraying his own class interests and going against his own class consciousness. Grant must walk the tightrope of defending privilege and heredity in a self-conscious democracy, and he uses racism to keep his balance. One might predict that one's own class allegiance should determine the intensity of one's beliefs in racial determinism, upper-class conservatives holding extreme racial opinions and lower-class leftists proposing universal brotherhood. Reality, of course, is not so simple: anti-Semitism has been practised by both extremes, and internal racial conflict has disfigured the progress of labour movements in times of economic stress.[4] However, as a general principle, class allegiance often is reflected in the attitudes of writers in the same privileged yet threatened position as Grant. The clear facts of class protection, showing through the transparency of his desperate racial rhetoric, point the way to a better understanding of some Canadian writers who later fictionalized similar situations, Charles Gordon ("Ralph Connor") being the best example.

Two other points raised in *The Passing of the Great Race* which appear in the 1920s in Canadian literature are the suggestion of polygenism and the claim that certain races, notably Jews, could never become good "white" Americans because of their inherent disqualifications. Particularly antagonistic towards "the Polish Jew, whose dwarf stature, peculiar mentality and ruthless concentration on self-interest are being engrafted on the stock of the nation,"[5] Grant laid the foundation of fears that certain races could not possibly be assimilated into the American dream, and could only be a sore on the body politic. This attitude, imported with some enthusiasm, was to persist selectively in Canadian letters, making a notable and influential appearance in James S. Woodsworth's *Strangers Within Our Gates* (1909). Polygenism, which Hannah Arendt has noted as an increasingly important theme in nineteenth-century English racial ideology,[6] was crudely represented by Grant as the diluting effect of miscegenation, which invariably left a product inferior to both original "strains," thus causing degeneration and eventually "race suicide."[7] This idea occurs frequently in

---

4 See William M. Tuttle, *Race Riot* (New York: Atheneum, 1970), pp. 16, 114.

5 Madison Grant, *The Passing of the Great Race* (New York: Charles Scribner's Sons, 1916), p. 14. John Higham uses Grant's book and its convoluted rhetoric as an example of nativism taken to the extreme of racism. Higham, *Strangers in the Land*, p. 157.

6 Hannah Arendt, "Race-Thinking Before Racism," *Review of Politics* 6, No. 1 (1944), 64.

7 Grant, *The Passing*, pp. 64-65, 69. Despite the "indigestible mass of French-Canadians," Grant went on to write, "Personally the writer believes that the finest and purest type of a Nordic community outside of Europe will develop in Northwest Canada" (pp. 72-73).

later Canadian literature, notably in Charles Gordon's novel, *The Gaspards of Pine Croft* (1923).

Grant's influential book is neither original nor very truthful, but it did define a North American white Anglo-Saxon Protestant ideology of race that assumed the respectability of anthropological science to exploit fears that could be better defined in terms of economics and class conflict. Another American, Emerson Hough, had taken it upon himself seven years before Grant's book to bring the same kind of fears and solutions to the attention of Canadians. In *The Sowing* (1909), subtitled "a 'Yankee's' View of England's Duty to Herself and Canada," Hough referred to the American experience as leading "through unsupervised immigration and through the guidance of personal greed, directly to the extermination of the American race."[8] Much as Grant was to do, Hough defined this American race as pioneer heroes of Nordic ancestry, about to commit race suicide. Most of his racial argument is actually about economic competition, "foreign" labourers being blamed for underpricing the more deserving true Americans. Despite the fraudulent logic of much of his book, Hough is important because he imported the new American model of racism into Canada, appealing to established Canadians to protect their basically Nordic culture (he ignores French-Canadians) from the inevitable deterioration that more immigrants would bring. It is an ostensibly anti-socialist message, an appeal to preserve an economic status quo, and its first publication serially in *Canada Monthly* must have propagated its ideas widely.

Deepening interest and speculation about a truly Canadian race is expressed in many books and numerous articles in the popular and scholarly periodicals from 1900 on. A few prominent writers virtually appropriated this subject, relating it to their own various personal concerns with immigration, religion, economic conditions, and Empire. Some of their individual studies are referred to below in the appropriate chronological contexts, but certain individuals should be considered here in the context of European and American race literature. The English-Canadian view was much milder on the whole than the alarmist rhetoric of Hough and Grant. It supported English and Scottish immigration first, and followed a qualitative ranking system downwards thereafter.[9] While this was justified frequently on

8 Emerson Hough, *The Sowing* (Winnipeg: Vanderhoof-Gunn, 1909), p. 141.
9 Some examples of these ranking systems may be found in: E. W. MacBride, "The Various Races of Man," *McGill University Magazine* 5, No. 2 (1906), 294-319; J. A. Lindsay, "National Characteristics," *Dalhousie Review* 9, No. 2 (1929), 181-87; W. G. Smith, *A Study in Canadian Immigration* (Toronto: Ryerson Press, 1920), p. 179ff.; Eugene L. Chicanot, "The Foreign Immigrant in Western Canada," *Willison's Monthly* 4, No. 1 (1928), 32-34; more by implication than by direct statement, similar expressions may be found in: S. Leacock, *Canada the Foundations of its Future* (Montreal: Gazette Printing, 1941), p. 209ff.; E. J. Soulsby, "Why Britons Stay at Home,"

practical grounds such as the expense of educating non-English speakers, the fears of communicable diseases, and the desire to create a greater British Empire, blatantly racial judgements underlay these excuses in the assumption that alien races were as fixed in their inferior characteristics as the Nordic race was in its superior qualities.[10] The desire to see English farmers settle on the prairies and become Canadians presupposed that a new Canadian nationality (which was interpreted in racial terms by many) already existed as an ideal for them by 1900, and that ideal gained strength especially with the impetus of nationalist fervor during World War One. This Canadian race had its superiority guaranteed by its predominately English and Nordic content, which itself was considered to have been proven great by the undeniably unprecedented achievement of the British Empire. When Stephen Leacock set out his wildly impractical plans for millions of new immigrants, he specifically meant Britishers within this Imperial context.[11] His theory, if not his numbers, was supported by many prominent men of letters, including Andrew Macphail, who wrote in the *University Magazine* in 1920:

> Immigration is war,—war by the new comers upon those already in possession. . . . There are breeds of men as there are strains of animals and classes of plants. They have their own affinities and their own repulsions. . . . When all immigrants are equal before the law, and have the same power over government through the instrument of the vote; when mental attainments and physical courage count for naught, the lower breeds will prevail. . . . The lower races, of course, deny the validity of this law. Without a flag or language, without surnames save such as they assume for themselves, they are the great apostles of the brotherhood of man, and sentimentalists among ourselves encourage the delusion in the belief that they are giving assent to Christian doctrine.[12]

So much for the "brotherhood of man." Such an echo of Social Darwinism was not uncommon immediately after the Great War and the appearance of Grant's book (in 1916). In fact, it formed a considerable part of the

---

Canadian Forum 8, No. 95 (1928), 743-44; J. S. Woodsworth, *Strangers Within Our Gates* (Toronto: Frederick Clark Stephenson, 1909), pp. 50-94.

10 A fine example of this was supplied by L. Hamilton, who also, while ranting away in a self-contradictory manner about selective immigration, warned: "The 'Canadian Forum,' a monthly Toronto Journal, has Radical sympathies, and many of its contributors are Jews whose articles while being critical, are never constructive, and whose ideas are distinctly alien to those of the British and French-Canadians." "Foreigners in the Canadian West," *Dalhousie Review* 17, No. 4 (1938), 452-53.

11 S. Leacock, *Economic Prosperity in the British Empire* (Toronto: Macmillan of Canada, 1930), p. 29.

12 Andrew Macphail, "The Immigrant," *University Magazine* 19, No. 2 (1920), 136-37.

English-Canadian view of race, which then was simply the natural ethnocentric pride of the majority Canadian charter group multiplied by Imperial accomplishments and peculiarly North American anxieties concerning both American pressures and, increasingly, the threat of "alien" immigration. English-Canadians have never been a race, but clearly in the first part of this century many viewed themselves as one, closely related to Grant's Nordic-American ideal but without the stigma of republicanism. They defined themselves against their opposition—the aliens—who were induced to metamorphose into the labouring-class version of English-Canadianness, at which point they became acceptable immigrants in that they no longer threatened upper-class Canadians with their foreign and therefore inferior politics, religions, or customs. A qualified and limited version of Canadianness was made available to aliens, often presupposing their innate inabilities to ever fully approach the basically British ideal of intelligence and civilization. English-Canadian opinion was divided between extremists who saw alien immigrants as innately unassimilable and therefore a threat to the new Canadian race, and those who believed in the possibility of varying degrees of assimilation through the suppression of alien cultural qualities and the inculcation of essentially British ones. An uneasy compromise existed in practice.

The idea of British immigrants "leavening" the alien influx, thus exercising some control over the future, was quite popular, the term itself being widely used.[13] A few direct refutations of racism did appear to counter the above opinions, but they were rare and usually aimed at only the most rabid and obviously fanatical aspects of racism. John Murray Gibbon, author of several romantic novels and an administrator of the CPR (Canadian Pacific Railway) colonization scheme, and Robert England, a well-known prairie educator, both increasingly propagated pro-assimilationist views throughout the 1920s and 30s.[14] To them, and especially to Watson Kirkconnell, then on the staff of Wesley College in Winnipeg, must go much of the

13 It appeared notably in one short-sighted and narrow-minded article by Bernard Muddiman, "The Immigrant Element in Canadian Literature," *Queen's Quarterly* 20, No. 4 (1913), 411, and later it was used by F. P. Grove in "Canadians Old and New," *Maclean's* 41, No. 6 (1928), 56. It was also a favorite word of Eugene L. Chicanot, appearing in "The Foreign Immigrant," p. 34; "English Townsmen on Canadian Farms," *Willison's Monthly* 3, No. 10 (1928), 383; "Maintaining the British Element in Canadian Farm Population," *Willison's Monthly* 3, No. 5 (1927), 182.

14 See John Murray Gibbon, "The Foreign Born," *Queen's Quarterly* 27, No. 4 (1920), 331-51; J. M. Gibbon, *The New Canadian Loyalists* (Toronto: Macmillan of Canada, 1941); and Robert England, *The Central European Immigrant in Canada* (Toronto: Macmillan of Canada, 1929). England also wrote about ethnic literature in "The Emergent West," *Queen's Quarterly* 41, No. 3 (1934), 405-13. Watson Kirkconnell published much in the same vein, an example being "Western Immigration," *Canadian Forum* 8, No. 94 (1928), 706-7.

credit for defending and interpreting in a favourable light the cultural traditions of "alien" immigrants which were threatened with extinction by the selective melting pot many Canadians still insisted on. They countered the most blatant racism with a less potent strain which, while welcoming the cultures of Paderwsky and Tsevchenko, still insisted on socio-political subservience to their own established sense of Canadian norms. To them assimilation to the Anglo-Canadian norm meant, as Frederick Philip Grove astutely pointed out in *Maclean's* in 1928, the forced acceptance by aliens of the Anglo-Canadian socio-cultural status quo. Apart from the continuous controversy in the serious press on the subject of race relations, there is quite a lot of similar evidence throughout the more popular periodicals of English-Canadian patronization of aliens, their acceptance of and respect for the "white man's burden," their anti-Semitism, and their general smug ethnic complacency. What little *rabid* rhetoric did achieve publication usually referred to what was considered the absolute necessity of excluding Asiatics from the West Coast.[15]

Religious intolerance, frequently defined and expressed in racist terms, was largely directed against Mennonites and Doukhobors, whose settlements en bloc aroused the hostility of the assimilationists, despite the welcome these immigrants had received on arrival and the promises made to them concerning freedom of education and exemption from military service. As cohesive groups physically and culturally, these and other religious sects had more power to resist the Canadian economic pressures which had prompted their importation in the first place in the West. Religious settlements had the same practical effect within their proto-communities as unions, and thus created political and commercial anxieties which in the press were actually represented more strongly than religious objections.[16] Aliens, whether distinguished by colour, language, nationality, or religion, attracted persecution for sticking together and defending their cultures, as if in little garrisons. Such persecution resulted in, for example, the Federal Government's breaking of promises made to the Mennonites, which led to the renunciation of and emigration from Canada by large numbers of them, later described in Rudy Wiebe's novel, *The Blue Mountains of China.*[17]

15 Although Leacock participated in this, referring to the "Asiatic peril" in *Canada the Foundations of its Future*, p. 209, a more emotional example, by John Nelson, may be seen in "Shall We Bar the Yellow Race?" *Maclean's* 35, No. 10 (1922), 13.

16 George Woodcock and Ivan Avakumovic, in *The Doukhobors* (Toronto: McClelland and Stewart, 1977), quote a newspaper headline "Protect Yourself Against the New Chinese" (p. 145).

17 For a contemporary view of this situation, see C. C. Jenkins, "The Mennonites' Trek," *Maclean's* 35, No. 4 (1922), 23-24, 36-37.

II

This brief view of the ideological history of racism emphasizes the economic causes of ethnic prejudice, which appear to be more important than other sociological, psychological, or historical factors. An analysis of ethnocentrism from the modern point of view is necessary to explain its appeal and its influence in contemporary literature.

Van Loon and Whittington, the political scientists who wrote *The Canadian Political System* (1971), define politics as "a process of conflict resolution achieved through the authoritative allocation of the scarce resources of a society."[18] The economic nature of ethnocentrism arises from the formation by individuals of groups for the purpose of guaranteeing their survival and prosperity by means of acquiring enough political power to affect if not control this allocation. When these groups seem to be composed of individuals of the same ethnic type, broadly defined as a mixture of similar linguistic, physiographic, and cultural qualities, then an ethnic group is perceived. When a theory of race is subscribed to also, then the ethnic group, alone or allied with other similar groups, may be raised to the status of a race, viewed in competition with other races. In *The Anatomy of Racism: Canadian Dimensions*, Hughes and Kallen explain this in a more political manner: ". . . within an ethnically stratified society, racism implies the idea of differential power, utilized by the dominant or majority ethnic group(s) to effectively prevent members of ethnic minorities from gaining access to power, privilege, and prestige."[19] Darwinian theory, interpreted simply as the survival of the fittest, defined by oneself, becomes an excuse for "man's inhumanity to man." John Porter, in his definitive study, *The Vertical Mosaic* (1965), clearly established the existence of a closed elitist controlling group in Canada, with ethnicity as a determinant of membership, as well as a series of ranked and relatively closed ethnic groups being exploited from above.[20] This elite has sanctioned the importation of waves of alien labour in attempts to provide basic labour, while making it difficult for immigrants to gain access to positions of power sufficient to control their own destinies.

The history of Canadian immigration can be seen as a conflict: the efforts of established Canadians to keep the "foreigners" in subordinate positions have conflicted with the struggles of immigrants to free themselves from such roles.[21] The history of ethnocentrism in Canada is closely associated with this ongoing conflict.

18 Richard Van Loon and Michael Whittington, *The Canadian Political System* (Toronto: McGraw-Hill of Canada, 1971), p. 6.
19 David Hughes and Evelyn Kallen, *The Anatomy of Racism: Canadian Dimensions* (Montreal: Harvest House, 1976), p. 109.
20 John Porter, *The Vertical Mosaic* (Toronto: University of Toronto Press, 1970), pp. 60-103.
21 Neils Braroe discusses the conflict between the ostensible social system and the perceived

Most modern explanations of racism are economic and Marxist, but there is a strong case to be made for psychological causes as well, especially one explanation peculiar to colonial situations. O. Mannoni studied colonial psychology in Madagascar, but much of his analysis is as applicable to the Canadian social psyche as it was to expatriates in the Sudan, where Margaret Laurence applied it.[22] For Mannoni, "Racialism . . . is a pseudo-rational construct—a rationalization—to justify feelings the source of which are imbedded deep in the unconscious." He based his interpretation of the extreme form of black-versus-white racism prevalent in Madagascar in the 1940s on the emotional immaturity of the colonizers.[23] Much race hatred, Mannoni claims, is caused in part by sexual guilt. He presses Freud into service and claims that "the exploitation is mainly a matter of repressed tendencies towards sadism, rape, or incest, the image of the misdeed which both frightens and fascinates us being projected onto others."[24] The Freudian concept of the reversal of values within the unconscious, particularly sexual mores, and the projection of these reversed desires onto perceived "non-persons" identified by different "racial" features, provides some help in understanding the frequent appearance within ethnic confrontations, real and fictional, of sexual tensions. This theory of race, less obvious and probably less significant than the economic explanation, remains practically unexplored consciously by most writers, some of whom nonetheless display a convoluted and possibly self-consciously disguised interest in the sexual abilities and customs of other ethnic groups. It is not uncommon, for example, to see white writers assign less inhibited sexual behaviour to characters of other groups. By describing different groups as being sexually freer and more powerful, they are possibly projecting their own individual or group fears of inadequacy.[25] Clearly there is a social aspect of racism

"moral value" (or self-worth) of those at the bottom of the system, and the phenomenon of protest that can overturn the system. *Indian and White* (Stanford, Calif.: Stanford University Press, 1975), p. 189.

22 Margaret Laurence, *The Prophet's Camel Bell* (Toronto: McClelland and Stewart, 1963), pp. 227-28.

23 O. Mannoni, *Prospero and Caliban* (New York: Frederick A. Praeger, 1964), p. 119.

24 Mannoni, *Prospero and Caliban*, p. 111. For a fine Canadian example, see *The Black Candle* by (Judge) Emily Murphy, especially the photographs opposite pp. 30 and 47 where the degradation of white women by drugs is associated visually with non-white men.

25 Examples of such contrasts on the sexual level may be found between the prejudiced Anglo-Saxon Brooke and the Métis Jules in Laurence's *The Diviners*, Dr. Hunter's frigid Anglo-Saxon wife and the Ukrainian Anna in Ross's *Sawbones Memorial*, and Theo and Norah in Richler's *Son of a Smaller Hero*. John Moss discusses this issue briefly in *Patterns of Isolation* (Toronto: McClelland and Stewart, 1974), pp. 105-8. The difference between the authorial attitude, which in each of these examples is basically anti-racism, and various characters' attitudes, which may embody popular and

which derives from sexual desires and fears, which may be individually explained by Freudian theory. It is reflected in literature in ways that occasionally betray an author's biases beyond his or her intentions.

Another psychological point of view is the romantic idealization of race. Linked with the eternal desire to return to a mythical past when peoples were pure and different and fought glorious wars to prove it, the romantic view of race can be seen in the work of Kant and Fichte. Associating the qualities of the soul with local landscape, and incorporating anti-Semitism almost as an afterthought, this mainly Germanic romantic view developed via Nietzsche into *Mein Kampf*, attracting various English writers along the way. Although Gobineau had denied that environment determined the greatness of nations, the theory gained credibility among Victorian race-conscious thinkers: Hippolyte Taine made it the basis of his theory of literary criticism in *Histoire de la littérature anglaise* (1863-64), and Matthew Arnold employed it in *On the Study of Celtic Literature* (1867). Presupposing that qualities such as intellect, valour, and nobility are racially innate and distributed unequally among various ethnic groups, this justification of racism perpetuates stereotypes, imprisoning groups of people within preconceived static expectations. Reinforced by the British Empire's military and technological advances, this view had infiltrated nineteenth-century English literature even before Taine's time, and had immigrated to Canada before Thomas Carlyle defended it in his famous 1849 essay, "The Nigger Question." Ethnocentric superiority does appear to be an ubiquitous belief and one that demands an evaluative ranking of other ethnic groups beneath one's own, thus contributing to emotions already raised by economic pressures.

The romantic view of race revived ancient myths as representative of a period when differences were thought to have been factual and obvious, as opposed to the vague and confusing distinctions of the present, whether it be Gobineau's pessimistic present or our own. Gobineau's racial determinism, bolstered by subsequent Social Darwinism, has been seized upon by people wanting a world view consistent with their own inflated ethnocentric pride. This partly escapist attitude can be seen in the twentieth century in Nazi Germany as well as in the extreme Imperial views of Kipling, best expressed in Canada by Robert Stead. By plaintively entitling his 1918 volume of jingoist poetry *Why Don't They Cheer?* Stead may consciously and sadly have written the epitaph for this view in Canada. However, it lingers on.

A final psychological explanation for racism has been provided by Mannoni, who suggested that a colonist in leaving his or her native country

psychologically significant prejudices, must be kept in mind, although it may not always be evident.

creates a vacuum of self-confidence which can be offset by lording it over the peoples already in the new country.[26] Clearly this suggests a psychological rationale for the oppression (or suppression) of Canada's Indians, quite apart from economic reasons. Equally it might contribute towards an explanation for the popular prairie caricature of genteel English homesteaders who would not work their land as they should, but who nevertheless behaved in an arrogant manner to their neighbours, producing the Canadian counter-reaction of "No English Need Apply" qualifications in advertisements for labour.

III

Close links can be seen between ethnic tension in Canada and the histories of immigration, economic booms, and depressions. It is axiomatic that periods of depression have produced public protest against further immigration, and such opposition has been explained as much by ethnocentric arguments as by economics. Canadian periodicals and public opinion polls show that such protest relaxed in intensity during more prosperous periods, when correspondingly immigration would be supported the most by business and government. Political controls over immigration seem to have attempted to compromise between the constantly changing opinions of labour and business, the fewest immigrants in this century being admitted during the Great Depression.[27] Nevertheless, governments have consistently promoted immigration as an economic incentive and as a panacea for slumps, and more recently to ensure the electoral support of Canadians with family ties abroad.[28]

Porter provided the English and French ethnic groups with the title of "charter-groups," justified by their composing almost 90 percent of Canada's population in 1881.[29] His use of the term reflects their control of the nation based on their historical and numerical preponderance. The great

26 Mannoni, *Prospero and Caliban*, p. 102.
27 Statistics are provided by W. Kalbach, *The Impact of Immigration on Canada's Population* (Ottawa: Dominion Bureau of Statistics, 1970), which seems reliable enough for such a general statement, although the DBS records have been questioned by D. M. McDougall, "Immigration into Canada, 1851-1920," *Canadian Journal of Economics and Political Science* 27, No. 2 (1961), 162-75. Feelings concerning immigration during the Depression may be gauged by the closed-door speech of the Minister of Immigration, W. A. Gordon, "Canadian Immigration," *Addresses Delivered Before the Canadian Club of Toronto 1930-31* (Toronto: Warwick Bros. & Rutter, 1931), vol. 28, 177-84.
28 Ministers responsible for immigration openly declared these reasons as the basis of their policies when the economy was prosperous enough to make it advisable. For example, see Guy Favreau, "The Values of Immigration," *Studies and Documents on Immigration and Integration in Canada* 8 (Sept. 1965), 4-9.
29 Porter, *Vertical Mosaic*, p. 64.

influx (3,371,000) of immigrants in the first two decades of the twentieth century threatened that control and altered the ethnic balance of Canada, as it developed into a population of which over one fifth was foreign born.[30] This enormous influx was a product of official government policy and was encouraged by recruiters in Europe. Large numbers of these immigrants were English and French, but increasingly Ukrainian and other Central Europeans were recruited to settle the prairies. As Laurier's Minister of the Interior from 1896 to 1905, Clifford Sifton was largely responsible for the great numbers of immigrants from continental Europe. Although he preferred Britons, he wanted farmers used to rough conditions. Defending his policy against the charge of "open doors," he wrote in *Maclean's* in 1922: "I think a stalwart peasant in a sheepskin coat, born on the soil, whose forefathers have been farmers for ten generations, with a stout wife and a half-dozen children, is good quality."[31] Eugene Chicanot, later editor of *Rhymes of the Miner* (1937), but in the 1920s a journalist who wrote frequently on immigration matters, put Sifton's case more clearly six years later in *Willison's Monthly*, damning the continental immigrant with biased praise:

> He is essentially a primary worker in the territory, the hewer of wood and drawer of water, working close to the natural resources of the country. He is to be found in the lumber camp and in the mine, and in the most laborious phases of agriculture. He undertakes work the Britisher or native-born Canadian would not and could not do.[32]

Until the Depression, this policy of bringing in millions of "agriculturalist" immigrants, preferably from the United Kingdom, was supported and carried out by the two national railways, other businesses, and the various governments. The desire to place a western farming class *beneath* the industrialized East, the plan to "nail people down on the land,"[33] was an economic strategy. The English-Canadians who moved west, following the initial pioneer waves, had higher expectations and ambitions than the Ukrainian peasants to whom free title to land meant so much. These English-Canadians expected to exploit the non-charter-group labour, fulfilling administrative and logistical functions of power, and they believed in their right to such positions because of their superior status either as established Canadians or as Britishers in a British colony.

The first large-scale racial confrontation in Canada in this century took place in Vancouver in 1907 when a race riot occurred. The situation had

30 Kalbach, Impact of Immigration, p. 84.
31 Clifford Sifton, "The Immigrants Canada Wants," *Maclean's* 35, no. 7 (1922), 16.
32 Eugene L. Chicanot, "The Foreign Immigrant in Western Canada," *Willison's Monthly* 4, No. 1 (1928), 34.
33 Charles A. Magrath, "Organization for Immigration," *Willison's Monthly* 1, No. 2 (1925), 53.

been developing for some time, the blatantly racist fears of the white population being aggravated by the continuous influx of cheap Asiatic labour, regardless of Laurier's head taxes and his sensitive agreements with the Japanese government. Mackenzie King headed a Royal Commission to investigate the situation, his solution being more subtle restrictions on immigration at the international level. Severe restrictions on Asiatic immigration (such restrictions already being in force with respect to blacks[34]) were incorporated into Federal foreign policy to pacify regional hostility. The Asiatic problem surfaced again in 1914 with the "Komagatu Maru" incident in Vancouver. This ship, carrying 376 Indians, directly challenged the Canadian policy by attempting to expose the restrictions as clearly racist. After sitting in the harbour for a month, these boat people were refused entry and escorted outside territorial waters by a Canadian cruiser.[35] British Columbia thus proved itself the most ethnically protectionist province in the Dominion (with the possible exception of Quebec). Here developed the political agitation which continued to deny citizenship to certain immigrants, and this background produced Canada's most racist work of fiction, Hilda Howard's *The Writing on the Wall* (1922).

The problem of the non-assimilation of the Doukhobors and the Mennonites in Western Canada originated before World War One, although its consequences became most apparent in the 1920s and 30s. While both are primarily religious groups, both exhibited collectively "foreign" behaviour to such an extent that they attracted ostensibly racist prejudice. Both groups were victims of religious persecution in Europe, and both had come to Canada after the Federal Government had promised them freedom of education and exemption from military service. These qualifications of citizenship eventually aroused concern that these groups would turn out to be permanently unassimilable and a liability, if not a threat, in wartime. Furthermore, both groups practised old-fashioned, simple farming methods and settled en bloc, thus avoiding much of even the then primitive prairie consumer requirements and the charter-group commercial superstructure erected thereon. While these groups were independent and introverted, aloof from non-members, their work-ethic, simple style of living, and large communal holdings provided the appearance of wealth which aroused their neighbours' jealousy. The fear of their inability to assimilate was in large part political—a fear that in their blocs they could exercise some control over themselves, whereas as individual farmers their votes could be more easily lost in the amorphous maneuvers of democratic

---

34 Surprising examples of this are provided by Trevor Sessing in "How They Kept Canada Almost Lily White," *Saturday Night* 85, No. 9 (1970), 30-32. See also Howard Palmer, *Patterns of Prejudice* (Toronto: McClelland and Stewart, 1982), pp. 35-37.

35 This entire incident and more is well described by Peter Ward in *White Canada Forever* (Montreal: McGill-Queen's University Press, 1978).

electoral practice.[36] Their high visibility as a "foreign" element attracted labour protests on conventional ethnocentric grounds. However, the fact that they were different and intended to stay different, coupled with radical anarchist acts by extremist Doukhobors, led to more discrimination and the reneging by governments on the initial promises.

Nationalism in Quebec is outside the scope of this work, as is the entire French-English confrontation. From André Siegfried's *The Race Question in Canada* (1906) to Pierre Vallières' *White Niggers of America* (1971), there is enough material for a separate study of equal significance. In the interests of thoroughly evaluating the English-Canadian reaction to non-charter-group immigrants, the question of their attitude towards French-Canadians (and vice versa) has not been attended to here. To indicate the depth of feeling present, however, and to identify that feeling as consciously employing racist terminology, mention should be made of l'Abbé Groulx, who raised Québecois political consciousness in a racist manner with a number of studies of French-Canadian history. In particular, *La Naissance d'une race* (1919) organized *Canadien* history defensively in a way that explicitly repudiated English-Canadian hopes of assimilation. Most English-Canadians who wrote in the early years of this century on assimilation discussed the problems posed by Central Europeans and ignored the problem of Quebec and Groulx. The deliberate suppression of *Canadien* concerns reflected their belief that eventually Québecois would follow the example of the English and acculturate themselves out of habitant backwardness. The arrogance of the true English-Canadian assimilationists of the time, believing that future Canadians would eventually all conform to a homogeneity based on themselves, would not make an exception of Quebec.

The Great War saw a focusing of ethnic feeling against so-called enemy aliens. Germans have consistently been the third most numerous group of immigrants since 1871. Their potential for trouble in wartime was less than it appeared, as many of these Germans, perhaps as many as 50 percent, actually came to Canada after generations of residence in Russia, the United States, or other countries.[37] The "Austrians" posed a different problem, the term then embracing Poles, Ukrainians, Germans, Czechs, Hungarians, Slovaks, Galicians, and many smaller groups. Not all had been loyal to the Austro-Hungarian Empire when they lived there, nationalist sentiment being strong among them. In 1914 Bishop Budka of the Ukrainian Catholic

36 This was stated directly at the time, for example, by C. B. Sissons, "What Can We Do With the Doukhobors?" *Canadian Forum* 4, No. 46 (1924), 299.

37 Joseph A. Boudreau, "Western Canada's 'Enemy Aliens' in World War One," *Alberta Historical Review* 12, No. 1 (1964), 1-4. Helen Potrebenko has also raised this fact, paraphrasing Frank Oliver, in *No Streets of Gold* (Vancouver: New Star Books, 1977), p. 121.

Church in Winnipeg issued a letter advising expatriate reservists to return to Austria to fight for Franz-Joseph, but he was persuaded by his more peaceful congregation to repudiate it.[38] Because of this letter and general fears of sabotage, registration of enemy aliens was enforced and some 9,000 people were interned in camps until 1916. The problem of Galicians, who came from an area split by the 1914 Austro-Hungarian borders with Germany and Russia, was handled by treating all as enemy aliens. Throughout Canada employers, including the CNR (Canadian National Railways), patriotically fired enemy aliens, and in some places where they did not, strikes occurred.[39] Even German professors at the University of Toronto were attacked. In Manitoba, the novelist F. P. Grove claimed to be Swedish instead of German, in order to avoid such prejudice, although he did defend Germany in his classroom during the war.[40]

The propaganda war contributed to the racial aspect of the normal fears of a populace in wartime. In Britain writers were mobilized under the control of Sir Gilbert Parker to spread propaganda about German atrocities, with the ultimate aim of encouraging the U.S. to enter the war. The best example of this type of work in Canada is Gordon's *The Major* (1917) which complemented his own speaking tour of the U.S. in 1917 after his return from France. Stephen Leacock ridiculed German stereotypes in his wartime fiction, especially in *Further Foolishness* (1916), and later in *The Hohenzollerns in America* (1919). Anti-German feeling was itself probably not so much the aim or the result of this propaganda; rather, Prussian militarism and German imperialism were seen as evil forces tyrannically imposed upon a stolid, primitive peasantry. Whatever the intention, the use of these stereotypes implied the encouragement of ethnic prejudice on the part of those who should have known better.

Slavs in Canada were a more sensitive subject, some being from enemy territory and some from allied nations. The Galicians in Canada were considered to be Austrians, and suffered thereby. Their troubles did not end with the Armistice, however, as Joseph Boudreau has noted:

> Shortly before the end of 1918 German and Ukrainian language newspapers were first suppressed and then compelled to publish English translations in columns parallel to the original articles. The "red scare" that followed the Bolshevik revolution in Russia soon replaced the German threat after the Armistice and Slavic immigrants were still suspect in many quarters.[41]

38 In 1918 and subsequently, the Bishop's congregation repudiated him, and he returned to the Ukraine in 1927; Norah Story, *The Oxford Companion to Canadian History and Literature* (Toronto: Oxford University Press, 1967), pp. 807-8.

39 Boudreau, "Enemy Aliens," p. 4.

40 Margaret R. Stobie, *Frederick Philip Grove* (New York: Twayne Publishers, 1973), p. 33.

41 Boudreau, "Enemy Aliens," p. 9. See also H. Palmer, *Patterns of Prejudice*, pp. 28-30, for the reaction to Galician immigration into Alberta.

The 1920s saw little overt racial conflict in Canada, prosperity covering up the immediate economic stimuli. In 1919 the practice of deporting labour agitators who had not yet become citizens (and of some who had) began, to be escalated during the Depression.[42] Links between communism and certain ethnic groups, notably Jews and Ukrainians, were suggested in prominent periodicals, encouraging discrimination against them. The Ku Klux Klan, associated loosely with provincial Conservative parties in the West, attracted large memberships on the prairies, especially in Saskatchewan.[43] Canadian fascist sympathizers emerged in the 1930s, following the successes of Hitler, Mussolini, and Oswald Mosley in Europe. The Canadian Nationalist Party in Ontario and the West, and the Parti National Social Chrétien, led by Adrien Arcand in Quebec, were both violently anti-Semitic. The Montreal Jewish poet, A. M. Klein, poeticized Arcand's efforts in "Hormisdas Arcand" and the oratory of his supporter, Camillien Houde, mayor of Montreal, in "Political Meeting," which ends with the bleakly memorable image:

> The whole street wears one face,
>   shadowed and grim; and in the darkness rises
>   the body-odour of race.[44]

Arcand and his English-Canadian counterpart, John Ross Taylor, were both interned in 1939. The European connection between fascism and the brutal persecution of Jews in the late 1930s quickly made even anti-Semitism unfashionable in Canada. It became possible for a novel about a Jewish/English-Canadian romance to succeed in Canada, to be followed by other post-war novels describing Jewish adaptation to Canada. This war too saw its share of anti-enemy propaganda, which took its toll upon people who only desired to be allowed to be Canadians. The Japanese in Canada suffered particularly when white British Columbia took this opportunity for economic revenge, achieving the internment and eventually the forced repatriation to Japan or resettlement outside the province of most Japanese and Japanese-Canadians in the country, recently described in fiction by Joy Kogawa in *Obasan* (1982) and in non-fiction by Ken Adachi in *The Enemy That Never Was* (1976).

42 Clive Cocking, "How did the Canadian Mounties Develop Their Unfortunate Habit of Deporting People They Don't Happen to Like?" *Saturday Night* 85, No. 6 (1970), 30.
43 Tom Henson, "Ku Klux Klan in Western Canada," *Alberta History* 25, No. 4 (1977), 1-8; An Observer, "The Ku Klux Klan in Saskatchewan," *Queen's Quarterly* 35, No. 5 (1928), 592-96. This is also mentioned in R. Winks, *The Blacks in Canada* (Montreal: McGill-Queen's University Press, 1971), p. 322, and in H. Palmer's *Patterns of Prejudice*, pp. 92, 100-10.
44 A. M. Klein, "Political Meeting," *The Rocking Chair* (Toronto: Ryerson Press, 1948), p. 16.

The third generation of the original flood of non-charter-group immigrants of 1890-1914 appeared to have more time to write and a greater facility with English, so that tales of their situations now began to appear. More refugees and "DP's" (displaced persons) from Europe arrived in a Canada which had become more outward looking and which was more aware internationally. A relaxation of racist restrictions on immigration in the 1960s saw larger numbers of Asians and Caribbean islanders arriving, creating new conflicts in the urban areas where they congregated. The 1965 *Report of the Special Committee on Hate Propaganda* (to which Pierre Trudeau contributed) exposed the sensational propaganda disseminated chiefly by American right-wing extremist groups. At this time too, Canadian neo-Nazi groups revived anti-Semitism, the 1965 Allen Gardens riot in Toronto being an example of their activity. With the development of provincial and federal human rights agencies for the investigation and rectification of incidents of racial discrimination, and with the acceptance of refugee contingents such as the Ugandan Asians and Vietnamese boat people, Canadians achieved a new level of international maturity which, although officialized in theory, has yet to be fully accepted at the grass roots level, and is balanced by events such as the resurgence of the KKK and the Western Guard in Ontario. While great advances have been made in the suppression of racism in Canada, public opinion is fickle, and the history of racism reveals its dangerous recuperative powers. It is an omnipresent force which must be controlled by a better understanding of its workings. Literature can help to fulfil this function.

IV

The more or less concrete facts of history do not record the all too common incidents of racial discrimination which characterize Canadian life at the grass roots level. Their presence can be indirectly assumed from sociological studies and public opinion polls, but it is only literature that properly presents their scope and their meaning in context, and it is significant that it is chiefly the literature of the "newcomers" themselves in the 1960s and 70s that does so. Early Canadian literature in English is not surprisingly almost entirely by writers with obvious English-Canadian backgrounds. More recent Canadian literature is not. The atmosphere of ethnic prejudice in Canada has been increasingly described and protested by authors from minority groups, whereas in the past it was tacitly or even unknowingly supported or tolerated by authors from the English-Canadian charter group. Acts of racial prejudice against visible minorities are facts in Canada now as in the past. Although it has never reached the proportions achieved by the United States or the Republic of South Africa, it involves subtle but practical forms of discrimination and is a fact of life in Canada for many people.[45]

For Gobineau, race was the single most important determinant of history. Few writers of fiction have ever approached this single-minded attitude. Whenever pressed into service as a vehicle to convey any kind of racial dogma, imaginative literature has usually done so in a less specific manner, by presenting a more rounded and comprehensive view of society. Ethnocentrism is only one aspect of human interaction: to be faithful to reality, fiction must include it in the larger societal contexts.

In the analysis of ethnocentric thought in literature, three types of presentation may be seen. The first type gives the impression of the author's unconscious repetition of prevailing popular beliefs and myths, and is closely related to unconscious ethnocentric pride. The stereotypical treatment of "the Jew" in Charles Gordon's fiction, as in F. P. Grove's, is an obvious example of this. Literature which deals with ethnic stereotypes so openly and simplistically often does so incidentally to other issues or aims or, as in the twentieth century because of increased public awareness of the sensitivity of the issue, is frequently romantic literature designed as light entertainment. In a 1946 study, "Majority and Minority Americans: An Analysis of Magazine Fiction," Berelson and Salter reduced 198 American short stories published from 1937 to 1943 to their ethnic bases, establishing a cutaway model of (presumably) unconsciously ethnocentric fiction. The study linked the appearance in the stories of ethnic minority Americans to stereotyped lower-class roles, serving a Nordic American elite. Characters were usually stereotypes—not necessarily ethnic stereotypes but stock types with ethnically identifiable characteristics—which must have simplified the writing. The study concluded that literature is elite-oriented, directing readers' desires, ambitions, and respect toward a model of superiority which in this case was represented by Madison Grant's American race.[46] The danger of such subtly transmitted ethnocentrism supporting fiction obviously lies in the casual reinforcement of stereotypes which perpetuate prejudice.

Stereotypes are the building blocks of much light literature but can be detected in some serious work as well. They are simple to use, and when marshalled along ethnic lines they can confirm attitudes of elitist superiority. Noting alterations in the ethnic mixture as more immigrants flooded

45 This point has been emphasized by Austin Clarke, in "A Black Man Talks About Race Prejudice in White Canada," *Maclean's* 76, No. 8 (1963), 18, 55-58. It also appears in an article by Lennox Brown, "A Crisis: Black Culture in Canada," *Black Images* 1, No. 1 (1972), 6. More recently it has been restated by Bharati Mukherjee, "An Invisible Woman," *Saturday Night* 96, No. 3 (1981), 36-40.

46 B. Berelson and P. Salter, "Majority and Minority Americans: An Analysis of Magazine Fiction," *Public Opinion Quarterly* 10, No. 2 (1946), 168-90.

the American melting pot in this century, Berelson and Salter provided a third reason for their use: "As the types of readers in an audience increases in diversity, both the variety and complexity of communicable ideas decrease. Heterogeneity breeds generality and thus the leading characters become members of the dominant and presumably the best recognized group."[47] Possibilities of ethnic characterization therefore become more restricted. This sociological view sees literature tending toward the general and away from the individual. As this view is derived from a study of the most simplistic type of popular serial fiction, its applicability to more serious work which may investigate unique psychological perspectives is questionable. While some literary characters are obviously stereotypes and others probably "true" originals, the difference between them may not always be recognizable to all, because individuals may be plotted into stereotypical situations, and, as these stereotypes themselves are taken for reality, individuality becomes more difficult to attain, and reality and originality more difficult to identify. One might expect serious literature in modern times to eschew stock characters and plots. However, stereotypes are so strongly implanted in the minds of writers as well as readers that they continue to appear, sometimes apparently in spite of themselves. It is this unconscious incorporation of ethnic stereotypes into fiction that is of concern here. It pervaded much of nineteenth-century fiction in England and the United States, notably H. Rider Haggard's African tales, and was retained in the work of Bret Harte, G. A. Henty, and John Buchan. Perhaps its presence is at least in part responsible for the lack of profundity in this work.

Some form of unconscious or indirect racism can be found in most literature which reflects authorial ethnic perspectives to any degree. It seems it must be expected, and often it also seems natural and relatively harmless. However, once exacerbated by economic conflicts, and possibly the associated personal troubles of writers, it easily expands into racist hostility. It invests literature with subtle traps that once identified may be disarmed, but which otherwise may pass unnoticed into the consciousness of readers. In reading the romances of Charles Gordon and John Murray Gibbon, for example, one comes to expect an evil "alien" character to be vanquished by a superior English-Canadian hero. One learns to identify aliens with evil and, in the absence of contrary evidence, continued discrimination is the result.

The second category involves fiction in which a racial theory is openly presented as part of a more comprehensive philosophy. To borrow a British example, Disraeli's *Coningsby* (1844), which tried to popularize the political theory of the "Young England" movement, employed Sidonia as spokesman and exemplary representative for a potential Anglo-Jewish power base for England. Sidonia united the best of the pure Hebrew race with the promis-

47 Berelson and Salter, "Majority and Minority Americans," 187-88.

ing vigour of the English. A complete racial theory, with qualitative levels, was explicitly laid out.[48] Kipling's sense of the white man's burden similarly revealed a theory which implied racism behind imperialism. This type of fiction, deliberately espousing racist theory as one aspect of an ideology, is not as common as the other two, especially in Canada.

The third category contains works written specifically to deal with discrimination. Whereas in the first category ethnocentrism is mere background noise, and in the second it contributes to more important themes, in the third type of work it is a major theme if not the only one. This category has grown considerably in this century. Especially after 1945 racial conflict has emerged as an accepted and frequent theme in literature throughout the world, as nationalism, with all its ethnic implications, multiplied. In South Africa, Alan Paton's *Cry the Beloved Country* (1948) and *Too Late the Phalarope* (1955), and Laurens Van der Post's *In a Province* (1934) courageously confronted legislated racism and set the stage for similar work by Nadine Gordimer, Dennis Brutus, and Alex la Guma. Disproving the race myths which still support the elitist white ruling class there, they employed literature in a moral leadership role, accepting the necessity of change instead of conforming to their own charter-group regulations and status quo. As African literature in English has developed, a priority has been the re-evaluation of European history in Africa, and in particular the definition of colonial racist acts as such. J. P. Clarke's *America Their America* (1964), S. Samkange's *On Trial for my Country* (1966), E. Mphahlele's *The Wanderers* (1971), and Y. A. Maddy's *No Past, No Present, No Future* (1973), among many others, have presented white racism in unpleasantly clear terms. Xavier Herbert's *Poor Fellow My Country* (1977) provides a monumental post mortem on Australian aborigines, condemning the white racism that has destroyed them. In the United States, J. Toomer's *Cane* (1923) and J. Spivak's *Georgia Nigger* (1926) preceded the work of James Baldwin and Ralph Ellison, who have powerfully presented the Afro-American reaction to white racism. In Britain, Enoch Powell's bitter protectionist oratory has been countered by Sam Selvon's humane and sad tales of Caribbean immigrant life. The question of race is increasingly a concern of literature.

Nineteenth-century Canadian literature belonged entirely to the first category. It included racist statements and beliefs that were incidental to other concerns. For example, Major Richardson's offhand denigration of Indians was only part of the setting for his romance, *Wacousta* (1832). Leslie Monkman has pointed out the double standard by which Richardson judged the Indians, an awkward paradox which encompassed a Rousseau-like respect for the Noble Savage combined with a blunt disgust for their savage and uncivilized behaviour.[49] As the Indian threat to European

48 B. Disraeli, *Coningsby* (Boston: L. C. Page, 1904), pp. 267-68, 302-8.
49 Leslie Monkman, "Richardson's Indians," *Canadian Literature* 81 (1979), 86-94.

colonization was reduced, their ennoblement could be safely commenced, concealing their inevitable extermination as a race. Like Richardson, T. C. Haliburton did not have a racial axe to grind, yet his offhand comments about the blacks of Nova Scotia are callous and complacently arrogant. Susanna Moodie's contempt for the American and Irish settlers she encountered, in *Roughing it in the Bush* (1852), might be seen to be balanced by her self-righteous repudiation of British prejudice against blacks and Indians. The latter in particular are well treated by her, although displaying more ostensibly "racial" differences from her than the white Yankees and Irish. Not such a villain in this respect nor surely as unconscious of her opinions as Ronald Sutherland has suggested,[50] she expressed her opinions in a way that probably reflected a *weltanschauung* based more on class than on race. In much the same way that many of Haliburton's sketches promoted Maritime business interests from which he was likely to profit directly, Susanna Moodie was hoping to recreate the cultured society of England in her backwoods area and by her writing to assume her rightful place near its top and earn the wherewithal to live up to it. Haliburton's condescending views of blacks and Moodie's disgust with Irish immigrants in the first chapter of *Roughing it in the Bush* were reactions to the potential threat of groups they preferred to see remain as labouring classes. Their fiction enforced a charter-group point of view on the reader. This perspective of urbane sophistication and elitist arrogance can be seen in a diluted form in later works, such as Gordon's *Corporal Cameron* (1912). It imbues such a book with the conceptual format of ethnocentrism tailored to the Canadian situation. Insofar as English literature produced in Canada before 1939 was largely the product of charter-group writers, describing a society controlled by a certain self-conscious group (which thought of itself as a race) hoping to maintain that control, it can be said to be ethnocentric to the point of racism. Yet it must be appreciated that English-Canadian writers, producing a self-congratulatory literature for their own group, recognized little need to even include others in their work, except for local colour, or to provide extra proof of their own superiority, until, the pressures of immigrants' indignation and self-assertion building with their growing numbers and increasing command of English, they faced a literary reaction produced by "alien" writers. However, not all English-Canadian writers seem to have required this pressure. Ethel Wilson's *Swamp Angel* (1954), set in the same area as Hilda Howard's viciously racist *The Writing on the Wall* (1922), is a novel that simply dissolves such distinctions. The protagonist, Maggie, argues: "I can't see what difference race can make . . . if you like a person. . . ."[51] Such a positive and clear attitude, expressed with such confi-

50 Ronald Sutherland, "The Body-Odour of Race," *Canadian Literature* 37 (1968), 50-51.
51 Ethel Wilson, *Swamp Angel* (London: Macmillan, 1955), p. 108.

dence and simplicity, does much to counter Mrs. Howard's savage and blatant racism.

The ethnic background and loyalties of Canadian novels can too often be predicted on the bases of their authors' biographies. Nationalist and ethnocentric sentiment continues to appear in literature, at times escalating to the level of racism, in the popular sense of the word. For an author to rise above a personal ethnic affiliation and become sufficiently free and detached to evaluate all groups and group loyalties (and not just in Canada, which would only be promoting another, larger group) is a rare achievement in Canadian literature. Charles Gordon thought he was doing this, but his failure is obvious at this distance. English-Canadian writers of Gordon's time provided a narrow view that demanded conformity. Non-charter-group writers, their voices increasingly being heard during the inter-war years, developed their own systems to which they conformed, and which they compared in various ways with the main, English model. Later Canadian writers in English made allowances for these alternative systems, seeking a humane synthesis that would accommodate a multicultural population without ethnocentric friction. For Canadian writers of all origins, the period after 1939 has been one of calculated compromise, negotiated suspiciously but with the goal of a united Canada urging them on, providing a larger nationalist ideal as a more attractive grouping. In times of prosperity, group expansion from the ethnic minority to the national level was natural, but as prosperity has decreased, this expansion has slowed down. Some shrinking back into smaller groups has given ethnocentrism the opportunity to revive. Much of Canadian prose fiction in English in this century has included comments, directly or indirectly, on ethnocentrism.

Of the three ways in which ethnocentrism can be categorized in literature, most early twentieth-century Canadian examples fall into the first category—that of the unconscious or semi-conscious repetition of popular ethnic stereotypes. The second category—of deliberate racial theorizing—has largely been ignored in Canada. The third category—of works countering ethnocentrism—contains fewer than two dozen novels and a few plays, poems, and short stories, but they are significant. They reflect the increasing liberalism of ethnic attitudes in literature as a whole as well as in the practical realities of their domestic settings, and the theory and the practice do not always match. They have also contributed to the raising of the level of public consciousness concerning racial issues and definitions.

This is a study of those works in the first and third categories, and of the chronological development from the first to the third. The study concentrates on those works that have grappled with the phenomenon of ethnocentrism in significant ways. It is more a study of those works than it is a study of authors, although at times biographical material has helped to explain certain attitudes. Certain quite prominent authors have been excluded simply because—as far as I know—their opinions on this theme have not been expressed in prose fiction within the time period studied.

In the first category I have concentrated on those writers whose work was in part influenced by the great influx of immigrants early in this century—Gordon, Gibbon, and Stead. Similarly, in demonstrating the reactions of immigrants, Western writers again are examined for they were the ones most under pressure—Grove, Salverson, and Lysenko being the important figures. Eastern Canada, having had longer to settle, has produced little literature on this theme in this century, but Central Canada has been fictionalized by Austin Clarke, Mordecai Richler, and Fred Bodsworth, among others. Where the entire canons of authors have been examined, it is because those authors—such as Margaret Laurence and Rudy Wiebe—have demonstrated a consistent concern in their work for ethnocentrism. Other authors, particularly more recent authors, who have emphasized their concern in single works, are represented here by those works.

Chapter Two

The English-Canadian Attitude, 1905-1939

I am not here to proselytize. My church is not in that business. We are doing business, but we are in the business of making good citizens. . . . We tried to get Greek Catholic priests from Europe to look after the religion and morals of these people. We absolutely failed to get a decent man to offer. . . . We had offers, plenty of them, but we could not lay our hands on a single, clean, honest-minded man with the fear of God in his heart, and the desire to help these people.

Mr. Brown, in *The Foreigner*, by Charles Gordon

I

The racial attitudes expressed in Canadian fiction in English in the first quarter of this century were mainly those supporting the supremacy of English-Canadian upper-class interests and reflected a static, conservative view of society. As well, non-fiction in periodicals and books largely presented the same view: this view became increasingly apparent as racial theorizing became more popular after 1900 when immigration reached proportions which some Canadians viewed as threatening. The pressure of immigration channelled through Winnipeg was described in *Strangers Within Our Gates* (1909) by J. S. Woodsworth, later the pacifist founder of the C.C.F., but then the superintendent of a Methodist mission in the city. In this hastily written pseudosociological study Woodsworth sought to describe the entire immigration situation in Western Canada, hoping both to help deal with current problems and to direct the future course of Canadian society. His book neatly summarized and in part attempted to

25

reduce charter-group fears and opinions about the newcomers, while presenting a purified Christian religious solution that proved rather impractical. This book is a good example of early twentieth-century Canadian prejudice and, although non-fiction, deserves mention here because of its open display of attitudes which infest contemporary fiction less overtly.

There can be no doubt that Woodsworth was sincerely moved by the real suffering he witnessed in the immigrant sheds and conclaves in Winnipeg, and his zeal in attacking the problem from a religious standpoint is admirable and understandable given his faith and energy. A prerequisite for his book and attitude was that a Canadian national identity had already been achieved, that "there is a certain indefinite *something* that at once unites us and distinguishes us from all the world besides."[1] At this time still a supporter of the British Empire, Woodsworth hoped to see Canada grow to become a stronger component within it, and to that end he pointed out the need to maintain the British majority by selective immigration: "We need more of our own blood to assist us to maintain in Canada our British traditions and to mould the incoming armies of foreigners into loyal British subjects."[2] This was the cornerstone of the English-Canadian attitude—the maintenance of the British political, economic, and cultural system that ensured their social superiority as not only the rule-making group but the commercially pre-eminent group as well. The initial inability of immigrants from other language groups and political systems to infiltrate the Canadian parliamentary systems and achieve effectual representation meant that they could be politically as well as financially exploited. The English-Canadian view accepted immigration as necessary for the continuous provision of lower-class labour, principally by 1910 to clear and farm marginal lands, in support of the established charter-group commercial superstructure. The English-Canadian theory of race evolved to explain and justify this division of labour by imputed racial characteristics, and accepted the so-called "alien" immigrants as a necessary weakness in the Imperial plan. Professor W. G. Smith put it concisely in *A Study in Canadian Immigration* (1920): "Of course, many a timorous heart may lament the fact that the elect of the earth, that is, the British-born Canadians with an ancestry of genuine Anglo-Saxon lineage, have to sojourn in the midst of peoples of every clime, but a similar situation prevails to some extent even in the British Isles."[3] It should be noted not only that Central Europeans were accepted but that under Clifford Sifton's administration as Laurier's Minister of the Interior (1896-1905) they were rigorously recruited, not because they were consid-

---

1 James S. Woodsworth, *Strangers Within Our Gates* (Toronto: Frederick Clark Stephenson, 1909), p. 13.
2 Ibid., p. 50.
3 W. G. Smith, *A Study in Canadian Immigration* (Toronto: Ryerson Press, 1920), p. 349.

ered so desirable in themselves, but because not enough Britishers could be enticed to supply the labour needed for the many schemes and booms organized by Canadian business.

In *Strangers Within Our Gates* Woodsworth supplied a qualitatively ranked survey of possible immigrant groups. They were evaluated on the basis of their potential for assimilation, estimated on the grounds of their assumed intelligence and undesirable features. Asiatics were at the bottom of the list. His approach was mainly theological; to him the Protestant religion stood for progress, civilization, and enlightenment. Judaism and Catholicism were only slightly better than paganism because of what he saw as the deliberate attempts of their church leaders to keep their followers in ignorance for their own material gain. To be truly Canadian one had to become Protestant, and when Woodsworth speaks of assimilation he implies conversion as its beginning, with the exception of French-Canadians whom he ignores. His concept of race superseded the biological to depend upon the cultural, as religion is employed to justify Anglo-Saxon Protestant supremacy in Canada.

It is important to distinguish between Woodsworth's ideas of cultural and racial attributes because the same views appear in subsequent fiction. On the cultural attributes of different peoples, he is explicit and voluble, energetically promoting Methodism; on racial attributes, his ideas are furtive and implicit, as if he were ashamed of them; linked together they can be seen to form a logical outgrowth of his religious egotism. The attitude of English-Canadians in 1909, so clearly expressed by Woodsworth, was that they were the most progressive and most civilized group of people in the world. Other related groups, including Doukhobors and Italians, for example, had fallen behind but might by education be raised up to the level of successful assimilation. This is not so much racial prejudice as inflated ethnocentric arrogance and cultural prejudice. It does not deny assimilation to "aliens" because of racially innate disqualifications, but instead generously admits their potential for eventual equality. It would appear to be a benign and tolerant sort of ethnic pride, and certainly it is a considerable improvement over some previous ideas. There is a difference between claiming another ethnic group to be backward but educable and claiming it to be genetically inferior. Woodsworth had no doubts about the first position. His complacent belief in Anglo-Saxon superiority is presented with no apologies. He admitted the possibility of some cultural contributions being made to Canadian society by immigrants, adding an exotic flavour here and there, but his view of the future was that of a solidly unified nation controlled by its English-Canadian founders.

Such xenophobic cultural prejudice inevitably verges on racism. Woodsworth discreetly avoided the direct expression of racism, but in circling the subject so much he often revealed a more protective and less generous aspect of his religion. Racism is a group-defence mechanism, and Woodsworth was defending the ideal Anglicized future of Canada against the assimilation-resistant groups that threatened to alter that ideal. Native Indians and blacks, he was happy to note, did not pose such a problem, being numerically small and relatively compliant. Asiatics he *did* see as a threat, writing shortly after the anti-Asiatic riot in Vancouver, and he covertly urged their rejection under more restrictive immigration standards. On Orientals in general he wrote: "There is, no doubt, a national prejudice that should be overcome. On the other hand, the expression, 'This is a white man's country,' has deeper significance than we sometimes imagine."[4] Neither the depth nor the nature of that significance is explained, but he did proceed to declare Orientals unassimilable and to demand their exclusion in future.[5] This was and is racial discrimination, of a type that may appear mild because of its confusing qualification and gentle tone, but which nonetheless is relentlessly exclusive. In the end, there is little *practical* difference between the racist ideas of Woodsworth and Madison Grant.

Woodsworth's attitude seems confusing. He qualifies most of his statements so well that he could retreat to either side if necessary. It now seems paradoxical to entertain ostensibly religious and liberally tolerant attitudes towards immigrants simultaneously with firm racist and discriminatory convictions. This is a dichotomy that permeates early English-Canadian literature. Woodsworth's idea of cultural retardation and assimilation justified his tolerance of white non-British immigrants, and could be extended to Indians and blacks as long as they seemed non-competitive with British ideals. He feared Orientals for their immense numbers and their capacity for economic rivalry, specifically as proven by their success in the West Coast fishing industry. Where a non-white group was declining in its potential to affect the British standards, then that group could be safely patronized, and the act of patronization could be used as evidence of one's racial tolerance. Where a non-white group was actively attempting to increase its population and ultimately its power to influence social change, then it was opposed on grounds that were fundamentally racist. The denial of the franchise to Orientals in British Columbia until after World War Two was a blocking of access to such power, exercised at the provincial level. Woodsworth's book concentrates on the details of the system without examining those in control. In a similar book published a year later, the prominent Western politician Charles A. Magrath let slip his concern with power quite nakedly in an offhand reference in praise of Doukhobors: "I certainly have never noticed any attempt on their part to get control of the legis-

---

4 Woodsworth, *Strangers*, p. 276.
5 Ibid., pp. 189, 276-78.

lature."[6] Anglo-Saxon control must not be threatened, and Woodsworth's defence of that control is implied throughout *Strangers Within Our Gates*.

Woodsworth was the self-appointed champion of the immigrant in Winnipeg in 1909, both in print and in his parochial work. Paradoxically his book, while drawing attention to the magnitude of the real problems caused by massive immigration, legitimized the ultimately despotic concept of social homogeneity on English-Canadian terms and the predestined exclusiveness of the white race in Canada. His crusading vision of Methodist evangelism converting aliens not only from their corrupt religions but also from their old and inferior lifestyles became a popular theme in the then important church press, and was probably one of the more popular points of the fiction of Gordon and McClung. The tacit assumption that all races would do best to follow British ways, and that some races could not and perhaps were never meant to do so, reinforced in the national consciousness racist developments of simple ethnic pride—a result Woodsworth could neither have foreseen nor desired.

This view of race was disseminated throughout the periodical press of the first two decades, frequently by prominent English-Canadians. Anyone surveying the press of that time would gain the impression that it was the only valid Canadian attitude of race, immigration, and assimilation, as few other views found their way into print. Their concern for these issues was mirrored in literature, which further publicized these racist beliefs. For example, Robert Stead's first book of poetry, *The Empire Builders and other poems* (1908), mixed the styles of Service and Kipling to defend charter-group interests from alien immigrant greed. In "The Mixer," a poem celebrating the transformation or "mixing" of assorted immigrants into fully assimilated Canadians, each stanza concludes with the abrupt refrain: "As I turn 'em out Canadians—all but the yellow and brown."[7] Such blatant flaunting of the colour bar has seldom appeared in Canadian literature, for more subtle phraseology could serve the same function, as Woodsworth proved. Nevertheless Stead's rhetorically blunt statement stands, and his desperate protectionism may best be understood when linked with Gobineau's response to class dispossession, in that Stead's main objection to immigrants of any origin was their potential threat to displace his charter group's position in the West:

> The land our children's sons will need,
>   That land we have wide open thrown
> To heathen knaves of other breed
>   And paunchy pirates of our own:

6 Charles A Magrath, *Canada's Growth and Some Problems Affecting It* (Ottawa: Mortimer Press, 1910), p. 121.
7 Robert J. C. Stead, "The Mixer," in *The Empire Builders and other poems* (Toronto: William Briggs, 1910), pp. 17, 19.

We give away earth's greatest prize,
And pat ourselves, and call us wise.[8]

Both Woodsworth and Stead were defending what they saw as their superior class position in racist terms, the former stressing religious differences and the latter emphasizing Imperial greatness. Both often employed words such as "breed," "stock," and "blood" in a racial sense, imposing livestock terminology and value judgements upon races. Anglo-Saxons were thoroughbreds who must be guarded against adulteration by inferior breeds, an agricultural point of view which seems to have been quite popular in the West, both as a simple but misleading form of speech and as the scientific theory known as eugenics. These words appear frequently in the works of John Murray Gibbon and Charles Gordon as well. Indeed in Gibbon's *The Conquering Hero* (1920) one of the positive characters, Dr. de Brémont, "was celebrated as a pioneer in the science of eugenics, that is to say, in the theory that only the physically fit should be allowed to marry."[9] Like the concept of race, eugenics had and still has enough scientific validity to qualify its negative aspects. However, its objections to miscegenation were made unscientifically on purely racist grounds, and its presence in the fiction of these authors is a constant reminder of the conceptual restrictions under which they wrote and which by writing about they reinforced.

II

Woodsworth's subtle racial complacency, which occasionally was surpassed by outbreaks of rhetorical hostility inspired by regional tensions, of which Stead's 1908 volume of poetry appearing a year after the anti-Asiatic riot in Vancouver is the best example, sums up well the English-Canadian racial philosophy just before 1914. The first major work of fiction in Canada to express the strength of that philosophy was Charles Gordon's *The Foreigner* (1909), which is basically a fictionalized version of *Strangers Within Our Gates*.

Gordon's work before 1909, including the best-selling books which had made his reputation, had largely ignored aliens and concentrated instead on Anglo-Saxon pioneers. In *Black Rock* (1898), *The Sky Pilot* (1899), *The Prospector* (1904), *The Doctor* (1906), and to a lesser extent in *The Pilot at*

8 Stead, "The Prodigals," in *The Empire Builders*, p. 95. It is interesting to note how closely Stead's protectionist remarks resemble Kipling's observations in 1907 on alien immigration into Canada. See Rudyard Kipling, *Letters to the Family* (Toronto: Macmillan of Canada, 1908).

9 John Murray Gibbon, *The Conquering Hero* (Toronto: S. B. Gundy, 1920), p. 135. For a further discussion of eugenics, see Terry L. Chapman, "Early Eugenics Movement in Western Canada," in *Alberta History* 25, No. 4 (1977), 9-17.

Swan Creek (1905), heroic missionaries are seen redeeming from sin "the best blood of Britain."[10] As well as physical dangers the frontier contains the risk of moral degeneration. Virile missionaries worked alongside upright matriarchal women to counter this threat. In Gordon's early fiction, written before non-charter-group immigration had grown to alarming proportions, his West was populated almost entirely by Anglo-Saxons. They were the only ones who counted. French-Canadians and Indians were suppressed into background colour, for they were not an active part of the dream and could only flaw the romance. This view of the West as the playground for an extended British civilization is Stead's and Emerson Hough's as well.

Gordon's response to the situation of the Indians at this time was logically incomplete, confusing, and ambivalent. He did believe in the inevitability of the beneficial assimilation of Indians into the dominant charter-group order, but still displayed a lingering admiration for the hypothetical Noble Savage of the past, as he wrote in *The Pilot at Swan Creek*:

> A few miles farther on brings us to St. Paul's, where stands the Indian school, where young Indians are taught all soberly their three R's and other things, with the hope that they may grow into mechanics and farmers, and so become citizens of our country. Shades of the red men of the plain and the canoe, of the rifle and hunting knife! I can fancy how your bones shudder in your moulded graves in rattling horror at the degeneracy of your sons. But what else is left to the Indian after he has lost his great plains and his rivers, his buffalo and his deer? What else but tailor-made clothes and shingle-roofed houses, and days of humdrum work, with plenty to eat and drink.[11]

On the one hand he was pleased to see their education proceed, and anticipated the benefits this would bring them when they were taught, as Gordon put it apparently with no awareness of the irony, to "become citizens of our country." On the other hand he lamented the extinction of a heroically adventurous and romantic way of life. While this dichotomous attitude underwent some change as his career progressed, his Indian characters remained a picturesque backdrop to the more important struggles of whites, usually serving them in menial roles of devotion.

Certainly Gordon had a strong British (and particularly Scottish) ethnocentric sensibility based upon Imperialism and Presbyterianism. His English-Canadian stereotypes are virile, God-fearing supermen and women, capable of immense achievements and great emotional control.

10 Charles W. Gordon (pseud. Ralph Connor), *The Sky Pilot* (Toronto: Westminster, 1902), p. 26.
11 Charles W. Gordon, *The Pilot at Swan Creek* (London: Hodder & Stoughton, 1905), p. 41.

They are physically brave and prove it constantly in a surprising number of fights. They are unreal characters, stereotypes inflated beyond credibility, with larger than life ideals of human behaviour, and they populate an imaginative world having little to do with realistic human nature. They are opposed by malignant characters who inevitably fail. These are usually Indians or half-breeds, sometimes French-Canadians, and often, after 1916, Germans or German-Americans. Gordon's aim was ostensibly religious, but for him Presbyterianism was a determinant of culture which was itself an attribute of race. English-Canadian culture was a class monopoly in Canada, and racism is mostly a product of class rivalry expressed in ethnic terms. In Canada, as John Porter has shown, religion has been an indicator and a governor of class. It is no accident that the upper-class characters in almost all of Gordon's fiction are not only English or Scotch, but Protestant and usually devoutly Presbyterian as well, while the lower classes and those characters requiring redemption are Catholic, pagan, or lapsed Protestants. Gordon focused on an Anglo-Saxon hegemony because that was the future he desired for Canada: when he became aware of the threat to that future posed by the mass immigration described in *Strangers Within Our Gates*, he faced the challenge characteristically not by adapting his dream to the incoming alien cultures, but by providing a recipe by which the aliens might be adapted to his ideal. The result was *The Foreigner*.

The Foreigner concentrates on Galicians, who were probably the most looked-down-upon group of white immigrants at the time. Certainly Gordon looked down upon them, but not without the hope of raising them from their supposed superstition-ridden ignorance and filthy habits. The inevitable exemplary missionary character, Mr. Brown, who appears late in the book but provides the means to a successful resolution, sums up the Galician "problem" for Gordon when he states: "These people here exist as an undigested foreign mass. They must be taught our ways of thinking and living, or it will be a mighty bad thing for us in Western Canada."[12] Taking one family as his example, Gordon showed how the oppression of the past could be forgotten, in the person of the once-revolutionary father, and how the unhealthy Slavic customs could be upgraded, in the person of the once slovenly mother, and how, in the absence of both parents, and under the benign influence of cultivated Protestants instead, the children could grow up to be true Canadian heroes, indistinguishable from all of Gordon's others. The son, Kalman, succeeds so well that he is to be rewarded by marriage to a British lord's daughter. The book promised that Galicians could assimilate to the point where they would disappear as a separate group, if only they are treated properly and are provided with an education in British civilization.

12 Charles W. Gordon, *The Foreigner* (Toronto: Westminster, 1909), p. 255.

Gordon operated from the reasonably enlightened premise that Galicians were not innately inferior but only suffered from cultural retardation. Despite his poor factual knowledge of them, he described their historical situation with some sympathy and he condescendingly tried to explain their custom of rowdy wedding parties with some understanding of their lonely state in an unfriendly land.[13] Their backwardness he blames on religious weaknesses: "It was the East meeting the West, the Slav facing the Anglo-Saxon. Between their points of view stretched generations of moral development. It was not a question of absolute moral character so much as a question of moral standards."[14] Denying absolute qualities in this case, Gordon endeavoured to convince his Canadian readership that Galicians were redeemable by education. This is cultural but not racial discrimination, which, though it callously excludes the Galician parents from the "civilizing" process which benefits their children, at least allows them the freedom to advance themselves.

Gordon often used words loosely, apparently without giving much thought to their consequences. His use of the word "race" itself was frequently vague, and similarly his use of loaded words such as "blood" at times implies more than he could have wished. The word "barbaric" appears throughout *The Foreigner*, as the Galicians are depicted as a primitive people not far removed from barbarism. It is, however, a word that qualifies negatively whatever it describes, presenting the Galician society as the opposite of British civilization. Gordon equated civilization with his own church, and offered it as the antidote for his medieval sense of Central European barbarism. Yet it must be noted that he recognized the primitive passions underlying all humanity, which appear at times of violence. Such recognition is shown by his description of the drunken half-breed, Mackenzie, when his murderous attack on Kalman is halted, "the fiendish rage fading out of his face, the aboriginal blood lust dying in his eyes like the snuffing out of a candle. In a few brief moments he became once more a civilized man, subject to the restraint of a thousand years of life ordained by law."[15] The epitome of Gordon's system of race classification was a Scottish Highland gentleman, but even one of those could regress to the same barbaric level of Canadian half-breeds and Galicians. The violent assault by Barney upon Dr. Bulling in *The Doctor* indicated that Gordon knew that

13 Gordon's errors are pointed out by Frances Swyripa in *Ukrainian Canadians* (Edmonton: University of Alberta Press, 1978), pp. 12-16. His lack of real sympathy for Ukrainians in *The Foreigner* is also mentioned by Tamara J. Palmer in "Ethnic Character and Social Themes in Novels about Prairie Canada and the Period from 1900 to 1940," unpublished M.A. thesis, York University, 1972, p. 46. It is compared unfavourably with Lysenko's treatment of them.

14 Gordon, *The Foreigner*, pp. 24-25.

15 Ibid., p. 234.

Scots were not far removed from such violent passions either. Such aware-ness of shared human failings among peoples suggests that Gordon was less race-concious than he actually was. There is in fact little difference between the ideology expressed by Emerson Hough and J. S. Woodsworth (at this early date in his career) and that which appears in *The Foreigner*. Most significantly, where Woodsworth had deplored the appearance of Jewish middlemen acting dishonestly as interpreters and business agents for less educated immigrants, the villain in *The Foreigner* is such a character. Rosenblatt, a greedy, conniving, and immoral Jew, is the antithesis of the Christian missionaries. He exploits the simple Galician community in Winnipeg both financially and immorally, whereas the Presbyterians main-tain a financially disinterested concern for the immigrants. Rosenblatt is seen as attempting to recreate the discredited system of European oppres-sion in Canada while the missionaries offer individual freedom and democ-racy. Rosenblatt is a product of the popular belief, evidently accepted by Gordon, that Jews controlled European finance by nefarious means. As far as Gordon was concerned, such manipulation and exploitation by Jews was not going to be permitted in Canada. Rosenblatt's evil plans are foiled and he dies a violent death suitable to his designs.

Rosenblatt is identifiable as a Jew by appearance, behaviour, and name. He is beyond redemption, Gordon apparently not considering it credible to extend the idea of conversion to Presbyterianism to include a Jew. His death is not mourned and provides a convenient climax as well as a moral lesson. There is no place for the old oppressive European ways in Gordon's Canada. It would seem, too, at this time at least, that there is no place for Jews.

Gordon's ideal Canada had been firmly established in his fiction before the threat to its successful attainment by alien immigrants was perceived. Suddenly determined to deal with emergent social problems, Gordon began with *The Foreigner* to employ non-Anglo-Saxon major characters. Neverthe-less his condescending attitude, that of a missionary paternally tending wayward children, reveals his inbred cultural discrimination. His habitual use of stock ethnic characters, with English-Canadians as heroes and aliens as villains, moves this cultural prejudice into the area of racial prejudice. Gordon consistently assigned racial attributes to various ethnic groups, beyond the simple type-casting *The Foreigner* contains, including "the alert Polak, the heavy Croatian, the haughty Magyar, and occasionally the stalwart Dalmation. . . ."[16] His Irishmen are usually colourful drunks, his French-Canadians are usually emotional clowns, and both always speak in tediously appropriate dialects. However, they are white and therefore redeemable, just as the Catholics Carroll and Perreault are brought to the point of being virtuous Presbyterians in all but name by Shock in *The Prospector*.

16 Ibid., p. 14.

Rosenblatt is Gordon's first Jewish character. After 1909 he ignored Jews until compelled to turn to them in 1917 when he was forced to scrape the bottom of the barrel (as he must have considered it) to find recruits for Canada's Army. The English-Canadian attitude towards Jewish immigrants at this time was one of suspicion. Madison Grant certainly had no hesitation in describing them as a physically inferior race, anthropologically. The more religious writers who broached the issue seemed to be jealous of Jews. For Gordon and Woodsworth, both ordained ministers with an intimate knowledge of biblical history, the idea of Jews being God's chosen people contradicted their own claim for predestined Anglo-Saxon superiority in Canada as in the world. Theirs was a narrow national (if not regional) and unhistorical view, so ethnically egotistic that racism was its inevitable result. Two separate poles of assumed superiority could not be tolerated. Furthermore, it was popularly believed that Jewish immigrants would not go on the land, but would instead compete in business with the WASP entrepreneurial superstructure. The appreciation of their unassimilability led to continued anti-Semitism in Canada, and although specific economic and religious reasons were put forward to justify it, in the end racism was its only real justification.

Three years after *The Foreigner*, Gordon produced *Corporal Cameron*, a romance about the pacification of the West combined with a guide for the successful way a "white" immigrant could make good in Canada. The success story of Cameron unfolds as he prospers as an immigrant, as a policeman, and as a Presbyterian to take his place finally in the fictional Western tradition which had become Gordon's trademark. This West is more civilized than that of earlier works. The NWMP is no longer corrupt, as it was in *The Prospector*, and now has taken on the appearance of a winning football team. Although this is not a novel about Indians, it is Gordon's first to deal with them at any length. Its point of view may be summed up by one simplistic and wishful statement: "The natives soon learned to regard the police officers as their friends."[17] There is no evidence that Gordon personally ever had much to do with Indians, which may excuse his ignorance. There was little more need to include Indians in this book than in his previous work, in which their absence is noticeable. In *Corporal Cameron* they remain background material, but they are also utilized to set up certain statements which Gordon must have wanted to make about them, and without which any book about the pacification of the West would have been incomplete.

As Cameron travels from Montreal to the Rockies, he encounters several villains who must be bested. Perkins, the love-mad farmhand, and Dick Raven, the possibly Scottish whisky-trader, are pale villains beside Raven's criminal cohort, Little Thunder, a "hideously ugly" and unbalanced Indian

17 Charles W. Gordon, *Corporal Cameron* (Toronto: Westminster, 1912), p. 334.

thug. This devilish figure is stopped from killing Cameron by Raven: "He seized by the throat and wrist the Indian, who, frothing with rage and snarling like a wild animal, was struggling to reach Cameron again."[18] However, this passage describing the Indian's animal violence is no worse than the one earlier in the novel presenting Perkins's jealous rage, or that one mentioned above in *The Doctor*. The difference here is that Gordon goes on to make Little Thunder the arch-villain of the novel, and his capture (at a Sun Dance, the institution of paganism for the missionaries[19]) is a colourful flourish to the climax, the police putting an end to Indian barbarism in the West. Such criminally committed and presumably spiritually doomed Indians must be punished, but Gordon makes it clear that for the majority of Indians there is a better way: they can become Christians. The NWMP provide the stick while the missionaries hold out the carrot. Cameron at one point is kidnapped by the whisky-traders and has to accompany them to a Stoney Indian camp where, from a hiding place, he observes a Mr. Mac-Dougal, "the aged pioneer Methodist missionary who had accomplished such marvels during his long years of service with his Indian flock and had gained such a wonderful control over them."[20] It is their *control* that Gordon was interested in. He goes on to sentimentalize the converted Indians at prayer:

> the circle of dusky worshippers, kneeling about their campfire, lifted their faces heavenward and their hearts Godward in prayer, and as upon those dusky faces the firelight fell in fitful gleams, so upon their hearts, dark with the superstitions of a hundred generations, there fell the gleams of the torch held high by the hands of their dauntless ambassador of the blessed Gospel of the Grace of God.[21]

The Stoneys, who evidently are not as placid as Mr. MacDougal would like, buy whisky from Raven and the idyllic scene is temporarily destroyed, but the reader is left with the vision and the hope that when the bootleggers are put out of business the missionaries will triumph and the Indians will be saved once and for all.

Gordon admired the NWMP's justice and firm methods of controlling the savage Indians. "Savage" is another example of an unfortunate choice of word, the negative meaning of which is intensified by frequent repetition. In this novel there is no nonsense about the Noble Savage. The converted Indians are placid and dull, vacillating between Christianity and liquor. The unconverted ones are dangerously "savage," although their danger is diminished by their admiration for and subservience to the police. It is a

18 Ibid., p. 328.
19 The use of the Sun Dance by other authors has been noted by Leslie Monkman in *A Native Heritage* (Toronto: University of Toronto Press, 1981), p. 18.
20 Gordon, *Corporal Cameron*, p. 342.
21 Ibid., p. 346.

simplistic interpretation of a historical process that, stressing religious sentiment at the expense of realism, could only have encouraged a patronizing and racially superior attitude towards the Indians. There was no pity for those holdouts who preferred their own old way of life to Presbyterian confinement.

Gordon, however, did not press the point to any logical extreme. Indeed it seems unlikely that he could have, for what shallow logic does exist in this book is shared uneasily by the two sides of a paradox that results in a logical cul-de-sac. In the sequel to *Corporal Cameron*, *The Patrol of the Sun Dance Trail* (1914), this paradox is even more obvious as Gordon simultaneously praises the primitive utopian Indian way of life before the advent of the whites, and condemns them for their slovenly, dishonest habits after it. In this sequel he explicitly blames the whites for corrupting the Indians with whisky, almost portraying the Indians as innocent victims. At the same time, and consistently employing the term "race" to differentiate the two groups, he presents most of the Indians in such a disreputable and villainous light, compared to his unreasonably noble and heroic Anglo-Saxons, that what pathos they have attracted is lost to an overwhelming sense of disgust and distrust. Being Indian seems to be an almost irredeemable fault. Even religion's saving grace is denied them now, and the heavy-handed and questionably legal methods the whites use to control them are presented as quite justified.

When war broke out in 1914 British writers were mobilized to write in support of the war effort. Much of this work by British and Canadian authors was anti-German, playing up emotional issues such as atrocities in Belgium with the dual aim of encouraging recruitment and morale in the Empire and inducing the U.S.A. to enter the war against "the Hun." Germany was generally presented as being infected with militarism and it was this dangerous societal infirmity rather than innate racial malice that was usually the argument of such writing. However, as the war progressed and the situation became more desperate, it became fashionable to write simply of beer-swilling brutal oafs conscripted en masse to defend clever and insufferably arrogant militaristic opportunists.

Gordon joined this crusade, specializing in the exposure of the Germans' supposed Godlessness, arguing that men who had deliberately made such a war could not be considered religious. As early as 1905 in *The Pilot at Swan Creek* he had given evidence of an antipathy towards Germans. In "Ould Michael," a story set in the late Victorian period, a German settler in the West insults the Queen in a bar and brawls with Ould Michael, an aged Irish veteran and alcoholic who nevertheless stands up for his monarch. The German is beaten up by another man and is revealed not only as disloyal but, equally bad in Gordon's canon of manly qualities, as a quitter. He is contemptible for his unsportsmanlike conduct in fighting a pathetic old man whose loyalty is meant to be inspiring. A clear prejudice against German settlers is expressed in this early story. Perhaps some of this prejudice was personal, arising from his brief travels in Germany while still a student in Scotland. Perhaps some was positive and Imperial, protecting the development of the Empire in the Canadian West. Certainly Gordon went on to become the most extreme anti-German novelist in Canada.[22] Other writers generally left the German settlers alone, as they were white, Nordic, Protestant, and they made good pioneers and stayed on the land. Next to Britons, they were considered ideal immigrants, questionable only in terms of loyalty.

As his autobiography, *Postscript to Adventure* (1938), makes clear, Gordon's reaction to the war in 1914 was immediate support for the defence of the British Empire. In his subsequent fiction the organization of military units in Western Canada is depicted almost as a crusade, with entire families enlisting and with ministers such as himself leading the way into battle. Despite his age Gordon went off to France as chaplain to a Winnipeg unit recruited in part from his own congregation. His firsthand experience of trench warfare, with its concomitant duties for chaplains such as writing the letters home to bereaved mothers whom he knew personally, must have cumulatively contributed to the intense anti-German feeling which pervades his work thereafter. Before the war he was aware of the German commercial challenge to the Empire and the potential threat German settlers posed to British rule in Canada. During and after it he tended to see Germans as evil. His ignorance of Germany and the many good reasons for German immigration (not to mention the fact that many of the German settlers in Canada were actually from Russia) led him to an extreme view and one that deserves the description of racism.

In 1917 Gordon was recalled from France and sent on a lecture tour of the U.S.A. His one wartime book, *The Major*, was published the same year and had the same aim as his tour—to induce Americans into declaring war against the enemy. It is the literary equivalent of a recruiting poster, aimed both at slackers in Canada and sympathizers in the U.S.A. The thin romantic plot weakly struggles under the heavy weight of a series of speeches by various spokespeople of both sides. The Germans are allowed to have their say but are always defeated in oratory and their physical descriptions are always far less appealing than those of the English-Canadians who oppose them.

The book is based in Alberta, although the setting shifts as far afield as Chicago, and it begins in the summer before the war. In an Albertan farming community the loyally Imperialist English-Canadians have as neighbours the long established German-American settlers, the Switzers,

<hr/>

22 Sara Jeanette Duncan produced some surprisingly propagandistic and insipidly melo-dramatic plays along the same lines. These unpublished plays are kept in Special Collections, D. B. Weldon Library, the University of Western Ontario.

whose son, Ernest, is in love with Kathleen Gwynne. Jack Romayne, former attaché to the British Embassy in Berlin and active in warning Canadians of Germany's war plans, visits the area, and scores a number of rhetorical points off Ernest as he competes with him for Kathleen, winning her after an unexplained shooting accident. Ernest had been a true Canadian youth, like his more docile sister, until he was sent to Germany for an education: "He came back here a year ago, terribly German and terribly military, heel-clicking, ram-rod back, and all that sort of thing."[23] Ernest had absorbed the militaristic spirit that, according to Gordon, controlled Germany completely with the aim of world domination, to be achieved deliberately and wickedly by war. Gordon disallows race prejudice in his condemnation of Ernest as the personification of German faults. Two English-Canadians actually speak against racial categorization and prejudice in Canada. Yet the fact remains that the use of the word in that context affirms that Germans are considered as a separate race. The objections to Germans that Gordon puts into the mouths of his Anglophone spokespeople are transparent excuses for that very prejudice he claims to reject. These objections seem mainly concerned with German manners. Ernest represents his people by acting as if they were superior, and by being insensitive to the labourers who work his coal mine and to women in general. German men are alleged to mistreat their women, forcing them to work in the fields as well as totally dominating them socially, thus precluding the cosy family scene which was so important to Gordon. Ernest has a violent temper and cannot control himself emotionally, in contrast with the cooler demeanour of Jack. One can reluctantly accept such a negative depiction of Germans produced in 1917 at the height of the submarine war when the situation looked very bleak for the Empire. However, it was a habit Gordon kept up. As late as 1925, in *Treading the Winepress*, the two German-American Cottman brothers were created along very similar lines to Ernest Switzer. It is their "haughty sense of superiority to the rest of mankind" that is their greatest fault, one that Ernest shares as well.[24] The expression of superiority that Gordon objects to in Germans, and that J. S. Woodsworth objected to in Jews, is a natural enough expression of ethnocentric pride. Only one superiority complex would be allowed in Canada and it would be that of the WASPs. An additional point Gordon makes against Germans in *The Major* is made by showing two German-Americans, Meyer and Professor Schaefer, greeting the news of the outbreak of war with blasphemous gratitude and excitement. By using this ugly scene to prove that the war had been desired and planned in advance by the Germans, Gordon makes them out to be unscrupulously evil criminals.

23 Charles W. Gordon, *The Major* (Toronto: McClelland, Goodchild & Stewart, 1917), pp. 95-96.
24 Charles W. Gordon, *Treading the Winepress* (New York: George H. Doran, 1925), p. 98.

As well as Germans there is one other non-English group presented in *The Major* (if one excludes for the present Joe Gagneau, the French-Canadian truant). One of the English-Canadian girls, Jane, while a student at the University of Manitoba, rather surprisingly defeated a German-Jewish student for the German prize that year before the war. Jane is said to be popular and socially active on campus: "Kellerman, on the other hand, was of that species of student known as a pot-hunter, who took no interest in college life, but devoted himself solely to the business of getting for himself everything that the college had to offer."[25] At the outbreak of war, however, Kellerman immediately enlists and is discovered by Jane and her friend Ethel marching with his regiment in Winnipeg. Kellerman explains to Jane that he is actually Polish and that his enlistment was prompted by a righteous desire to revenge his father's murder by a German officer in German Poland. Ethel asks afterwards: "Is that little Kellerman, the greasy little Jew whom we used to think such a beast?"[26] Jane's indignant defence of the man shows that Gordon was pointing out to Jews in Canada how to metamorphose into true Canadians. Joining the army is the cure for anti-Semitism. In fact, Jane comes to prefer Kellerman to Lloyd Rush-brooke, an English-Canadian slacker who calls Kellerman: "that greasy little Sheeney," "the little Yid," and "that little Hebrew Shyster."[27] Rushbrooke's crude prejudice, and the later indictment of him as a slacker and potential profiteer, displays Kellerman in the best possible light. However, like most of Gordon's clumsy attempts to treat other "races" well in spite of themselves, this one does not succeed very well. The adjective "little" is almost always qualifying the word "Jew," and any other euphemism for the word. It is accepted that Kellerman is a small man (although he is big enough to join the army), but the repetition of the "little" that constantly diminishes his stature as a person seems unnecessary. It is a patronizing qualification of his character, the more appreciable when one sees that the figure of Nathan Storm, the sophisticated Jewish father in *The Gay Crusader* nineteen years later, also is referred to several times as "the little Jew." Also of interest is the fact that while the other university men are commissioned as officers, Kellerman is in the ranks. Gordon's favourable presentation of Jews is unconsciously qualified and conditional upon their participation in the war as combatants.

In *The Major* and two years later in *The Sky Pilot in No Man's Land* (1919) Gordon established in print a teleological foundation for racial animosity towards Germans. His implicit denial of exactly this in the former novel was buttressed by an explicit denial he found necessary to include in his autobiography:

25 Gordon, *The Major*, p. 255.
26 Ibid., p. 342.
27 Ibid., p. 343.

the chief and dominant cause of the conflict, in the main, must be discovered in the blind, militaristic spirit of the Prussian Junta which cowed and forced the great German people, fully half of whom were thoroughly socialistic and antimilitaristic in their modes of thought, into that criminal adventure for the conquest of the world. Even in those days of war, however, I am now glad to think that never was I conscious of any feeling of personal hatred for the German people. . . .[28]

Yet the evidence in his novels proves otherwise, and the paradox suggests that he was being as fair as he knew how to other "races," and that his prejudices which seem so obvious now were then so much an accepted part of life for English-Canadians that they passed unnoticed. Partly the problem lies in loose semantics. Towards the end of *The Major* Larry explains to Jane his reasons for renouncing his former Quaker and pacifist beliefs and enlisting: "I have come to see that there is no possibility of peace or sanity for the world till that race of mad militarists is destroyed."[29] Surely Gordon meant the German leadership only here, and not the common people who had been conscripted into a mad dream. Certainly he left the impression that Germans might not be completely and innately evil, and that settlement in Canada could release some from their bondage. Yet the fact remains that Gordon was making statements about races, that he viewed the German concept of themselves as a superior race as a direct challenge to the British Empire, and that with little intellectual understanding for the true roles of either side he emotionally supported his own ethnic group and devoted his skills (and a good part of his integrity) to the attack on the other group. He was making statements about race, conducive to racism as an extreme version of British ethnocentric pride. The Anglo-Saxon sense of race did prove confusing to him for a while. In *The Sky Pilot in No Man's Land*, an American industrialist refuses to sell oil to Germans during the war: "'No stuff of mine,' he said, 'shall go to help an enemy of the Anglo-Saxon race.'"[30] Six years later, in *Treading the Winepress*, Gordon switched to the phrase "the Anglo-Keltic race" instead, which had the advantage of excluding Saxony to make room for his own Scotland.[31] It is obvious that he was aware of the consequences of his references to various races, particularly his own, although he was undoubtedly sincere in disclaiming any personal feelings of racism and in branding it unchristian and un-Canadian. Yet in his demands for aliens to assimilate into the English-Canadian culture, he is intolerant and discriminatory. His novels are

28 Charles W. Gordon, *Postscript to Adventure* (New York: Farrer & Rinehart, 1938), p. 313.

29 Gordon, *The Major*, p. 370.

30 Charles W. Gordon, *The Sky Pilot in No Man's Land* (New York: George H. Doran, 1919), p. 194.

31 Gordon, *Treading the Winepress*, p. 184.

indirectly full of racism and must take some of the blame for passing it on as a pseudolegitimate idea, for he *was* the most popular Canadian novelist at the beginning of this century.

To pin Gordon down on race is difficult because of his increasing awareness after 1919 of the dangers of blatantly racist philosophy. His post-war novels, both the historical romances and the economic studies, deal variously with Scots, Indians, French-Canadians, and Germans. Concerning the last, he never forgave the Germans their war guilt and he harped on their menacing nature for the rest of his life. The French-Canadians he dealt with in his customary patronizing way, yet he was aware of the urgent need for "a new national unity that would wipe out forever from true Canadian hearts all the racial and religious jealousy and hate that has darkened the future of our Canadian life."[32] Despite such good intentions, French-Canadians emerge as second-class citizens in his novels. In *The Major* Joe Gagneau is, among the schoolboys, the habitual lazy truant in much the same way as "Fusie" is in *Glengarry School Days*. In *To Him that Hath* a French-Canadian boy and an English-Canadian boy grow up together as inseparable childhood companions, but differences emerge as they age. Jack, the English-Canadian, acquires education, becomes an officer in the army, and heroically settles a nasty labour situation in his father's mill. His friend, Tony, leaves school early, enlists in the ranks during the war, and returns to become a drunk, an irresponsible worker, and a bitter labour agitator. French-Canadians do not succeed in Gordon's novels except under WASP supervision, as in *The Runner* (1929). Few other writers have depicted French-Canadians so clearly as "white niggers of America" just as few have provided such a grandiose dream of Canadians as superheroes.[33] His view of Indians altered over the years as their control became more of a certainty. With the removal of the menace they still represented when he first went west in 1890, he developed a professed admiration for them.[34] In *The Runner* he contrasted the absolute savagery of European warfare in nineteenth-century Upper Canada with that of the more gentlemanly and honourable Indians to express an "indictment of the white race."[35] Although his motives were probably different, his attitude towards "tame" Indians is quite similar to that of Susanna Moodie, expressed seventy years before. Gordon eventually came to the point where he could write in 1929: "It is a sad and cruel story, the story of the march of Christian culture upon

32 Gordon, *Postscript to Adventure*, pp. 286-87.

33 As Peter Buitenhuis has noted about Parker, "his specialty was the endearing French-Canadian habitant, for so long the sentimental stereotype, the white nigger as it were, propagated by the English in Canada." P. Buitenhuis, "Writers at War: Propaganda and Fiction in the Great War," *University of Toronto Quarterly* 45, No. 4 (1976), 279.

34 This idealization of Indians at a safe distance after their threat was removed has been noted also by Monkman in *A Native Heritage*, p. 68.

35 Charles W. Gordon, *The Runner* (Toronto: Doubleday, Doran & Gundy, 1929), p. 180.

the simplicity and barbarity of a people in whose uncultured heart burned the passionate fires of liberty, justice, and truth."[36] That the Indians were a problem no more must in part be due to the merciless imposition of European cultural requirements which Gordon had supported in his fiction. Made somewhat cynical by the war and its aftermath of sudden labour problems upon which he was consulted, Gordon shows signs of yearning for the mythical, uncomplicated Golden Age. However, it is improbable that he ever relented concerning the necessity of the assimilation of all non-charter-group immigrants and natives.

One of the most peculiar and interesting of Gordon's novels is *The Gaspards of Pine Croft* (1923). In one sense its theme is that of a man's immoral past catching up with him and destroying his life, just as it did for the Don in *The Prospector*. A terrible nemesis strikes down Hugh Gaspard too, but in another sense this book is Gordon's statement about half-breeds.

The book opens with Hugh Gaspard, ethnically a French-Scotch combination, living happily with his Scotch wife and three-quarters Scotch son, Paul, in a remote valley in British Columbia. Suddenly his Chippewayan mistress of over half a decade before appears to confront him with his half-breed son, Peter. Onawata came for help for her son but as soon as she discovers that Hugh is married she considerately leaves. She is no savage but a sensitive woman with dignity and integrity—in part because of her mission education, for she had before that been "an ignorant squaw whose rights and wrongs could be estimated in terms purely materialistic."[37] When Hugh's wife discovers these remnants of his past she dies of shock, forgiving him on her deathbed and loading him unbearably with guilt. In despair the escapist Hugh runs off, leaving Paul to be brought up very properly by the patrician British family of Colonel Pelham, his neighbour. Three years later Hugh returns with Onawata as his wife, and another baby, Timma. He becomes a drunk and is contrasted with his upright son. Hugh's downfall and death is partly caused by his own moral weakness, partly by his renunciation of Presbyterianism, and partly by his own half-breed make-up. This last can hardly be underestimated as a factor in the plot. Gordon supports the then popular notion that miscegenation inexorably lowers the innate standards of the superior race to the level of the inferior—the race suicide that Madison Grant warned against in *The Passing of the Great Race*. Gordon has Hugh muse on the gloomy prospects of his own half-breed son, Peter:

> Too often inheriting the weaknesses and vices of both races, he was the derelict of the borderland of civilisation. Settled down upon the land, as in the Red River Valley, he could climb to strength and honour

36 Ibid., p. 164.
37 Charles W. Gordon, *The Gaspards of Pine Croft* (New York: George H. Doran, 1923), p. 34.

among the white race. Roving the plains and the woods with the tribes, he frequently sank beneath their level, more easily accessible to the vices of the white man, unable and unwilling to attain to the splendid and unspoiled nobility of the red man in his native wilds.[38]

For Gordon, half-breeds are racial cul-de-sacs, errors in the divine scheme. There is little understanding of the social prejudice against half-breeds, especially Indian half-breeds, which he is reflecting and which created their unfortunate predicament. Instead Gordon implied that half-breeds are innately inferior and fated to be unhappy failures, and that people should stick to their own kind. Neither Peter nor Timma ages enough in this novel to contribute to this lesson, but the one other half-breed in the cast is a vicious murderer.

The Indians and the whites (with the exception of Hugh, who is part French, and the by now inevitable Germanic villain whose name, Sleeman, is so sinister, represent the two racial polarities which may not be connected. Gordon rules out miscegenation for both sides, refusing even to consider the positive benefits it might be presumed to bring to the Indians. The "pure" Chippewayans, who receive very sympathetic treatment at Gordon's hands in this novel, are fugitives in the bush, maintaining their own integrity only at a distance from white civilization. Gordon praises Onawata's noble father, a chief who tried to minimize contacts between whites and his people: "He permitted no mingling of blood strains in his tribe, no half-breed could find a home in his wigwam."[39] The nobility of these Indians is undercut by their acceptance of their defeat, and their convenient removal of their own remains. It is safe to rhapsodize over them at a distance, and Gordon does so as he posts his warning that the children of interracial love are doomed. He does admit that, while these Indians are pagans (except Onawata), they have a right to worship the same God in their own way, a considerable advance for him and one that probably reflects the anthropological respect for Indians that resulted from the work of Jenness and Barbeau, which began to be published during the 1914-18 war. However, he still assigns Indians unfortunately chosen adjectives such as "savage," a practice which further undercuts his odd insistence on native nobility. It is noteworthy that Hugh's ranch-hand, Indian Tom, is a faithful servant and bushcraft mentor for Paul as he grows up, just as Black Hawk was for Rene La Flamme in *The Runner*. Gordon's Indians remain henchmen, cast in various menial roles to support their white masters.

38 Ibid., pp. 36-37.
39 Ibid., p. 51. In a short story published a few years later, "Red and White" (1926), Nellie McClung picked up on this theme, implying that contacts with whites could only degrade and ultimately destroy the Indians, whose only hope for survival lay in retreat to the bush. N. McClung, "Red and White," in *All We Like Sheep* (Toronto: Thomas Allen, 1926), pp. 128-75.

In his last novel, Gordon tried to come to terms with anti-Semitism, once again against the German threat, but his ubiquitous prejudices undermined what was probably a sincere attempt to help Jewish-Canadians rise above discrimination. In *The Gay Crusader* (1936) he included positive Jewish-Canadian characters (refugees from Germany) and even entertained the possibility of a Scotch Presbyterian-German Jewish marriage. He deliberately contrasted German brutality against Jews with British and Canadian acceptance of them. Gordon emphasized that anti-Semitism was unchristian, and he associated it not surprisingly with Germany, in the person of Schmelling, an obnoxious German-American journalist. However, Gordon's depiction of the Jewish Storm family in Canada is awkward and stereotypical, particularly stressing their over-emotional reactions. The father, Nathan, states that in his fifteen years in Canada he has never encountered anti-Semitism personally, and that he believes it to be alien to the Canadian character. However, in an apparent contradiction, his daughter, Judith, is supposed to have been made quite aware of it throughout her life. A marriage between Judith and Paul MacDonald is potentially prepared but falls through because of religious objections (from the Protestant side) and, conveniently, Paul's love for another—an English Protestant. Gordon thus avoids capping his career as a minister by marrying a Jew and a Christian. The point that such a marriage could have made, as indeed it would make in Gwethalyn Graham's *Earth and High Heaven* (1944) eight years later, is considerably diminished by Gordon's lack of courage to see it through. It is further undermined when he ends the book by strangely comparing the Americans' responsibility for the Depression with the Jews' responsibility for their own Diaspora: "The sin that drove the Hebrew people into eternal exile was not that they crucified their Messiah, but that in their mad lust for wealth and in their proud scorn of other peoples, they completely ignored that eternal law of co-operation."[40]

Gordon's attitude towards Jews was not just ambivalent. It was quite as illogical, confusing, and incomplete as most of his views, especially concerning race, and this failure of logic is complemented by his ignorance of other peoples and his negligent propensity for employing stereotypes which too often conformed to popular opinion and thus reinforced racist myths and theories. Disapproving of events in Germany, and conscious of the basic humanity of the Jews, and even more conscious of the need for Canadian society to accept the slow-to-assimilate Jews, he produced this extremely tolerant (for him, and for his time) novel which nonetheless indirectly reveals his patronizing and qualified perspective. The Storms are acceptable as Canadians because they do nothing that English-Canadians would not do

40 Charles W. Gordon, *The Gay Crusader* (Toronto: McClelland & Stewart, 1936), pp. 337-38.

and there is no sense of their religious culture at all. They are virtually Anglo-Saxon Protestants, as it is only as such that Gordon would accept them as potential Canadians.

III

The popularity and sheer quantity of Gordon's work doubtless meant that his ideas reached a good many people, but he was not the only one to express English-Canadian race-consciousness or anti-Semitism in Canadian literature. John Murray Gibbon, in 1921 the first President of the Canadian Authors' Association and later the manager of the CPR's immigration scheme, took a great deal of interest in what is now called multiculturalism. Unlike Gordon, Gibbon felt that immigrants added spice and interest to Canada, and that some allowance should be made for their cultural traditions while they assimilated politically into the English-Canadian system. A conservative politically himself, he drew upon his student experiences in Europe to defend continental immigrants against charges of immorality and unhygenic customs. One of his articles, "The Foreign Born" in *Queen's Quarterly* (1920), attempted to allay charter-group fears about their new neighbours and, like Woodsworth, he called for more enlightened assistance for them, particularly in cities where Bolshevism was considered to be a threat. Gibbon wrote several studies describing an ideal multiculturally unified nation, in which he set out the advantages of having such disparate cultures fusing together in Canada. His role in organizing the exotic Handicraft Festivals in Western Canada in the early 1920s plus his European residency gave him considerable knowledge in this area. Yet in his historical and sociological studies as well as in his less successful fiction he consistently displayed a vehemently anti-Semitic attitude as well as the sympathy for eugenics mentioned above. Most notably, in the middle of *The Conquering Hero*, an otherwise conventional and mediocre novel, Gibbon unnecessarily inserts a scene of powerful anti-Semitism quite unrelated to the plot. While travelling by train to New York, Hector, a stereotypical manly English-Canadian businessman, confronts a Jew:

> a bagman of hyphenated Hebrew ancestry whose efforts in worming himself ahead had not escaped Hector's watchful eye, tried to slip past them. Hector, however, successfully intervened his burly form, so the Hebrew tried to bluster—
> "I am a shentlemans just as you, and I have a friend who is keeping a seat for me, I tell you."
> "Nothing doing," said Hector, and held his ground.
> The Hebrew became more noisy until Hector remarked loud enough for everyone to hear:

"All right, Ikey. This is the breakfast car, not the Promised Land."[41]

This short and senseless interjection is the most blatant expression of anti-Semitism in this early fiction. It accomplishes nothing but the perpetuation of interracial animosity. Gibbon maintained these feelings long after Nazi persecution of Jews made anti-Semitism unfashionable in Canada. In *The New Canadian Loyalists* (1941), a wartime survey of immigrants' fidelity to the Allied cause, he continued to imply the unassimilability of Jews.

The word "white" had a meaning in the novels of Gordon, Gibbon, and Stead beyond colour. To call a man "white" was to praise him as a fair and honest man of integrity. Their use of the word implied that Britons had a monopoly of such virtues and that such behaviour could hardly be expected of non-whites. Jews and certain Mediterranean peoples were generally not considered truly white, in either sense of the word. In Gibbon's *The Conquering Hero* Donald, the English-Canadian hero, when asked if his friend the Polish princess is Jewish, replies bluntly: "No, white."[42] The use of this word casually or deliberately further stressed the subdivision of humanity below the British ethnocentric standard.

Prejudice against immigrants was not restricted to non-Britons. There was considerable feeling expressed by the English-Canadian community against newly arrived British immigrants that can now be explained by reference to class. The class of immigrant, British or not, that was desired was lower-class farm workers, or at least people who would and could farm. The arrival of other classes with more cosmopolitan and urban ambitions was resented. The protectionist platform was re-designed to obstruct upper-class and unsuitable immigrants. They were ridiculed for habits and expectations inconsistent with pioneer life. The remittance man became a Western joke, but the "No English Need Apply" qualifications in job advertisements testified to the seriousness of the feeling. It was suggested, by Stead in "The Son of Marquis Noodle," by W. Jarvis in *Letters of a Remittance Man* (1907), and even by F. P. Grove in a very uncharacteristic short story, "The Extra Man," that the manual labour of homesteading was the proper way for such Britons to acquire the manly attributes which constituted Canadian nationality. It is worthwhile noting that those three authors as well as J. S. Woodsworth and Charles Gordon had not homesteaded themselves and were in fact members of the post-pioneering superstructure in the West, providing education, religion, and journalism. They would profit from encouraging the toil of others. Of course, this is not racism but class tension; it becomes racism when it deals with ethnically diverse peoples, but even then its roots in class rivalry are obvious.

41 Gibbon, *The Conquering Hero*, p. 106.
42 Ibid., p. 148.

Robert Stead's fiction was strongly protectionist, elaborating on the theme of his early poem, "The Mixer," quoted above on page 29. In his novels *The Homesteaders* (1916) and *The Cow Puncher* (1918) the lament for the handout of valuable Canadian land to unknown and unworthy immigrants is continued. After the war, however, his antagonism to non-British newcomers appeared to moderate, and by 1922, in *Neighbours*, he could describe a Russian settler's chances of success optimistically:

> Sneezit was on the road to independence! The drab curtain of oppression which had hung about the Sneezits since the beginning of their race he had torn in two, and through the rent his grizzled face beheld a world of hope and promise, a world in which he was as good as his neighbour![43]

Despite his mockery of Sneezit's unmanageable real name, this pioneer "sheepskin" family is sincerely praised for its industry, asceticism, and adaptation to the demands of pioneer life in Western Canada. The Sneezits, however, are white, untainted by the semi-white status accorded popularly to Italians and Turks, for example. Russians, like Galicians, were generously accepted as whites *and* as victims of centuries of tyranny and despotism which had prevented them from keeping up with their more progressive fellow-whites in Britain. While Stead's formerly staunch Anglo-Canadian and British standards had relaxed enough to thus enlarge his definition of whites after the war, he still drew a line at Orientals. In both *The Cow Puncher* and *Denison Grant* (1920) he depicted Chinese houseboys in the service of wealthy WASPs. In *The Cow Puncher* the servant is described in strikingly negative terms:

> Dave pressed a button, and a Chinese boy (all male Chinese are boys) entered, bowing in that deference which is so potent to separate the white man from his silver. The white man glories in being salaamed, especially by an Oriental, who can grovel with a touch of art. And the Oriental has not been slow to capitalize his master's vanity.[44]

Such derogatory statements are part of the low background level of contempt for foreigners that persists throughout Stead's work. The employment of Oriental and black domestics is frequently seen in Canadian fiction of this type and time, and probably reflects accurately one aspect of their place in Canadian society then. This reflection is from the point of view of English-Canadian wealth which required not only servants but, in true Imperial fashion, exotic coloured servants. One seldom finds such servants "of colour" in later works of realism, as the focus shifted away from the plutocracy to the servant class itself, and eventually in an about face in

43 Robert J. C. Stead, *Neighbours* (Toronto: Hodder & Stoughton, 1922), p. 166
44 Robert J. C. Stead, *The Cow Puncher* (Toronto: Musson, 1918), p. 169.

the 1970s we find Austin Clarke writing novels from the perspective of a black maid. In Stead's case, when he goes out of his way to provide coloured stereotypes and accompanies them with overtly racist remarks, then something other than mere historical and sociological accuracy is being attempted. Stead's work not only contains but also proselytizes his racially discriminatory beliefs about non-whites, and when he used the adjective "white," as he did increasingly after 1916, it must have been with this in mind.

Doubtless the most vitriolic example of racist fiction ever to appear in Canada was Hilda G. Howard's *The Writing on the Wall*, first published under the pen-name of Hilda Glynn-Ward by the *Vancouver Sun* in 1921 and reissued in 1974 by the University of Toronto Press as a historical curiosity. A Welsh immigrant to British Columbia herself, she took up the defence of this the white man's country by attempting to expose the terrible habits and machinations of Orientals seeking to take over the land for themselves. Set entirely in Vancouver and along the coast northwards, the novel is in three unequal parts. The first is set in the past (1910) and shows how the Orientals undermined white society by playing on the greed and vices of various leaders. The second part is in the present (1920) and shows events leading up to the question of granting Orientals the vote in British Columbia, the actual issue which seems to have driven the author to take up her pen. The sell-out of land, resources, and power to the wily Orientals is practically accomplished. In the third part, largely a nightmare in the mind of the Lieutenant Governor who is under pressure to sign a bill permitting Oriental landowners the right to vote, a vision of the future is constructed in which the province is entirely controlled by Chinese and Japanese who ignore the now hapless whites and fight among themselves for power. The Lieutenant Governor wakes up to the dangers of the bill and, inspired by his enthusiastically racist wife, vows to do all he can to keep British Columbia white.

This poorly written but well-organized novel elaborates on popular opinion on the West Coast for complete exclusion of Asiatics. Howard was far less concerned with the Christian or moral dangers of outright racial hatred than Gordon was, and she lacked either the will or the ability to conceal her prejudices as he tried to do. Her opinions were extreme, alarmist, and desperate. The main factual objections she raised against Orientals included their unhealthy habit of fertilizing their vegetable gardens with night soil, their white slavery, their opium dens, and their general immorality and duplicity. The Japanese are shown illegally landing immigrants en masse in isolated coastal areas and charting the coast for military purposes. The Chinese are shown bribing the authorities to overlook large numbers of new arrivals in collusion with short-sighted capitalists who require cheap labour. However, these and other similar arguments, some of which were based on rumours and actual events current in the public mind, were less important than the primary one that Canada was and should be a white man's country and that Orientals could never be Canadians.

In emphasizing the dangers of the Oriental presence in British Columbia Mrs. Howard went too far and her warning loses ground in part because of its fanatical irrationality. If the book is to make sense the Orientals must be a credible menace, but she makes the whites seem like foolish children, easily manipulated and despoiled. In fact, almost all the white Canadians in the novel are weak and gullible individuals, whereas the clever Orientals are credited with showing more natural intelligence and industry than whites, as one white character complains bitterly:

> They were bad enough when they were kept under as labour, but now they're getting education along with our own, they're a million times worse! They're uppish now, you even see that in the yellow brats coming out of school; they're cleverer than us and they know it and *you and I know it too*! Specially the Japs, you'll see them at the top 'o the class and the white kids at the bottom every time.[45]

The objection to their becoming "uppish now" is the same as Gordon's objection to Jews above for their "proud scorn of other peoples"; it was reprehensible for it competed with opposing feelings of English-Canadians. However, in Howard's book there is no claim to innate white superiority, apart from suggestions of a higher morality. The intelligence and common sense of the whites is minimized in every way, and were it not for the malicious and sinister ways of the Orientals this book would raise little sympathy for the whites ensnared in their own greedy enterprises. The hostile climate of opinion at the time in British Columbia must account for the acceptance by the *Vancouver Sun* of a dogmatic book so excessively rabid in expressing its points that from this distance it seems to destroy its own case by overkill and to actually promote the opposition.

Mrs. Howard's obvious bias creates an extremely interesting situation in the third part. The hypothetical future (with its surprising prerequisite of an independent British Columbia) shows Vancouver taken over by Orientals. Chinese control the city officially and even hold down positions of authority on road gangs. They own the best houses and monopolize the commercial life. Whites are reduced to working under them as manual labourers, can expect no help from the police (who are also Chinese), and are being forced out of the country. This invented dream situation was meant to shock those who could take it seriously. Interestingly, however, the dream actually reverses the actual roles of whites and Orientals then. In postulat-

---

45 Hilda G. Howard (pseud. Hilda Glynn-Ward), *The Writing on the Wall* (Vancouver: Vancouver Sun, 1921; rpt. University of Toronto Press, 1974), p. 85.

ing the total white subservience to Orientals in British Columbia, Howard was unconsciously describing in the manner of a photographic negative the actual inequitable situation of the Oriental immigrant. The injustice of her one-sided view escaped her entirely. There is no sense of any real understanding of Orientals as people. There is only a blind and desperately protectionist set of apprehensions quite similar to those which motivated Gobineau. This, the most racist book in Canadian fiction, provides the low water mark against which any positive achievements of literature in the area of race relations may be measured.

In contrast to Mrs. Howard's negative work, Nellie McClung provided a positive study of non-charter-group assimilation in *Painted Fires* (1925), a novel that comes close to being an updated post-war version of Gordon's *The Foreigner*. The title refers to illusions which fail to satisfy. Canada is shown to be full of them.

The novel concentrates on a single Finnish girl who leaves Finland to emigrate to the New World, ending up in Winnipeg. Suddenly deprived of the help she had expected from relatives, this character provides McClung with the opportunity to philosophize on the plight and perils of the single girl. Helmi is a very capable young woman whose subsequent troubles are largely because of her slow acquisition of English, her exaggerated sense of honour, and her lack of understanding of Canadian ways. McClung also blames Canadians for misunderstanding and exploiting immigrants.

The official scapegoat for the labour unrest in Canada which culminated in the Winnipeg General Strike in 1919 was the foreign agitator. A number of immigrants from Russia and the Ukraine were deported, while Finns were suspected of Bolshevik contamination as well. Helmi's slow rise to success, despite its sad setbacks, is contrasted with the failure of Anna, a truly Marxist Finn who also is against more immigration because of its depressing effect on wages. Anna ends up in jail for assaulting a policeman and Helmi learns that Marxism is only a "painted fire." As a democrat she disproves her Canadian friend's idea that "Finns are naturally red. . . ."[46] Helmi is certainly not a socialist and her character is presented in such strong and positive terms that it makes up for the difficulties in which her poor English lands her. Despite these troubles, such as being sentenced to three months in a reformatory on a false charge by a magistrate who seems incredibly prejudiced against "foreigners," Helmi (suddenly in perfect English!) immediately and patriotically declares for Canada on the outbreak of war: " 'Canada is my country,' Helmi replied, with flashing eyes, 'and I would fight for it if I could. I wouldn't hang back like a big coward.' "[47] Like Gordon, McClung seems to have evaluated Canadian spirit by the extent of a person's belligerency and combativeness. Helmi is prodigiously

46 Nellie McClung, *Painted Fires* (Toronto: Thomas Allen, 1925), p. 69.
47 Ibid., p. 200.

strong, humble, morally upright, and quite clean. These characteristics McClung presents as Finnish qualities to show how desirable Finns are as immigrants and how wrong prejudice against them is.

Painted Fires is a good attempt at defending immigrants against unfounded prejudices, despite its weaknesses as literature, but it shares some of the weaknesses of Gordon's *The Foreigner*, notably the unconvincing characterization of immigrants. Negligible information is provided either about Finland or the Finnish people. After her arrival in Winnipeg Helmi shows few signs of ever having been Finnish. Her problems could be those of any immigrant with a minimal command of English. She arrives alone and remains independent and even ignorant of the Finnish-Canadian community. Her religion is ignored and her eventual success is dependent upon her marriage with an English-Canadian. Her experience seems atypical.

The book has positive aspects in that, at a time when Finns were attracting undue attention as socialist agitators, a popular novelist made a heroine out of one and showed her to be a woman much the same as English-Canadian women. Nevertheless, like Kalman in *The Foreigner*, Helmi turns her back entirely on her European past in favour of the ideal Canadian life. Like Gordon, McClung disinfected her immigrant protagonist in order to appease English-Canadian anxieties about their future.

The English-Canadian concept of Canadian society was definitely a uniquely Canadian product. Although the British were the most favoured ethnic group, there was enough prejudice against them too to make evident the fact that English-Canadians were conscious of vague differences between them. Some of this was class consciousness, and some was the result of an emergent sense of ethnocentric pride. In *Home is the Stranger* (1950) Edward McCourt illustrated his title by writing about the "strangeness" experienced by an Irish-English war bride brought to a prairie community. By this time an author could suggest that Canadians had finally produced for themselves an original temperament consistent with a new type of land and living conditions. This contrasts noticeably with Gordon's dream of a virile, new, classless nation which he nevertheless described along the lines of too many Old World customs of the past. In *The Foreigner* Canadian society was assumed to have achieved a more or less unchangeable form to which non-charter groups would have to adapt, and that form is scarcely distinguishable from the idealized Scotland which appears in some of Gordon's other novels. There is a strong feeling of stagnation in Gordon's work, suggesting that although the society is growing it is not changing, as in fact he did not want it to change. The English-Canadian point of view tried to immobilize the dynamics of social change, in part to maintain their privileged position and in part doubtless out of a sense of comfort with established ways. Furthermore, this attitude depended upon ignorance of other peoples, and the desire to simplify external complications which did not directly appear to affect local circumstances. The automatic extension of suspicion of Bolshevik sympathies to all Russians and Ukrainians as well as to Finns, after 1917, is such a simplification. In part this seems to be the product of a desire for clear-cut definitions, of ethnicity as well as everything else. Writers such as Gordon accepted Galicians as Russians, whereas they were just as likely to be from Germany or Austria-Hungary, and were certainly different from Russians. The demand for simplicity and stasis and English-Canadian supremacy, in all social and political ways, constituted a narrow-minded upper-class attitude peculiar to the Canadian situation in the first quarter of the century. Yet after the 1914-18 war the old order changed quickly and a new sense of national identity emerged, one which did not ignore or superciliously suppress non-charter-group cultures but which had to take them into account just as the new nation states of Central Europe had to be respected. The English-Canadian monopoly was infiltrated from below by the very process of assimilation it had tried to supervise, and new voices began to be heard.

Chapter Three

The Immigrant Reaction Before 1939

The Wasp is *everyone's* target now. Or didn't you know it? According
to you—or according to what you do on the program—every Wasp is
guilty until he's proved innocent.

> Esther, in *Voices in Time*, by Hugh MacLennan

The literature produced by English-Canadian writers such as Gordon,
Gibbon, and Stead may be viewed as a literature of defence, erected to
protect class interests that superseded definition merely by class to include
qualities of ethnicity which themselves were viewed as aspects of race.
Definitely hostile to outsiders, these writers at times took the offensive (in
every sense of the word), producing literature promoting political, social,
and moral ideals in a comprehensive cultural package which was to be
arbitrarily imposed upon all inhabitants of Canada, ostensibly for their own
good. The English-Canadian attempt to monopolize literature as a step
towards monopolizing Canadian society began after 1919 to be opposed by
immigrants increasingly articulate in English. In many ways this English-
Canadian view of race, its condescending racism having been unchallenged
for the first two decades of the century, now came under attack from its
victims. A vigorous literature of defence, in the same way that Gordon's
fiction was essentially defensive by its fundamental protectionist foundations, began to appear. This new literature presented a fragmented defence,
in that the various immigrant "groups" each had their own sense of
superiority which competed with the same feelings held by English-
Canadians. Self-defence became a more visible characteristic of Canadian

55

literature as a whole. The New-Canadian defence led towards a dialectic between the two opposing ideals which eventually forced a synthesis. The allegedly inferior races began to speak for themselves in print, compelling the establishment of much-needed communication links between both sides and doing away with self-appointed interpreters such as Gordon. Canadian literature began to fulfil its potential as a catalyst for the eradication of racism. Until then the silence of non-charter-groups had been taken as evidence of their inferiority, in the same way that lack of defence is always considered a sign of weakness and an opportunity for exploitation. With the work of Grove and Salverson before World War Two, and with that of Lysenko, Richler, and Clarke after it, the entire set of assumptions that English-Canadians had publicized about non-charter-group Canadians were challenged. The prejudices were not quickly overturned, but they were so sufficiently discredited and weakened that they played less of a role in society than before. Prejudices combatted each other, and as a result a composite sense of Canadian identity began to emerge.

The publication in non-fictional works and periodicals as well as in fiction of evidence of "alien" capabilities in areas thought to be the preserve of Anglo-Saxons corroded the old biases. The sanctimonious view that immigrants from everywhere except Great Britain must be wildly happy to leave their impoverished and oppressed homelands gradually gave way before the testimonials to the cultures, the history, and the people left behind. Because of books such as Laura Salverson's *The Viking Heart* (1923), English-Canadians began to realize that not all immigrants arrived humbly ecstatic about escaping from their homes. While the English-Canadian concept of farming (often presented in fiction by men who had never farmed) largely downplayed environmental hardships, the new voices of immigrants who could express themselves in English complained volubly about the unsuitable land they had been given and the terribly hard living conditions they had not expected to encounter. It became known that Canada was not good enough for some New Canadians, as thousands left. Until the twenties most English-Canadians seemed to have looked down on many immigrants (depending on their origins) as simply "hewers of wood and drawers of water," who must be force-fed British ideals in the hope that they might change. The cultural baggage that many immigrants brought with them, again well described by Salverson in *Confessions of an Immigrant's Daughter* (1939), began to be better known by English-Canadians who had formerly seen little cultural or intellectual behaviour on their part. In Canada the struggle for respect by "ethnic" writers soon became sufficiently vigorous to resist surrender to these pressures.

Frederick Philip Grove was one of the first of these writers who acted as spokesmen for the immigrants. It was not a priority for him, as he certainly concentrated on other, more important themes, but it was a role he did attempt to fulfil. His noble-sounding conclusion to *A Search for America* indicates his awareness of the problems of immigrants and the valuable assistance that an altruistic middleman such as himself could provide:

> When I arrived there [Winnipeg], I had a number of interviews. I wanted to go to foreign settlements and help recent immigrants to build their partial views of America into total views; I wanted to assist them in realizing their promised land.[1]

His interest was probably sincere, and not entirely a literary pose nor an acceptance of the inevitable with gracious hindsight. If *A Search for America* and *In Search of Myself* can be believed at all, his own difficulties in acclimatizing himself to the New World had given him some firsthand experience of the treatment of immigrants and the prejudices of Anglo-Saxons. His change of name and assumption of a Swedish ethnic alias, although doubtless prompted mainly by a natural desire to escape from his disreputable past, may indicate also his appreciation of anti-German prejudice in Canada, while his marriage to a Mennonite must have broadened his appreciation of the problems of minorities in Canada as elsewhere.[2] The number of immigrants in his prose testify to his concern with their plight, as well as to his refusal to support the romantic English-Canadian interpretation of settlement and assimilation, possibly because of the notable absence of realistically portrayed immigrants in Canadian literature as a whole at the time he arrived in Manitoba and until after *Settlers of the Marsh* (1925). To Grove must be given the credit for breaking the English-Canadian monopoly in Canadian literature by validating the experiences of "aliens" as equal to those of charter-group Canadians in terms of their significance collectively as human beings. He did it largely from an assumed British point of view which he coated with enough layers of continental European sophistication that ingratiated him with the English-Canadians who suffered from a cultural inferiority complex. As far as Grove was concerned, humanity could be divided into two categories— austere pioneers working their land directly, and non-pioneer consumers dissipating their lives in luxuries. Yet complementing this simplistic and somewhat spartan ontology was a more or less conscious philosophy of race. Like Gordon, Grove not only expressed a conscious attitude towards race in

---

1 Frederick P. Grove, *A Search for America* (Ottawa: Graphic Publishers, 1927), p. 448.
2 Grove's alias has been commented upon by D. O. Spettigue: "His early teaching assignments, at Haskett, Winkler, and Virden were all in German Mennonite districts, where Grove himself was recognized for a German. At the time of his marriage in 1914 to Catharine Wiens, herself of German stock, her family accepted him as German. She assured me that, because their marriage took place just before World War One began, he had had to claim himself Swedish in order to avoid suspicion—a move which was not entirely successful." D. O. Spettigue, Introduction, *In Search of Myself*, by Frederick P. Grove (Toronto: McClelland and Stewart, 1974), p. xi.

his writings with some deliberation, but also imbued his fiction with a subconscious and apparently contradictory attitude. Also like Gordon, Grove's attitude was often narrowly regional and limited, and the contradictions it contained revealed logical flaws rather than potentially significant paradoxes.

From *Settlers of the Marsh* onwards, Grove's West is populated with European aliens or non-native settlers, mainly Russo-Germans, Swedes, Icelanders, and Britons. In fact, the settlers of the marsh themselves are all aliens. However, it is in his short stories, including those never published, and in two non-fiction articles published in *Maclean's*, that Grove's attitude to race and his assistance to immigrants in carving a place for them in Canadian literature and ultimately in a multicultural Canada, can best be seen.

A concise summary of Grove's racial theory concerning established Canadians and immigrants is provided by two articles he wrote at the time of his popular speaking tours across Canada and published in *Maclean's* in 1928 and 1929. He wrote what amounted to sermons aimed at negating the Anglo-Saxon sense of superiority over aliens. He attacked the concept of pure races and encouraged the idea of blending different peoples in Canada. Somewhat prematurely in 1928 he claimed: "The Anglo-Saxon is constitutionally opposed to the narrow theory which places a value on pure racial strains." He recognized that English-Canadian ethnocentrism was the biggest obstacle to the successful integration (not "melting") of aliens into Canadian society as a whole.[3] In fact he chided the English for their aloofness, claiming that the en bloc settlements of foreigners were one result of this snobbish behaviour:

> The British will not mingle with them. Why not? From one single reason: from racial conceit. It is a very strange, and, to us New Canadians, very incomprehensible, but none the less indisputable fact that the average Anglo-Saxon considers himself superior to all the other races of the world, individually the more so the less reason he has. . . . I have lived in mixed districts where small Anglo-Saxon minorities sat like an army of occupation in conquered territory within solidly Ukrainian, Russo-German, or Scandinavian settlements. It was they—that is, the first generation of British immigrants—who held aloof, not the foreigners, unless they were provoked.[4]

3 Frederick P. Grove, "Canadians Old and New," *Maclean's* 41, No. 6 (1928), p. 56. Grove dismissed the melting pot theory, as he addressed the New Canadians further: "This country does not claim to be a 'melting pot.' What it does claim is that in it there 'are many mansions'—and one of them, undoubtedly, is the mansion that has been waiting precisely for you" (p. 56).

4 Frederick P. Grove, "Assimilation," *Maclean's* (Sept. 1, 1929), p. 75.

Grove exposed the English-Canadian ideal of assimilation for what it was—an attempt to force aliens into becoming English-Canadian copies and denying their antecedents. Critical of the melting pot's products, and acutely conscious of European cultural benefits made available to Canada by the immigrants, he espoused a vague plan for a "federation" of nationalities, possibly anticipating a politically defined form of multiculturalism. In all this he appeared to be promoting a tolerant and humane plan of internationalist accommodation which would suit his own future ideal of Canada—a strong community of ascetically industrious producers of necessities.[5] His plan was introspectively Canadian, even Western Canadian, in that it was qualified by certain racist reservations which he considered necessary but almost hypothetical because of their inapplicability to most of Canada and certainly to the prairies. While Grove felt that Europeans of differing nationalities were more or less equal, it is clear that some other races were believed to be unassimilable, but that fortunately the isolation of the prairies made the possibility of trials unlikely. In hypothesizing God's plans for Canada's future, Grove wrote:

> I will make that northern division [Canada] part of a great empire in which slowly, slowly the principle of federation is to work itself out among distant nations that have no immediate contact, among nations which are too different to admit of even the dream of assimilation: Hindus, Kaffirs, Afrikanders, and Malays.[6]

His view became more unpleasantly clear when he wondered further if perhaps the various white groups in North America would eventually be forced to join forces against "the menace held over it by a colored race; merging its national quarrels in a common enmity."[7] Grove's literary contribution to closer interracial relationships was restricted to the white race. Contemptuous of divisions within its limits, he remained nevertheless conscious of a threat to its supremacy from without. He seemed to be in agreement with his unnamed European friends whom he claimed in his essay, "A Neglected Function," to be "nearly all of them viewing the phenomena observable in any given country from the wider view-point of a leadership on earth of the white race, as opposed to the leadership of this or that special nation within that race."[8] He did not elaborate, as these ideas were superfluous to his own view of Canada as a white man's country, and were only expressed as asides. Even aboriginal Canadians were ignored

---

5 By the time of *The Master of the Mill* (1944), Grove had realized that utopian pioneer communities and even small farms had been replaced or made superfluous by new technological demands and inventions.

6 Grove, "Assimilation," p. 79.

7 Ibid. This article was written after a decade of violent race riots in the United States.

8 Frederick P. Grove, "A Neglected Function," *It Needs to Be Said* (Toronto: Macmillan of Canada, 1929), pp. 7-8.

completely in his fiction, where Canadian history begins with the first turning of the sod by a white pioneer. Grove's otherwise admirable sense of the spiritual wholeness and mutual responsibility of humanity was racially qualified to apply to whites only.

Grove's contribution towards the realistic presentation of the alien immigrant in English-dominated society was considerable, opposing as it did the limited prejudice then current. This is most apparent in the unpublished short stories which, like their better known counterparts edited by Desmond Pacey and published under the title *Tales From the Margin* (1971), provide a degree of background for the novels.

Many of Grove's unpublished stories deal with Russo-German immigrants. (The term refers not to persons of dual nationality or mixed ethnicity, but simply to German colonists in Russia.) Possibly a Russo-German himself by birth, Grove made a point of distinguishing between German ex-colonists from Russia and Germans straight from Germany. His stories present mainly Russo-German and Swedish farmers and labourers in interaction with the established administrative superstructure. One unpublished story, whose title, "Foreigners," is possibly a deliberate contrast with Gordon's novel, is the most extreme example of such interaction. It describes the visit of an English-Canadian official (from Grove's point of view he might just as well have been called an official English-Canadian), Archibald Bryan, to a bush school in a "foreign" district to investigate the ratepayers' complaints against the teacher, a Miss Albright, whose cosmopolitan behaviour has provoked unrest.[9] Some of the ratepayers have little ability in English, and some had been disenfranchised because of the war, despite their being naturalized, as Grove takes pains to point out. Nevertheless they know exactly what they want, and their demands are

9 Frederick P. Grove, "Foreigners," The Grove Collection, University of Manitoba, Box 13, pp. 60-70. The dissatisfaction voiced by such ratepayers against teachers who after all were representing English-Canadian ideals (similar to the communal fears the Mennonites develop against Razia in Wiebe's *Peace Shall Destroy Many*) is interesting as one side of the coin. Although it must be said that Grove did (as Wiebe would later) present both sides fairly and with some sensitivity, his sympathies were for the ratepayers defending their own cultural mores. This protest should be seen in the context of the crusade that Protestant religious leaders (Woodsworth and Gordon included) mounted against the foreign communities ostensibly to save their souls but actually to make them conform. Religious periodicals of the time glorified those English-Canadians who went to foreign settlements to teach (often because of personal financial concerns), while educators praised in secular terms the lonely teacher who singlehandedly could drag communities of aliens into Canada's century. For example, see W. G. Smith, *A Study in Canadian Immigration* (Toronto: Ryerson Press, 1920), pp. 397-98; Robert England, *The Central European Immigrant in Canada* (Toronto: Macmillan of Canada, 1929); Mary Howard, "This Work of Canadianizing. When Are We Going to Do It?" *Christian Guardian* 91, No. 3 (Jan. 21, 1920), 12; W. H. Pike, "Slavic Stock and the New Canadianism," *Christian Guardian* 90, No. 49 (Dec. 3, 1919), 10-11.

honest and reasonable. Bryan intolerantly overrides them and the meeting fails, as far as they are concerned. The issue is later settled, so that no one wins, when a brush fire probably set by the disgruntled ratepayers destroys the school and Miss Albright's house. Fire is the chief metaphor, symbolic of the destruction brought about by an unsympathetic bureaucracy arbitrarily oppressing foreigners. Hope is in the second growth, as it was for Gordon in his novel, *The Foreigner*, but this is so only because English-Canadians have refused to recognize the first growth. The story ends on a low note, as the destructive fire holds little promise for the future. One wonders how, without any school at all, the children of these ratepayers will ever be able to defend themselves constructively, but at least the parents have maintained their right to raise their children, instead of just giving in to English-Canadian ways, and the "lesson" of Gordon's novel is effectively countered. The story is a controlled complaint against unfair treatment of non-charter-group immigrants by the dominant group.

In other stories, notably "Lost" and "Water," the plight of German settlers unable to make a living on their marginal lands and barely surviving in hopeless poverty contrasted strongly with what could be called the "Canadian Dream": the myth of the successful pioneer. As the German character, Holznagel, recounts in "The Heir," "Here, most Englishers look down on us damn foreigners, even though they've asked us to come here. We're like cattle, good enough to do the hard work for them; but as for friendly intercourse, phew . . . they'd just as easy make friends with the horses and oxen they keep."[10] A related complaint is made by Kolm bitterly to Crawford in *The Yoke of Life*: "They tell us before we come to this country that they will give us free land. They don't tell us that what they really want is our free labour in clearing it and making it fit for human beings to live in."[11] Similar expressions of resentment appear also in "The Lumberjack" and especially in "The First Day of an Immigrant," in which Niels Lindstedt, just off the train, joins a threshing gang and earns their respect by his willingness to work hard. Still, he felt looked down upon:

> At dinner, in the house, he has become aware of a certain attitude towards himself, an attitude assumed by those who were unmistakably Canadian. After all . . . he is among strange people who look down upon him as if he were something inferior, something not to be taken as fully human. . . . He has heard Jim, the cynical, good-looking young fellow say something to a number of the men who, like Niels himself, were apparently recent immigrants. Jim had contemptuously addressed them as "You Galishans!" And it had been clear that they resented it. Niels does not quite see why they should; if they are

10 Frederick P. Grove, "The Heir," The Grove Collection, University of Manitoba, Box 15, pp. 15-19.
11 Frederick P. Grove, *The Yoke of Life* (Toronto: Macmillan of Canada, 1930), p. 56.

Galicians, why should they mind being called by that name? But he understands that what they really resent is the tone in which it was said.[12]

There is in this passage an appreciation of racism, but added to it eventually is the understanding that hard work in a pioneer community creates its own successes and acceptance, albeit to some extent qualified by one's attainment of English. In "The Marsh Fire," a story which expanded his fire symbolism to include the world war, Grove portrayed settlers of all nationalities co-operating to extinguish a threatening conflagration, their strength and endurance defining them as people beyond the luxuries of nationality.

In these stories Grove presented with considerable sympathy the Central-European immigrant's view of Canada and Canadians, which contrasts noticeably with the dominant view. He did so with considerable fairness, accepting the prefabricated English-Canadian sociological and cultural factors that dictated a certain authoritarian benevolence to their idea of assimilation. The European immigrants he wrote about were mostly farmers, better suited to represent his ideal of pioneer industry than the more flaccid and urbanized English, whose desperate protectionist fears are shown exposed in time of war. Grove did, in "The Deserter," suggest that German settlers in Canada were well aware of their good fortune in being out of the war, and had no intentions of treacherously sabotaging the Canadian home front. This is the closest he came in writing to protesting the wartime disenfranchisement of and discrimination against German-Canadians. It appears evident that he was attempting to counter obvious examples of unreasonable reaction against Germans, created by the British propaganda campaign, but he was too cautious to identify himself too closely with the situation, maintaining a detached and neutral perspective which befitted his assumed nationality. As in so many conflicts, Grove sought a superior synthesis and the freedom to judge in his original terms. Aware of the prejudice immigrants attracted, Grove moved to place himself above it. He did, however, describe the immigrants' predicament with controlled indignation, from a carefully chosen diplomatically affected Anglo-Saxon perspective.

When one becomes aware of Grove's sympathy for the immigrant, anti-Semitism seems an unfortunate oddity in his work, especially as there seems little enough reason to include Jews at all in his novels. When Grove, like Gordon, is seen to go out of his way to include negatively portrayed Jewish characters which remain unbalanced by positive ones, then anti-Semitism can be the only diagnosis.

12 Frederick P. Grove, "The First Day of an Immigrant," *Tales From the Margin*, ed. D. Pacey (Toronto: McGraw-Hill Ryerson, 1971), pp. 214-15.

A variety of Jewish businessmen populate the complete works. Two of the short stories, "Herefords in the Wilderness" and "Saturday Night at the Crossroads," contain the same man, Kalad, an Armenian Jewish rural storekeeper. In the latter, Kalad's crude enterprise is satirized for its weakly ironic imitation of the heroics of the pioneers it serves. The industry of his family is roughly denigrated by its obsessively materialist goals: "His wife, a short, fat Jewess, was his helpmate, shrilly driving her children to slave labour in the interests of material prosperity . . . her unsmiling voice spoke of one single aim in life, money. She was the personification of what the word 'hag' implies."[13] Their beautiful daughter flirts with a gentile but the narrator discounts the possibility of any union between them as he explains the apparent indifference of her parents: "There was no danger of leaving her free; for I divined in her that intense race-consciousness which is peculiar to Jews."[14] The second growth theory expressed in "Foreigners" is not large enough to include this girl, whose inherited avariciousness and clannish attributes seem enough to disqualify her as a Canadian. Greed and aversion to manual labour are also exemplified by Schweigel, "the Jew" who settles near Spalding's farm in *Fruits of the Earth* and who, it is implied, goes to offer Abe his vote in return for some fodder.[15] Mixing peddling with farming, and unashamed to beg for what he does not know enough to offer to work for, Schweigel is a grotesquely comic figure in the novel.

It is in *The Yoke of Life* (1930) that Jews openly present more menacing characteristics. The German settler, Kolm, is victimized by Jews who control the commerce of the entire area. They offer low prices for his crops and Baum, the unappealing storekeeper in the town, eventually maneuvers the honest farmer off his own farm.[16] The Jews are depicted as cunning vultures, taking advantage of seasonal weaknesses in the farmer's finances to exploit him mercilessly. While they do nothing illegal, the tone in which their mercenary activities is described casts them as villains. They are grasping and greedy. The hero, Len, at one point thinks of Baum:

13 Grove, "Saturday Night at the Crossroads," *Tales From the Margin*, pp. 53-54.
14 Ibid., p. 55.
15 Frederick P. Grove, *Fruits of the Earth* (Toronto: J. M. Dent and Sons, 1933), pp. 157-58. Abe makes no deal with Schweigel, simply providing charity, but "the Jew" offers to help in return with his vote.

    It is interesting to note that as much as Grove seemed repelled by the greed he attributed to Jews, he also found in them a degree of sensuality to admire. Schweigel himself is a physical caricature of a man, but his wife is very attractive, as is Ruth in "Saturday Night at the Crossroads," and as are Rosenbaum and Rosebaum in *The Master of the Mill* and "Jane Atkinson" (see note 19, below) respectively.

16 The scene after the loss of the farm, with Kolm defiant but defeated and reduced to where he had begun in Canada, is striking and almost mythical, in the modern cinematic sense of a poor family evicted by a wealthy (Jewish) businessman, with all their belongings in a cart and nowhere to go.

That man sat like an ogre on his money-chest. Len's whole being revolted.

Yet, the old Jew had sons; they were young. But even at that he felt repelled: racial prejudices gathered into an almost physical sense of aversion.[17]

Grove the author specifically explains this aversion in terms of "racial prejudices" in the same way that (Grove?) the narrator of "Saturday Night at the Crossroads" presents Kalad's daughter as protected by her "intense race-consciousness." Both sides are represented as victims of inherited antipathies related to their different races, and no solution which could bring them together is supplied or even admitted of. Grove limited himself to "the Jew" instead of Gordon's phrase, "the little Jew," consistently using it instead of names or even occupations to identify them as he does most of his other characters. Their importance to him was their Jewishness. It was not so much that he had a point to make about Jews (although in the process one was made), but that he used them in extremely negative ways to make positive points about non-Jews. His Jews are not farmers but urbanites and therefore second-rate anyway in Grove's estimation. They were somewhat foppish, often dressed immaculately and incongruously for the West. They were impolite and arrogant. They had superior education and manners. They appeared as parasites feeding upon the honest labour of real men. Just as much as Gordon had done in *The Foreigner* and *The Gay Crusader*, Grove perpetuated the popular myth of Jewish control over finances, in a particularly unpleasant manner. Even the vaguely unsettling characters of the Jewish bookkeepers in *A Search for America* and *The Yoke of Life* contribute to this impression.

In *A Search for America* it is clear that Jews are not the only social parasites, for Grove presents a variety of scenes of dishonesty and duplicity in which gentiles participate more than Jews. Miss Henders, the Jewish book agent, does no worse than the other canvassers, but Branden's sensitive conscience is particularly contrasted with her open cynicism. She is singled out from the others for this purpose. Branden walks out with her and listens to her confession of self-interest above all else. She has "beady black eyes" and a "harsh laugh," shouts "petulantly" and, as Branden delicately puts it, has "a face which could not conceal her emotions, and manners and movements which jarred a little on my sensibilities."[18] The

---

17 Grove, *The Yoke of Life*, p. 215. Gretl Fischer has complained about the paradox of Grove being awarded the Lorne Pierce Medal four years after producing "*The Yoke of Life* with its crude anti-semitism. The villain there has not even a name [he has—Baum]; he is merely referred to as 'the Jew.' The grotesquely sinister portrait in this book was certain to infect receptive minds with the plague of racial hatred." *In Search of Jerusalem* (Montreal: McGill-Queen's University Press, 1975), p. 126.

18 Grove, *A Search for America*, pp. 164-74.

distaste erected against such an unattractive character must be evaluated along with that which surrounds all of Grove's other Jewish characters.

Another type of Jewish character appears in Grove's later work. In *The Master of the Mill*, a Mr. Rosenbaum plays a minor role in the stock market maneuvering by which Edmund gains control of Canada's flour-milling industry. Rosenbaum, a millionaire from Montreal, is the only successful career financier presented in the novel, the man whom Edmund depends upon for his financing, which again indicates Grove's belief that finance was controlled by Jews. Once again there appear frequent references to "the Jew" and once to the "magnificent Jew," for Rosenbaum is not only dressed immaculately in a lush and dazzling style, but physically he is an impressive and attractive man. He is the one active man of culture among the Canadian characters, who are shown to have power and prestige and some wealth but no real appreciation of the European tradition of culture. He alone gallantly pays attention to Edmund's wife as a complete woman.

The character of Rosenbaum seems to have been "lifted" from Grove's earlier, unpublished novel, "Jane Atkinson," in which Charles Rosebaum, also a millionaire from Eastern Canada, visits Jane's home and makes her aware of the social deprivations of prairie life. Another "magnificent Jew," Rosebaum's physical description exceeds that of Rosenbaum: "to Jane's surprise—for from Jim's words, 'an English Jew' she had expected a man with a poor physique—a tall myopic man of magnificent appearance, exceedingly good looking with his black curly beard and his impulsive notions which, however, were extremely Jewish."[19] Rosebaum flatters Jane with his extravagant consideration and sophistication. His attentions go to her head and for some time after his departure she dreams romantically of him. Finally a chance encounter with him and his family makes Jane aware of the potential immorality of her half-imagined flirtation, be it ever so sophisticated. Rosebaum is revealed as a childish sexual adventurer, a tempter careless of his own wife and children. Although in *The Master of the Mill* Rosenbaum's character is not developed as fully as that of his predecessor, much the same may be said for him. Both men appear incongruous in the Canadian settings, remaining oddly unsettled and very European. Both are urbanites and therefore in Grove's mind parasites. They are ultimately negative characters, and the necessity of their inclusion is questionable. Certainly in "Jane Atkinson" there was little need for a Jewish financier to be imported into the Western plot from the East (unless Grove wanted to make a point about Eastern financial exploitation of the West?) and the use of another in *The Master of the Mill* seems to reinforce Grove's sense of finance (in Canada, at least) being monopolized by Jews, parasitical dilettantes in the real world of work.

19 Frederick P. Grove, "Jane Atkinson," The Grove Collection, The University of Manitoba, Box 16, p. 96.

Laura Salverson was the other prominent Canadian writer to attack prejudice from the receiving end in the 1920s. She did so in defence of her own Icelandic background. If the Galicians were considered by English-Canadians to be at the bottom of the "alien" pile, then surely Icelanders must have been near the top if not actually at it. Nevertheless Salverson maintained that they were an endangered species and complained strongly in her fiction and in her autobiography about their gradual disappearance into the mainstream of Canadian society. Her defence might seem to be something of an overreaction, considering that Icelanders were of Nordic stock. Her vehement assault on anti-Icelandic prejudice reveals the extent of such feelings on the part of English-Canadians. If racism was such an important issue to Salverson and her Icelanders, then what must it have been like for less acceptable groups such as Galicians and Jews?

Like Grove, Salverson concentrated on Scandinavian and Germanic characters. Born in Canada of immigrant parents who turned to Norse culture to soothe them in their New World difficulties (she did not begin to learn English until the age of eleven), she became a fervent traditionalist herself, and while many Icelanders were assimilating for various reasons, she resisted such forces and argued for the preservation of the old ways. She operated from a position of superiority, believing that Icelanders, with their remarkable history of exploration and parliamentary government and their inspiring sagas, could only be losers if they assimilated into Canadian society. In *Lord of the Silver Dragon: A Romance of Leif the Lucky* (1927), and in *Immortal Rock* (1954) she connected North America and the Vikings together in an almost fanatical manner, asserting in the latter book, on slim evidence discredited by most experts even then, the Kensington Stone theory that Norsemen had penetrated overland from Hudson's Bay as far as modern-day Minnesota in the sixteenth century. In her books set in more modern times, her Icelandic immigrants are portrayed as continuing this saga of settlement: her people and not Columbus discovered America. All of her twentieth-century Scandinavian characters are presented as heirs of this pre-Columbian tradition of colonization in North America, and therefore had no need to take second place to anyone, as if the order of arrival had something to do with subsequent ranking. She served willingly as an interpreter, bringing Norse history and culture to the attention of Canadians who were unknowingly dismissing them as just more aliens requiring civilization and education.

Salverson considered the Icelandic cultural tradition to be superior to the vacuum she felt surrounding her by contrast in Canada. Aware of feminist issues (*When Sparrows Fall* was dedicated to Nellie McClung) and a firm pacifist, she wrote a sense of Christian Socialism into her books that co-existed unhappily there with her bleakly agnostic fatalism. She saw modern Europe as a chaotic disaster area, and Canada as a yet unfulfilled dream. Her writing was confined by her self-imposed limitations. She restricted herself to Scandinavian immigrants for all her fiction set in Canada, and it may be argued that she did so not so much because of her familiarity with and allegiance to them, but because of her belief in their superiority and therefore their priority in literature. She showed a little more awareness of Canadian history preceding the arrival of whites than Grove did, perhaps because her childhood in the West preceded his arrival by more than a decade, exposing her to more Indians and Métis than he encountered. One memorable Indian character appears in both her novel *The Viking Heart* (1923) and in her autobiography, *Confessions of an Immigrant's Daughter* (1939). Laughing Joe, who has every reason to weep instead of laugh, personifies the plight of the Canadian Indian. He is a disinherited vagabond who amuses idle whites with his imitation of their laughter as a form of begging.[20] The inclusion of his representative tragedy, coupled with her depiction of the Indians in *The Viking Heart* as "derelicts of a race once great in native splendor,"[21] and as objects to be used by whites but who still possessed traces of their former dignity and independence, shows her essentially sympathetic to the Indians' defeat as a fait accompli. It was over, she implied: this sad preface to the main drama of whites in a newly-emptied land. It serves to establish her sensitivity, but does little more.

In her first and best novel, *The Viking Heart*, Salverson drew heavily upon her own family's experiences as immigrants, the debt being in part acknowledged and in part obvious in *Confessions of an Immigrant's Daughter*, which appeared fourteen years later. In *The Viking Heart* she fictionalized the story of the mass movement of some 1,400 Icelanders to Canada after the eruption of Mt. Askja in 1875 and economic pressures had made emigration necessary. By starting her story in Iceland she was able to refute various myths that English-Canadians held about Icelanders and aliens in general. She showed the people content and happy in their native land, and sad to leave it. They were shown appreciative of living in the midst of a great cultural tradition. To show immigrants at home in their own element before transplanting them to Canada where they would inevitably look out of place was and remains a valuable educatory aspect of such fiction, establishing as it does the worth of alien cultures and, by extension, alien peoples. Salverson also attacked the ludicrously exaggerated rhetoric of Canadian recruiters overseas, which had falsely enticed immigrants, some of whom might otherwise never have come. The stories she has to tell of the harrowing experiences of Icelandic settlers, particularly the quaranteening for their first winter of a group in a swamp near Gimli because of smallpox,

20 Laura G. Salverson, *The Viking Heart* (Toronto: McClelland and Stewart, 1929), pp. 128-29; *Confessions of an Immigrant's Daughter* (London: Faber and Faber, 1939), pp. 50-51.

21 Salverson, *The Viking Heart*, p. 128.

support her claims that Icelanders had earned their right to be accepted as Canadians in full measure.

In *The Viking Heart* Salverson traced the history of one family, the Halssons, whose troubles of this sort were considerable. They persevered and suffered and at length came to terms with the land and with established Canadians by sharing bereavements. Death, and especially the burial of loved ones in Canadian soil in so many books by or about immigrants, marks the total acceptance—the decision point of no return—by them of Canada as their new homeland.[22] Second-generation Icelandic-Canadian Thor becomes a medical doctor and dies in France during World War One. His memorial service back in Canada is taken by an English Methodist minister who comforts Thor's mother afterwards. In a single sentence Salverson claims that the deaths of Canadians, regardless of their origins, unite all Canadians: "He was an Englishman and she an Icelander. But they looked each into the other's soul and found they had a common heritage."[23] Linking a Methodist cleric and a first generation "alien" immigrant in this way seems to be Salverson's answer to the enforced assimilationist policies proffered by Rev. Gordon in *The Foreigner*.

Salverson did not pursue the religious argument. Her vision of God as "The Dark Weaver," an intimidating balancer of events and indifferent guardian to man, makes conventional religion almost superfluous in her novels. *The Viking Heart* defends Icelanders from prejudice because they were Icelanders. It neither links them with non-Scandinavians against the common discrimination nor does it seriously criticize the English-Canadians for their attitudes to any but Icelanders. She wrote as if to rectify a simple mistake which could be made up for by admitting Icelanders into the inner circle of power where they had a right to be. She bitterly noted the prejudice directed at the first generation group. One of her characters, Bjorn, recounts it:

> You know the attitude that the people had towards us. Suspicion, distrust and contempt. A little of that faded when we proved our worth in the rebellion. . . . But we Icelanders are still a curiosity to many. They think us creatures of doubtful habit and uncertain intelligence. They tolerate us because we are useful—because we are doing what they refuse to do, being of such superior clay.[24]

Salverson's resentment concerning the class her people were funnelled into on their arrival, her bitterness at her family having been allocated to the lowest strata in the Canadian hierarchy increased by her personal pride in her own ancestors' high positions formerly in Iceland, is not unlike the

22 Examples may be found in *The Viking Heart*, Edward McCourt's *Home is the Stranger*, and Illya Kiriak's *Sons of the Soil*.

23 Salverson, *The Viking Heart*, p. 322.

24 Ibid., pp. 107-8.

resentment expressed by Gobineau. Grove rose above these class distinctions by reversing the hierarchy and preaching that pioneers were naturally superior to storekeepers and city-dwellers, but Salverson wrote to claim her place in the sun.

A later novel, *The Dark Weaver* (1937), is also the story of the immigrant experience, now enlarged to encompass a representative sample of Nordic peoples. The prologue introduces several sets of people: the Boyens of Norway (or possibly Iceland); the Marcussons of Denmark;[25] the Holmquists, Russian refugees from Copenhagen; and Dr. Hartman and Oscar Beaur from Germany. This is a multicultural novel even before it arrives in Canada. For various reasons these various characters immigrate and join together on the prairies, forming a spontaneous little community of their own. The characters represent not just an ethnic spectrum, but a political and philosophical one as well, ranging from capitalism to Marxism, and from insensitive self-interest to ultra-sensitive self-abnegation. Under the gloomy threat of the nemesis-laden God who presides over the plot, the personal tragedies of these people are played out. Their community is introverted, having little interaction with other Canadians. There are two experiences with the "outside." The first is Ephraim Marcusson's adultrous dalliance with Marie, an Indian half-breed, and the second is the participation of Manfred as an aviator and Greta as a nurse in World War One. Ephraim's indiscretion is solemnly judged by the neighbouring Indian band who decide he must take Marie's child into his own family. Oscar Beaur's negative reaction to this event merges imperceptibly with Salverson's:

> Those sanguinary faces staring out from the rim of firelight were as savage as a circle of wolves waiting to pounce upon their prey. Those horrible brutes, on whose faces cruelty and cunning marked the limits of intelligence, represented the sort of progeny Ephraim was asked to accept into his ancient line. Mein Gott! It was monstrous—so monstrous that Oscar felt as though the entire white race had suffered an intolerable affront. . . . In face and form, disposition and temperment Marie might be French, but that could not alter the disagreeable facts of dual ancestry. Endearing or not she was likewise the innocent and helpless repository of savage traits and instincts. Dark thoughts.[26]

Marie dies and her daughter is adopted by Ephraim's forgiving wife. The child's subsequent life is not followed, so the reader is left wondering what chances Salverson would have given her for a normal life as a Marcusson.

As in *The Viking Heart*, the war provides an opportunity for these immigrants to prove their worth to Canada by fighting for Britain. Salver-

---

25 The nationality of the Boyens and the Marcussons is not clear. Norway and Denmark are calculated guesses. Perhaps there are clues which would be recognized by Scandinavians.
26 Laura G. Salverson, *The Dark Weaver* (Toronto: Ryerson Press, 1937), pp. 95-96.

son hated war, but evidently recognized (perhaps from Gordon's novels) that English-Canadians judged Canadianness in part as the willingness to fight for the British Empire, and that if Icelanders were ever to gain their respect they too must participate, as indeed they did. Yet Salverson deplores this necessity in strong terms, as when Greta sails for France: "Behind her lay the beautiful shores of a young peace-loving continent, betrayed into carnage by the duplicities of the old world. Ahead lay the bloody arena dedicated to the slaughter of the innocents!"[27] Manfred's psychological crisis after his Christmas bombing raid of Mannheim, and on learning that Greta had been wounded, leads him first to shoot down his cousin Ricky (a German pilot and a school friend), and then to suicidally crash in protest against a world where his perfect love can be destroyed so violently.

Salverson's immigrants in *The Dark Weaver* are good pioneers as she understands the word. There is, however, little sense of farming in the Canadian style. Urban and commercial careers were what her fictional characters aspired to. Although in fact the Gimli Icelandic community was agricultural and truly pioneering, her personal experiences were urban and transient, leaving her with little knowledge of farming. She presented her immigrants as monied, capable, and courageous, little different from the Viking nobility of her *Immortal Rock*. They come as European speculators, never expecting to be made to start out at the bottom. They end up as much Canadians as anyone else, having paid their dues to the graveyard and done their "bit" in the war. They have earned their respect.

Salverson's weakness was for romance. Because the romance element in *The Viking Heart* is minimal, the novel is probably her best work. An excess of it in *The Dark Weaver*, not to mention *Black Lace*, is what flaws her subsequent work. *The Dark Weaver*, the third of her three immigrant novels, dissipates its energies in complicated romantic entanglements that do little for the plot and less for her didacticism. A prime example of the excess of romance is *The Dove of El-Djezaire* (1933), in which romance replaces realism in the narrative of the experiences of Icelanders kidnapped and sold into slavery on the Barbary coast (a narrative evidently based on a true event and a famous saga). The closest Salverson comes to writing about an Icelandic villain is in the person of Jan Klaus/Murad Reis, a renegade pirate who leads the slaving expedition against his former island home. He turns out to be really half-Dutch and half-Danish, however, and despite his adoption of barbarism he is touched as he watches one of the slaves weeping on his ship. As Salverson puts it, with a characteristic melodramatic exclamation: "Ho, Jan Klaus! Once again race betrays you. . . . Adopted of Islam, despoiler and thief, blood calls checkmate when it will. . . . Deeds are of the day, instinct of the centuries."[28] Also in *The Dove of El-Djezaire*

27 Ibid., p. 373.
28 Laura G. Salverson, *The Dove of El-Djezaire* (Toronto: Ryerson Press, 1933), p. 51.

the author has a Jewess (Esther) who keeps a tavern (Abraham's Bosom) patronized by the Moslems in Algiers. Salverson's only Jewish character, Esther is "true to her emotional race. . . ."[29] She does, however, contribute to the happy ending with some courage.

Salverson's attitude to ethnicity was very similar to the English-Canadian attitude. Her immigrant novels and her autobiography were in large part trying to establish Icelanders and other Scandinavians in the same superior category as Britons. She deplored the pressures of assimilation and yet was forced to record them as part of the history of Icelanders in Canada. Without actually making statements about racism as a theory, she employed the word "race" frequently in ways that implied racist beliefs. Her view of Icelanders was very one-sided and positive. Although at times they were shown as childish, they seem on the whole to have stepped in splendour out of the Norse sagas which were so important to Salverson as a child. It is clear that she believed that instincts developed and integrated over centuries had accumulated to form the ethnic character she proudly presented as Scandinavian. In her novel *When Sparrows Fall* (1925), which, although set in the United States, could with the omission of two or three sentences just as well be in Canada, the stalwart Ephemia reacts stoically to the news of a friend's injury: "All her Viking ancestry, manifested in her emotional restraint and clear courage, reacted to the thought. She was proud, as her forebears had been proud when their warrior dead were carried home on the shields of respectful retainers."[30]

Is this ethnic pride which, prompted by her own unpleasant experiences of being looked down upon, led to self-justification and over-compensation by the excessive gilding of her own type with virtues that seem absurdly out of place in North America? It must be said in her favour that, unlike Gordon, she looked down on no one except possibly the Indians, whom she regarded as a dying race anyway and to whom, despite their limitations as barbarians, she was willing to concede a certain degree of nobility and morality. Nevertheless, in most other ways associated with race, Salverson's work reproduces many of the same effects (and suffers from the same defects) as that of Gordon, and she was much closer in spirit to him than to Grove. Both Gordon and Salverson wrote out of an overbearing sense of the superiority of their own white kind and individually their own discrete groups. Now immigrant groups with their own sense of superiority had begun to challenge that of Gordon's group. Grove took his superiority for granted and did not feel obliged to emphasize it in his fiction. Salverson

29 Ibid., p. 173.
30 Laura G. Salverson, *When Sparrows Fall* (Toronto: Ryerson Press, 1925), p. 232. Like Gordon, Salverson viewed stoicism and emotional displays as opposites, the former identifying true Anglo-Saxons and the latter indulged in by Jews. "Emotional restraint" becomes a virtue, proving the connection between English-Canadians and Scandinavians.

wrote to claim kinship with the élite English-Canadians, doubtless with Gordon's romances before her as examples, and with the aim of joining the entrepreneurial class. It is significant that her most vehement complaints about the difficulties of upward social mobility for immigrants, in *Confessions of an Immigrant's Daughter*, coincided with her extended apologia for her father's failure to improve himself in Canada. Her democratic principles were not very socialist, and were doubtless inspired by the suffering of the first generation pioneers (which she was largely spared) and her own personal poverty which continued after her marriage. The feeling of being cheated, of deserving more because of her racial origins (not just for herself, but for her people) came as naturally to her as it had to Gobineau.

Before the Second World War Salverson and Grove were the two most prominent writers who drew attention to racial discrimination against immigrants in Canada, and their attitudes can easily be contrasted with those of English-Canadian writers of the same period. Both authors were encouraged in their careers by Watson Kirkconnell. As a university teacher and linguist in Winnipeg, he was in contact with a wide variety of immigrant groups in the two decades of peace. Kirkconnell championed their writers, as much when they wrote in English as when they did not, and he wrote articles industriously to confirm the value of their work to Canada. Further, and despite his fanatical prejudices against Communists, he defended every white immigrant group against the various charges that decades of discrimination had accumulated against them. In his books and articles he specifically refuted the concept of pure races, including the British or "Anglo-Saxon race" to which it might be assumed he belonged, and he optimistically looked forward to a successful blend of cultures in Canada.[31] Certainly Kirkconnell's work, and he produced hundreds of booklets and articles on the subject, must have contributed to the slowly changing attitudes as much as the new literature which it equally encouraged.

31 See Watson Kirkconnell, "Western Immigration," *Canadian Forum* 8, No. 94 (1928), 706-7. For examples of his work with non-English writers, see his contributions to the "Letters in Canada" annual surveys in the *University of Toronto Quarterly* from 1938 to 1966, as well as "Icelandic-Canadian Poetry," *Dalhousie Review* 14, No. 3 (1934), 331-44. For examples of his defence of New Canadians of all (white) groups, see *Canadians All* (Ottawa: Director of Public Information, 1941); *Our Communists and the New Canadians* (Toronto: Southam Press, n.d.) (an address to the Canadian Club of Toronto, Feb. 1943); and *Twilight of Liberty* (London: Oxford University Press, 1941). Unfortunately Kirkconnell's anti-racism only extended as far as the white "race," as he did refer to the Oriental menace as an argument for the speedy population by Europeans of Western Canada. See "Western Immigration," 706-7.

Chapter Four

The Immigrant Reaction,
1939-1980

Now, I'm a sort of James Baldwin reactionary, born too late for my style, a faggoty little nigger making up to white boys; so I got to come to a backward country like Canada where there's enough social lag for me to survive. I mean, you want to be *nice* to me, don't you? . . . I mean, I've only been in Canada a week, and the guilt here is just unreal, and you hardly got no niggers to make up to.

Boy, in *The Young in One Another's Arms*, by Jane Rule

I

The war, which brought so many racial and ethnic complications to the forefront of public consciousness by showing exactly where such thoughts eventually led, and which associated racism with the evils of Nazism almost archetypically, inspired English-Canadian writers to a re-evaluation of racism per se, a re-evaluation still made from the inside by the privileged looking out over those who admittedly were alien to Canadian charter-group standards. The influx of displaced persons and refugees added urgency to this process. As well, the "outsiders" were becoming increasingly vocal themselves about their own versions of Canada's future, and while Grove and Salverson had tried to alter instead of directly oppose British views on assimilation, each maintaining their beliefs in Nordic superiority, the post-war non-charter-group writers explored political, psychological, and religious possibilities beyond established Canadian conventions—the very thing most feared by Gordon—and indeed cited the

British-vaunted democratic liberties of Canada for their justification in pursuing such goals.

Spokespeople for and leaders of non-charter groups, in the West in particular, began even before the war to encourage their people to write, not necessarily in English, for translations were envisaged, foreseeing the value of ethnically identified literature as a weapon in negotiating acceptance and equality with the charter groups.[1] Self-exposure to the larger community was seen as an advantage, a way to prove their worth and give the lie to various accusations of cultural retardation, uncleanliness, and unchristian values that had been levelled at them, and which provided the basis for the development of more violent forms of racism. Books, it was hoped, could break through the barriers of prejudice and, by initiating communication, establish connections that would eradicate racism and lead towards a cohesive national identity. In 1960 Michael Luchkovich, the Federal M.P. for Vegreville from 1926 to 1935, a prominent Ukrainian-Canadian spokesman, and the translator of the 1959 English edition of Illia Kiriak's immigrant novel, *Sons of the Soil*, published in *Canadian Author and Bookman* an article entitled "Racial Integration and Canadian Literature" in which he described immigrant literature as a grass roots movement to publicize their contributions to Canada.[2] Specifically he recognized the potential of such literature to strengthen the resistance of all cultures to the threat of the melting pot, and to establish the concept of a mosaic. "Mosaic," of course, became the operative word in internal ethnic relations in Canada after 1960. His English translation of *Sons of the Soil*, although abridged, is an excellent example of this kind of work. Kiriak's novel traced the progress of one (fictional) Ukrainian pioneer settlement, stressing the importance of religion and crafts in the maintenance of cultural continuity, and also showing how discrimination could be overcome by working hard together with respect for the preservation of each other's cultures. The "mixed marriage" between a Ukrainian-Canadian and an English-Canadian at the end of the novel symbolizes the mutual acceptance that Kiriak felt could be achieved. Not for the first time was an identifiably Ukrainian voice heard in Canada's literary forum, protesting the discrimination of the past and proving how unjust it remained in the present, but *Sons of the Soil* provided a firsthand look at the feelings of an immigrant who had been through the entire pioneer experience. What had not been written about before simply did not exist in history. Kiriak proved the existence of the

---

1 An early example of such a pep-talk, made available to English-Canadians so that they would appreciate the intention, was Ivan Kmeta's "Literature and the Melting Pot," *Canadian Author* 15, No. 3 (1938), 12.

2 Michael Luchkovich, "Racial Integration and Canadian Literature," *Canadian Author and Bookman* 36, No. 2 (1960), 14-16.

Ukrainian pioneer contribution to Canada in a medium that, assisted by Luchkovich, English-Canadian readers could understand and appreciate.

Vera Lysenko preceded the English edition of *Sons of the Soil* in speaking for Ukrainians with her two novels, *Yellow Boots* (1954) and *Westerly Wild* (1956). Her first book, however, *Men in Sheepskin Coats* (1947), is a journalistic defence of the people English-Canadians looked down on variously as Galicians, "hunkeys," and "sheepskins." The factual material of this book provided the basis for her later novels. In it she condemned the widespread Anglo-Saxon prejudice towards Ukrainians and went on to associate it with economics and power:

> The greatest obstacle to the Canadianization of the Men in Sheepskin was not their clinging to the old traditions but rather the attitudes towards them of other groups who had preceded them in settlement; those who looked askance upon the newcomers as "ignorant, irresponsible foreigners in hordes," creatures of mud who must at all costs be made over in the superior British mould. Preachers ascended into their pulpits and in a thoroughly un-Christian manner warned against the perils of the "foreign invasion."[3]

This protest is almost identical in meaning and attitude to the one delivered by Grove which was quoted in Chapter Three. By Canadianization Lysenko meant not assimilation but mutual respect and tolerance of all by all, without any pressures towards change or conformity.

Indignantly Lysenko traced the history of anti-Ukrainian prejudice from the first reactions to their arrival through their repression during the 1914-18 war, and the political harassment of their semi-socialist community organizations in the twenties and thirties. The book is virtually a self-proclamation of ethnic liberty, as well as a lament for the unfair treatment accorded to multitudes of hard-working people. Writing after the 1939-45 war she still saw such treatment as widespread. She also deplored the lack (in 1947) of immigrant literature:

> Seldom indeed does one encounter a character of, let us say, Slavic origin, in Canadian fiction, except in the role of an illiterate, a clown, a villain or a domestic servant. One exception may be noted: the Ukrainian Canadian heroine, Anna Prychoda, of Morley Callaghan's novel, *They Shall Inherit the Earth*. Yet Anna . . . possesses no distinctively Ukrainian traits; she might as well have been of French, Irish or Icelandic ancestry; Callaghan made no attempt to limn out the particular characteristics and problems of the second generation to which his heroine presumably belongs. The magnificent drama of migration and assimilation to Canada's Western lands of a polyglot population has not appealed to Canadian writers, mainly for the reason that consciously or unconsciously they still prefer to think of the non-

3 Vera Lysenko, *Men in Sheepskin Coats* (Toronto: Ryerson Press, 1947), p. 98.

Anglo-Saxon as a comic or uncouth personage, unworthy of elevation
to the dignity of literary subject-material. . . . yet Canadian culture as
such will not come of age until it embraces in its entirety the manifold
life of all the national groups which constitute its entity.[4]

With this idealistic goal in mind, Lysenko turned from journalism to
fiction and wrote *Yellow Boots*.

An unprepossessing novel set in the West, beginning in 1927 on the
prairie and then moving with Lilli, the heroine, to Winnipeg, *Yellow Boots*
is not just about Lysenko's own Boukovinians, who inhabit most of its
pages. It depends on them for its start, but in an attempt to attain the status
of national epic which she felt was needed, she transcended her own group
to take in all immigrant groups including Britons. Lilli Landash is the
gifted daughter of Boukovinian immigrants. Her musical talent, grounded
in her people's cultural traditions and their closeness to nature, provides the
catalyst to unite the various ethnic groups scattered about the West. Lilli
becomes a singer and travels about, entertaining people with a repertoire of
folk songs gathered from Palestine to Japan. The common background of
folklore and song, which Lysenko suggests is shared in the primitive past of
all peoples, brings all Canadians together to enjoy each other's cultures in a
positive way. The new awareness of this common pool contributes to better
understanding all round.

Unlike Salverson, Lysenko spent little time complaining about prejudice
in her fiction. The superiority complex of Anglo-Saxons is deplored briefly,
but she spent her time more positively educating English readers to the
cultural traits of Boukovinians. She admitted their backwardness in areas
where science has helped Anglo-Saxons to progress, such as agricultural
science, but she showed how they could catch up in a single generation and
free themselves from the habits of centuries of oppression. Lysenko's main
achievement was in surpassing the narrow xenophobic habits of a single
group, which Salverson appeared unwilling or unable to do, and expanding
her mosaic vision to include all immigrant types, using a choir as a symbol
for Canadians uniting to sing each other's songs together. Her inclusion of
blacks marks the first time they appear (even if briefly and with minimal
detail) in Canadian literature on an equal footing with whites. They have
their place in Lysenko's choir and their songs are sung. A Japanese-
Canadian girl, "one of the most skilled workers in the factory" where Lilli
works, is included in the plot as if she were just as Canadian as anyone else.[5]
Again this is the first time for such an occurrence, and it is particularly
significant given the residue of post-war anti-Japanese feeling. The choir
director is Jewish and he brings a knowledge of and a feeling for music to the

4 Ibid., pp. 293-94.
5 Vera Lysenko, *Yellow Boots* (Toronto: Ryerson Press, 1954), p. 260.

amateur singers of Winnipeg, while his Jewishness is unimportant except that he too is a participant. Even the few minor archetypal habits of characterization that can be found in the novel dwindle in significance when compared with Lysenko's grandiose scheme for national unity.

In her second novel, *Westerly Wild*, Lysenko emphasized romance at the expense of ethnic didacticism. This story of a half-Polish half-French-Canadian teacher in the Saskatchewan dust-bowl is relevant only because of the author's use of a rural school as a catalytic factor providing the varied ethnic population with an important opportunity to mingle and learn about each other. The experience is seen as cumulative rather than as levelling in that the children (and ultimately the nation) are the richer for experiencing the sum total of all their backgrounds rather than simply conforming to the English-Canadian ideal. No one group is discriminated against for any reason. The prairie drought is used as a symbol for the intellectual drought of its inhabitants, and any and all contributions of a cultural nature are accepted as valuable.

Lysenko's major achievement as a writer was the impressive social study of Ukrainian immigration which constituted her first book. Her leftist perspective in it is important for its explanation of racially based exploitation of New Canadians, but it is considerably less extreme than Dyson Carter's, for example.[6] Her positive attitude and her enthusiastic nationalism supplied a vigorous alternative to the English-Canadian goal of assimilation and can be seen as a natural expression of the independence and dignity of immigrant groups which had been expressed more directly already by Grove in his *Maclean's* articles in 1928 and 1929.

A similar message is found in Magdelana Eggleston's *Mountain Shadows* (1955). Eggleston substituted a slightly more realistic approach to the resistance to the melting pot while assaulting racial prejudice directly and dogmatically. Like Lysenko, Eggleston reminded readers that all non-aboriginal Canadians are "foreigners" in Canada, and equal in that respect. The arrogance and the superiority complex of English-Canadians are displayed in several ugly episodes which also illustrate the effects of racism on its victims, all interpreted by the sensitive protagonist, Maggy Mileris, the adolescent daughter of Lithuanian immigrants. Maggy's situation evidently resembles the author's own life and, just as Salverson vindicated her own Icelanders, Grove the Russo-Germans, and Lysenko the Boukovinians, Eggleston offers a plot that rests upon a defence of Lithuanians. However, with that ancestral duty accomplished, again like Lysenko, Eggleston moved beyond her own ethnic viewpoint to embrace the rest of the thirty-

6 See Chapter Five. It is also less extreme than that of Myrna Kostash in *All of Baba's Children* (Edmonton: Hurtig, 1977) and Frances Swyripa in *Ukrainian Canadians* (Edmonton: University of Alberta Press, 1978), both non-fiction and somewhat resentful studies aimed at setting the record straight.

five ethnic groups who inhabit Maggy's home town in Alberta. Maggy is a vulnerable victim who is helped to a better awareness of her situation by the explanation of a sympathetic English-Canadian who encourages her not to lose pride in her Lithuanian past as she becomes more and more Canadian. The town is a Canadian microcosm at an early stage of development with people still getting used to each other. Friction and tension characterize the relations between different groups, with the English-Canadians, as usual, sure of the upper hand. Yet an awareness of common humanity comes upon the community during a mine disaster. Anxiety and death bring everyone together dramatically, conquering the prejudices that are viewed as belonging to the Old World. Eggleston describes a melting pot in operation, slower than the American model, but making progress despite the partly justifiable resistance of the newcomers. Her novel shows racial prejudice to be un-Canadian in spirit and the result of ignorance, and acknowledges education as the most important means of eradicating it. In a resolution not unlike Branden's noble statement concluding *A Search for America*, Maggy makes up her mind not to try to escape from Coaltown's ethnic chaos, but to become a teacher and devote herself to educating immigrant children. This to Eggleston is the Canadian challenge—the construction of a comprehensive new national identity which makes allowance for ethnically diverse cultures, rather than the destructive selfishness of racial discrimination which, as she shows, makes enemies of neighbours and perpetuates bad feelings.

II

Violent and tragic as the consequences of racism are shown to be in Canada, a growing awareness of the more catastrophic events in Europe during World War Two began to flood Canadian literature with indignation, disgust, and fear. The Holocaust slowly produced an impact on Canadian consciousness as it was revealed, not just by shocking photographs and sensational news reports at the time, but eventually by literature as popular as Leon Uris's *Exodus* (1958) which explored the human consequences of racism taken to an unnatural extreme. Henry Kreisel's *The Rich Man* (1948) and *The Betrayal* (1964) illuminated the gap between Europe, where urgent pressures forced desperate solutions, and Canada, the "peaceable kingdom" where larger human responsibilities may be neglected because they are so seldom invoked. The relative emptiness of Canadian life and the slower-paced pursuit of material success in a comparatively richer environment bury such potential responses so that when racism does flare up it is thought of as a foreign phenomenon, temporarily in transit. In Kreisel's *The Betrayal*, a Canadian-born Jewish professor of history is made to realize just how remote from European history he actually is:

> By an accident I had been born in a country in which, as Stappler had
> put it, it was possible without too much difficulty to be a decent
> human being, to decide what was morally right and to act accordingly,
> a country in which justice and law, though God knows often abused,
> were nevertheless very real.[7]

For a Canadian Jewish writer the awareness of Canadian insularity in the
face of historical events of immense moral significance can produce considerable guilt. Mordecai Richler's first novel, *The Acrobats* (1954), follows
the growing awareness of an English-Canadian character in post-war Spain
of the moral ruins left by the war, the psychological detritus that clogs the
channels of communication between survivors of all sides, preventing a
normalization (in the Canadian sense of returning to peace and comfort that
André, the protagonist, uses as his measure) of social relationships. Europe
is ugly and racism is a way of expressing its ugliness. Anti-Semitism lives on
after Hitler, at least in Franco's Spain.

Richler's second book, *Son of a Smaller Hero* (1955), deals with one
Canadian's struggle to break free of his Jewish background and become a
person rather than a category with a lifetime of group-imposed expectations
to fulfil. Noah Adler is not a Jewish anti-Semite nor a would-be "goy." He
is a searcher for values beyond group codes. Richler presents the St. Urbain
Street area of Montreal as nothing less than a ghetto, physically (with
extensions into Outremont) and conceptually: "The ghetto of Montreal has
no real walls and no true dimensions. The walls are the habit of atavism and
the dimensions are an illusion. But the ghetto exists all the same."[8] Richler
shows how the ghetto has an inside wall set in place by the inmates, as well as
an outside wall set in place by non-Jews. Anti-Semitism is presented as a
constant throughout the book and indeed throughout Richler's work, but
this is balanced by his portrayal of Jews themselves as anti-goyem and just as
virulent in their ethnocentric defensiveness as their opposition. To show the
"goy" side, Richler included an episode in which several Jewish boys steal a
sign reading "This Beach is Restricted to Gentiles" from a Laurentian
resort. In his work set in the Montreal area, Richler continually reminds his
readers that many resorts, hotels, and restaurants were off-limits to Jews.
The quota system at McGill University is also mentioned as still being in
effect there as late as 1952.[9] Written in 1955, this book was in part an
exposé of current and recent practices of anti-Semitism throughout
Montreal society. However, Richler did not limit himself to one side of the
story, as his Jewish characters are just as racist, if not more so, as the

---

7 Henry Kreisel, *The Betrayal* (Toronto: McClelland and Stewart, 1971), p. 46.
8 Mordecai Richler, *Son of a Smaller Hero* (Toronto: McClelland and Stewart, 1969), p. 14.
9 Ibid., p. 41. Richler attempts to describe and explain the general anti-Semitic attitude
  on campus at McGill, in *Joshua Then and Now* (Toronto: McClelland and Stewart, 1980),
  p. 208.

Christians. Moore, the Irish lush who becomes the token "goy" working for Adler's junk business, hates his employers for conventional anti-Semitic reasons, but is himself a contemptible person in their eyes, living testimony to their own superiority. His employer asks him: "Liss'n, Moore, why couldn't you be a nigger? Or still better a Chink? Who in the hell ever heard of an Irish chauffeur?"[10] The Jews are in their ghetto as much because they want to be as they are forced to be. Richler sees humanity retreating into camps which are all alike in certain ways in that they each organize people, they each demand that their peculiar conventions and standards be adhered to, and they each are by nature competitive with each other. Freedom then ceases to be a possibility. Noah's quest for individual truths independent of the collectivities which either artificially create impersonations of truth or which bend it to their own ends removes him from the Montreal Jewish ghetto and the encircling outer-ghetto of Canadian charter groups and sends him to Europe, which in *The Acrobats* has already proven to be full of ghettos too.

Richler's third novel, *A Choice of Enemies* (1957), developed further this theme of communities—racial, religious, or intellectual—which become orthodoxies unto themselves. Set in post-war London, it concentrates on a group of writers, many of whom are Americans in exile. They are a group because of a common distaste for McCarthyism and its consequences for freedom of expression. Their intellectual connection intensifies to the point where people represent ideas or camps and are no longer individuals. Dogma dehumanizes them. In his introduction to the 1977 New Canadian Library edition, Bruce Stovel succinctly summarized the theme: "The novel's title, then, is ironic: to choose one's enemies is choosing a state of conformity, of legislated acts and attitudes. A choice of enemies is a choice of unfreedom, and so, paradoxically, a rejection of choice altogether."[11]

The main character, Norman Price, tries to understand Ernst Haupt as an individual instead of as a reactionary ex-Nazi refugee from East Germany, which is how Norman's colleagues see him. Accepting Ernst as a human being instead of as a philosophical argument is Norman's undoing for it means that he leaves the wolf-pack of a conscious community to be a lone wolf. Hatred is a group bond. Participation in a group involves hatred of non-participants who are defined by their choice and not their character. In requiring conformity, they lose originality. The racial conflict which illustrated this same argument in *Son of a Smaller Hero* is here replaced by a political argument, but the point remains the same. In his first three novels Richler established a position which rose above ethnic quarrels and group conflicts to provide an overview of the unnecessary squabbling that is

10 Richler, *Son of a Smaller Hero*, p. 188.
11 Bruce Stovel, Introduction, *A Choice of Enemies*, by Mordecai Richler (Toronto: McClelland and Stewart, 1977), p. viii.

unfortunately so much a part of human life. A search for wholeness, for basic commonality that transcends ethnic and sectarian parameters and even national definitions underlies these three books, supplying them with integrity and vision.

The Jewish characters in Richler's first three novels are not very pleasant people, but neither are they villains. In *The Acrobats*, Chaim and Barney recognize their own vulnerability in each other. Both are victims, reduced respectively to material and spiritual poverty. Both are capable men, weakened in one sense by their sensitivity but also, in quite another sense, made stronger than others by the knowledge that such sensitivity imparts. *Son of a Smaller Hero* contains Max, the scheming lecher who exploits the dead for political gain, and Shloime the hoodlum. *A Choice of Enemies* includes Karp, the unscrupulous manipulator and survivor, as well as several unsavoury Jewish writers. The popularity of Richler's next novel, *The Apprenticeship of Duddy Kravitz*, a book based on the "pusherke" character who seemed to personify most of the classic qualities attributed to Jews by anti-Semites, produced a problem for Richler. He repudiated criticism that he was encouraging anti-Semitic attitudes in an interview with Donald Cameron:

> I've been accused of being an anti-Semite, I do hack away at the left—but these are the areas where I'm involved, and so that's what I'm most critical of. And besides, there's no point in addressing a novel to the Enoch Powells of this world. . . . I'm not an anti-Semite, I've never been one, and I don't think we could even discuss that seriously. However, I do agree that someone who was anti-Semitic could pick up *Son of a Smaller Hero* or *Duddy Kravitz* and say, You See, That's What They're Like. I don't care about that, I really don't *care*. They're beyond the pale, you know, one cannot argue with them, and to submit to that or be inhibited by that would be their ultimate triumph as far as I'm concerned.[12]

Richler goes beyond the comparison-shopping of ethnicity, the comparing of the cultural price tags arbitrarily attached to various groups, that had previously restricted non-charter-group writers such as Lysenko. He is capable of repudiating his own group as a basis for repudiating others and sees that as a fundamental necessity. Some of the cruellest (and funniest) examples of ethnic humour at the expense of Jews may be found in Richler's work. It is not Jews per se that Richler is mocking but groups. Black humour is his forte, and it is fairly well distributed. Cannibalism and the guillotining of the hero darken the humour of *The Incomparable Atuk* (1963). In it, Rory Peel and his father, Panofsky, represent the high points of the type of characterization suggested by Gordon, Gibbon, and even Grove.

12 Donald Cameron, ed., *Conversations With Canadian Novelists—2* (Toronto: Macmillan of Canada, 1973), pp. 117-18.

Peel changed his name to become an advertising executive, and only hired non-Jewish employees to prove he was not prejudiced. His employment of a German maid carries this compulsion to sanitize his image even further. Seeing anti-Semitism everywhere, he makes himself obnoxious by stressing simultaneously his Jewishness *and* his need to be accepted as a "white" Canadian. Panofsky is a fanatic, obsessively involved in a secret pseudo-scientific experiment to prove that all English-Canadians do look alike. He furtively switches name tags on babies at a Protestant hospital to confirm his thesis that they all have "no-faces" which cannot be told apart, all to support his claim that "the most boring, mediocre man in the world is the White Protestant goy, northern species, and in Canada he has found his true habitat."[13] The satire of Jews is achieved on two levels. While Peel and Panofsky make obvious targets, on a secondary level Atuk himself is an Eskimo Duddy Kravitz, an aboriginal on the make in Toronto, who eventually arranges to convert to Judaism, and who personifies the stereo-typical traits often assigned to Jews. However, the conniving of the Jewish characters is balanced by the equal treatment of non-Jews. The success story of swimmer Bette Dolan is satirized for the brutally affectionless way her father "coached" her across Lake Ontario. Others are put down for other weaknesses. It is not a book partial to any side; it satirizes Canadians of all types and sides (for it does not develop beyond types and sides) for their faults, anxieties, and greed, all of which are seen to combine to make them susceptible to the worst American influences. *The Incomparable Atuk* dis-plays Richler's concern for anti-Semitism and for the Jewish equivalent against non-Jews, and while both these forces are important facts of life they are satirized on equal terms as being divisive and weakening. Canadian social mythology is debunked and racial myths are only one part of it.

Richler's two latest novels merge his racial theme into more enriched structures of Canadiana. *St. Urbain's Horseman* (1971) renews the German-versus-Jew controversy that is found in *The Acrobats*, *A Choice of Enemies*, and *The Incomparable Atuk*, as Hersh in his imagination pursues a German war criminal because of his Nazi past and not his nationality. The bellig-erent mood that underlies Richler's work from *The Apprenticeship of Duddy Kravitz* on emerges in the person of Joey, Hersh's idol, who physically fought against anti-Semitism in Montreal, actively defending himself and his family. The anti-Semitism of Adrien Arcand and wartime Quebec is remembered again, but this time there is no retreat into a protective huddle and embittered invective. The horseman is Joey, Hersh's alter-ego, the Jew who fought back, repeatedly in Spain, with Trotsky in Mexico, and in Israel in 1948. Joey's defensive violence seems to be the logical result of perpetual persecution, yet Hersh resists those tendencies in himself in order to stay

13 Mordecai Richler, *The Incomparable Atuk* (Toronto: McClelland and Stewart, 1971), p. 130.

above the level of anti-Semitism. In one sense literature is Richler's battle-ground, in which he can attack the indifference and ignorance of Canadians to such anti-Semitic discrimination as the quota system at McGill. Segregation, he recognized, was negative, building up barriers of stereotypes. He reminisced about this in *The Street* (1969): "Looking back, it's easy to see that the real trouble was that there was no dialogue between us and the French-Canadians, each elbowing the other, striving for WASP acceptance. We fought the French-Canadians stereotype for stereotype."[14] Having graduated out of this dead-end street, Richler himself has set up and destroyed stereotypes by inflating them to ridiculous proportions whereupon their flaws become obvious and then valueless. By satirizing common stereotypes in his fiction he has exposed the gap between stereotypes and realistic characterization, implying that to be of any value in describing humanity in detail literature must renounce stereotypes. Thus in *The Incomparable Atuk* there is implied a critical theory which repudiates the concepts embodied almost naturally in the work of Charles Gordon, for example. Racial attitudes have been included with other associated attitudes and taken to their logical consequences; they stand revealed as narrow group xenophobia, and their stereotypes are seen as false and therefore of limited value. Gordon did not lie; he was deceived and deceived others in turn. Richler escapes deception by escaping group definition, and he gives to literature a new freedom to tell the truth, built upon the ruins of dismantled and exploded stereotypes.[15]

Herman Buller's first novel, *One Man Alone* (1963), was also set in Montreal and dealt with anti-Semitism, but it is far more closely related to Dyson Carter's *Fatherless Sons* (discussed in Chapter Five) than to any of Richler's work. Buller's leftist political idealism might have led him to the fanciful extremes that Carter's work shows, but it was inhibited by a corrosive cynicism that accentuated the negative rather than the positive. The story follows the life of Morrie Cohen, a Montreal Jew, as he grows up and tries to pursue a writer's career, eventually marrying a French-Canadian. It takes place mainly in the 1930s. Race and class are the two themes, and they are much more integrated here than in *Fatherless Sons*. The first part establishes the social background of the Montreal setting in which Jews and French-Canadians are pushed together by their common poverty which disallows the luxury of divisions. They don't "elbow" each other, but co-operate after much trouble and squabbling. Like Richler, Buller first defines the Jewish ghetto as a fact:

14 Mordecai Richler, *The Street* (London: Wiedenfeld and Nicolson, 1972), p. 56.

15 Yet the difficulty of completely escaping such stereotypes is hinted at by Richler in "The Holocaust and After," in *Shovelling Trouble* (Toronto: McClelland and Stewart, 1972), p. 84. Also in this collection is "Bond," an essay on the anti-Semitism inherent in Ian Fleming's spy novels. I am indebted to Professor Frank Watt for bringing these essays to my attention.

> The island of Montreal was actually a triad of islands surrounded not
> by walls of water, but rather by walls of prejudice and social separate-
> ness. The sectors of the City occupied by the three dominant races of
> French, English and Jewish were sharply defined.
>   Montreal's Jews lived in a Ghetto. The Ghetto, though not defined
> by law, nor enclosed by laws, nor barred by gates was circumscribed by
> an invisible wall of culture and isolation. The Jews lived a confined and
> constricted small town life within the large cosmopolitan city.[16]

The story is told from the point of view of the underdog, which Buller
defines as the working class people of both French-Canadian and Jewish
origins. The relationship between the two groups is explored at length,
with English-Canadians playing only a minor role. In fact their brief
appearances are mostly negative. The most obvious racist in the novel is
Miss Ogg, an English teacher who discriminates against both blacks and
Jews. One black youth, Colin, is included as Morrie's friend to show that
among the poor colour is unimportant. It is interesting to note that Colin,
later seen in St. Antoine as a pre-med student, hopes to become a doctor and
go to work with Dr. Schweitzer in Africa. However unimportant race *should*
be, Buller mirrors the realities of its actual rivalries, particularly between
French-Canadians and Jews. Again like Richler, he is fair about apportion-
ing the blame. Sam Levy is a small sweatshop owner who serves on the board
of "the Immigrant Aid and Family Welfare Societies" to be able to recruit
cheap labour for his factory.[17] His hypocrisy is used to show the relationship
between capitalists and racist behaviour. On the other hand, Buller sys-
tematically itemized the many complaints Jews had, such as a school system
which ignored their religious days and taught such books as *The Merchant of
Venice* ("curricular anti-Semitism"[18]), Mayor Houde's racist flirtation with
fascism, l'Abbé Groulx's call for boycotts of Jewish businessmen in 1935,
political gerrymandering to prohibit Jewish votes en bloc, and religious and
ideological censorship. Buller's main point, however, is economic. For
example, he explains that the boycott of Jewish stores "was started by the
middle class merchants for their own benefit. These anti-Semites demand
special privileges. They seek an economic monopoly behind the wall of race
loyalty at the expense of their own down-trodden workers."[19] As Sam Levy
has demonstrated, greedy businessmen are not limited to any one side.
Their race is insignificant before their class interests, yet they use race for
profit. Racism is shown to be almost a convenient business practice.

16 Herman Buller, *One Man Alone* (Toronto: Canada National Book Club, 1963), pp.
   38-39.
17 Ibid., p. 49.
18 Ibid., p. 59.
19 Ibid., p. 98.

In Part Two, which follows Morrie's involvement in a labour dispute at Asbestosville, Buller's anti-clericalism adds the church to the forces he blames for racism. The curé of Asbestosville, while trying to support his congregation in their struggle, resolutely follows race lines instead of class lines and is thereby seen as a brake on his own people's progress. Even interracial love between Morrie and the French-Canadian Philomine is first frustrated by the curé and later destroyed when Philomine is murdered for having married a Jew. The optimism of romance that sustained Graham's *Earth and High Heaven* in upper-class Montreal cannot survive among the earthy desperate conflicts of the working class. Yet a form of optimism does persist in the hope that a nationalist uprising in Quebec, fueled by better education and a developing class consciousness, will defeat American imperialism (the Asbestosville mill is owned by coldly indifferent Americans), and that "French Canada will find unity in identity of interests among French, English and Jewish workers . . . national unity through class identity!"[20]

One Man Alone is flawed by excessively didactic sermonizing. Each chapter is a little sermon in itself, with the plot being overwhelmed by the message which usually takes over by the end, and undercut by trite simplistic language which shows little awareness of the nuances and complexities of the interpersonal relationships it describes. It is a novel written to educate a certain class, to illustrate the consequences of divisions along race lines in the face of a class-defined opposition. French-Canadian merchants are as much to blame as Jewish merchants for the divisive conflicts at one localized commercial level, but also Buller presents American imperialism as the main enemy. With his own anti-WASP and anti-American biases, albeit on grounds of class rather than race, he seems to be encouraging the resolution of a localized French-Canadian versus Jewish-Canadian conflict in order to create a united Québecois front against Americans—an elevation of the ghetto situation into national dimensions. Nationalism in general as well as Buller's in particular may be seen simply as an upgrading of race consciousness.

Buller's second novel, *Quebec in Revolt* (1965), is a historical romance centred on the Guibord affair. Strongly anti-clerical, it stresses the natural class links between the poor Irish-Canadians of Griffintown and the poor French-Canadians of Montreal. His third novel, *Days of Rage* (1974), is virtually a re-write of *One Man Alone*, from a jailed French-Canadian guerrilla's point of view. It emphasizes some of its predecessor's points more clearly, as when the curé responds to the Asbestos Company strike by dogmatically declaiming: "I'm a nationalist, not a Marxist. I choose to view the strike not as a class struggle between exploited and exploiters, but as a

20 Ibid.

nationalist conflict between French workers and American employers."[21] For Buller, it is necessarily both, and his books are political statements which present racism as an integral part of the dialectic in Quebec and in Canada as a whole. While Buller shows the positive potential of natural class connections and sympathies among the poor of all backgrounds, he does not limit racism to the rich capitalists, as Carter shortsightedly does. Buller allows the tensions of racial hatred to filter through all social strata, explaining the infection of the very poor as well; whereas for Carter, to be poor almost automatically removed oneself from the possibility of racism, and to be wealthy or directly dependent upon wealth forced one to be racist.

None the less, Buller and Carter seem very much alike, the one concentrating on Montreal and Asbestosville in Quebec, and the other on Sudbury in Ontario. Both operate from the left, are anti-clerical, anti-American, and in favour of a national unity of the working class. Both put class before race as research tools for social analysis. Carter wrote essentially from the English-Canadian position (as far as race is concerned), using English-Canadian characters to show how society could be altered for the benefit of everyone, and because of his northern setting he used Indians as a victimized race. Buller focused on the anti-Semitism issue in Montreal in relation to French-Canadians, portraying English-Canadians simply as a wall of power, money, and indifference.

Adele Wiseman's *The Sacrifice* (1956) is not primarily a race-conscious novel, but rather a good example of what has been termed the immigrant novel.[22] When an immigrant novel deals with an ethnically homogeneous community of immigrants, then it can supply details of the pressures that lead to group protectionism and ethnocentrism. *The Sacrifice* shows well the establishment of groups within groups, as newly arrived Jewish immigrants are looked down upon by those already in place. Wiseman notes: "It was not often that the native girls paid much attention to an immigrant boy—as though their parents hadn't been immigrants themselves."[23] The grouping effect involves continuous mobility for self-improvement. It can even be stronger than family ties when the opportunities exist for extra-familial progress and such ties prove to be obstacles.

This choice between one's family group and a more successful group is the theme of John Marlyn's *Under the Ribs of Death* (1957), a novel about a Hungarian boy growing up in Winnipeg in the 1920s. Sandor Hunyadi is a protagonist tainted with a degree of villainy for renouncing his parents and his Hungarian past in a desperate attempt to become anglicized and

---

21 Herman Buller, *Days of Rage* (Toronto: October Publications, 1974), pp. 82-83.
22 Tamara Palmer supplies a convincing argument for the value of the term "immigrant novel" in "Ethnic Character and Social Themes in Novels About Prairie Canada and the period from 1900 to 1940," unpublished M.A. thesis, York University, 1972.
23 Adele Wiseman, *The Sacrifice* (Toronto: Macmillan of Canada, 1977), pp. 75-76.

overcome the anti-Hungarian prejudice which had made his childhood so miserable. Giving up a rich cultural tradition for the vacuous materialism of Canada is Sandor's decision. He places his faith in a change of name. Better equipped to penetrate the English-Canadian establishment as Alex Hunter, the conqueror-seeker, Alex tries to move beyond his roots, without the obnoxious drive that Duddy Kravitz would later display. Despite studying English and business courses at night school, Sandor/Alex is not accepted by English-Canadians who continue to discriminate against him because of his still apparent Hungarian origins. Left in a limbo between his parents' Old World lifestyle and that of the unobtainable New World, unemployed with a family to support during the Depression, Alex refuses to return even though he recognizes he can't go forward. His repudiation of his past impoverishes him without freeing him of its racial limitations in Canadian society.

Marlyn presents Alex's problems as being economic in nature, but such is the strength of the Canadian dream in the boy's eyes that he cannot admit its failure, and instead he blames racial discrimination for his personal failure. As a social force which prohibits his advance, racism is strongly delineated in the novel and would be a considerable impediment to anyone. But Alex inflates its dimensions, blaming it entirely for his situation, and failing to see that cutting himself off from his past and impersonating an Anglo-Saxon has defined him as an irresponsible person no one would want to employ because of his rootless shiftiness. Racism is his scapegoat. The love of his family supports him in the end, and it is not impossible that he will benefit by it and reassume the identity which would have some basis, yet admittedly be a handicap, in the English-dominated business world. Himself a second-generation Hungarian-Canadian, Marlyn showed the dilemma of such an individual looking from the outside in to where he thinks prosperity and security are, and prepared to sell his soul for them.

The conflicts of Marlyn's novel accentuate the proximity of racial, ethnic, and cultural concepts in a study of this nature. Obviously there are both positive and negative associations—not absolute characteristics but illusive and changeable associations—to the concept of ethnicity. The harsher term "race," with its implications of purity and immutability, depends upon real ethnic differences for its less real validation. Racism uses this already debatable justification for purposes of discrimination, which are negative to the victim but positive to the racist, who may thereby feel he is protecting whatever group to which he wishes to claim allegiance. Culture is also divided up, for although it is obviously not racially governed or restricted, attempts *are* made to connect its various forms with various races. Ethnocentrism, on a small group level as much as on the national and international levels, is the real problem, and when analyzed in terms of class and the particular demographic developments of Canadian history, it can be seen to bar the way to success for a white Hungarian-Canadian in Winnipeg as much as for a black Barbadian-Canadian in Toronto.

III

Austin C. Clarke is probably best known in Canada for his Toronto-based trilogy consisting of *The Meeting Point* (1967), *Storm of Fortune* (1971), and *The Bigger Light* (1975). A Barbadian by birth, Clarke immigrated to Canada in 1955, where the success of his first books, *Survivors of the Crossing* (1964) and *Amongst Thistles and Thorns* (1965), in which he fictionalized various themes in Barbadian settings, led to positions as writer-in-residence at several American universities as well as an appointment as Barbadian cultural attaché in Washington. Resettled in Toronto since 1977, he continues to be active in the expatriate Caribbean community.

Clarke's fictionalization of the situation of blacks in Canada is quite similar to the work of Sam Selvon, who followed the hordes of West Indian immigrants to the United Kingdom, describing their conditions of life there in a series of light yet bitterly serious novels.[24] In them, light-hearted optimistic West Indians are shown being ground down into dehumanized material by a cold and indifferent white society. Racial discrimination floods Selvon's work with unpleasant tensions, publicizing actual problems. In much the same manner in which Selvon was the self-appointed publicist of racism in England, Clarke has exposed equivalent issues in Toronto. The indignation which permeates his books arose from personal experience, as the first volume of his autobiography, *Growing Up Stupid Under the Union Jack* (1980), and the less autobiographical but still historically and personally authentic *Amongst Thistles and Thorns* implied. In an interview for *Maclean's* in 1963 Clarke claimed: "In my eight years in Canada I have been treated with prejudice and discrimination by most white people, in large and small ways." His anger was evident in the tone of the interview as he insisted that the practical situation of non-whites in Canada was little different from that in the United States.[25] Although he spoke of Canada in general, his experience is mainly limited to Toronto and its West Indian community which has grown so rapidly since 1945.

Clarke's Barbadian books, including *The Prime Minister* (1977), the setting of which is purposely vague, do not contain many instances of racism. The rich are white and the poor are black and the resentment expressed is more economic than explicitly racial. *Amongst Thistles and*

---

24 Selvon moved to Alberta in 1977. His best known books about blacks in Britain are *The Lonely Londoners* (1956) and *Moses Ascending* (1975).

25 Austin C. Clarke, "A Black Man Talks About Race Prejudice in White Canada," *Maclean's* 76, No. 8 (1963), 18, 55-58.

Thorns contains the only scene of real racial ugliness: when a white boy maliciously sets his dog on a black child, the victim is rebuked by an old black watchman for assaulting the dog! Generally, however, these books concentrated on the local troubles of the impoverished black population and their struggles to improve their situation. Whites are not really a part of their lives, living as they do separately in walled enclosures of luxury and idleness. Blacks do their laundry and cook in the hotels for them, but have little contact with them as people.

The Canadian books, particularly the trilogy and the collection of ten short stories in *When he was free and young and he used to wear silks* (1971), some of which are taken from the trilogy, show West Indians in unavoidably close contact with white Torontonians. The resultant friction is examined in detail not in an openly dogmatic or self-righteous manner, but definitely with the aim of exposing racism and offering suggestions concerning its eradication. Clarke writes from the point of view of black immigrants who are trying to find success in a cold, white country. In their colloquial language their world of poverty, humiliation, resentment, and loneliness is explored as it takes them to the point of masturbation and homosexuality, and a selfish repudiation of their past in their efforts to turn white. Clarke writes about their problems, of which racism is only one, and an externally imposed one at that. Cultural differences between English-Canadians or Jewish-Canadians and Caribbeans cause much of their troubles, but racism is always in the background.

The Meeting Point introduces the cast of Bernice Leach, a Barbadian domestic working for the wealthy Jewish Burrmann family in Forest Hill; her visiting sister, Estelle, who is made pregnant by Mr. Burrmann; her friends Dots and Boysie Cumberbatch; Henry White (who is black) and his Jewish girlfriend, Agatha; and Brigitte, the German maid who works for Mrs. Gasstein. To point out each person's colour or group membership may seem to be falling into the trap Clarke is trying to expose, but in fact it is necessary because of the emphasis Clarke places on his characters, having each one represent one point of view from an ethnic standpoint. These standpoints are not clear-cut and independent, but are vague and mesh together more and more as the trilogy develops, following the increasingly interconnected relationships of characters in all ethnic groups. Certainly the characters in Clarke's novels develop, Boysie being the best example as he progresses from being a shiftless cane cutter in Barbados through unemployment in Toronto to the point where he can and does leave his prosperous janitorial business there to explore the Black Power movement in the United States for his own personal edification. Most of the characters benefit from various harsh experiences in that they adapt to Canadian ways of life as much as is necessary for their material success, while retaining Caribbean ideas of pleasure and relaxation. They do achieve a level of prosperity through hard work, once they accept that work in Canada is as necessary as it was in Barbados, and their little successes provide them with some independence from various forms of racism so that they can then develop as people apart from ethnic prisons of definition. Clarke seems to be saying that money whitens, but that it can whiten too much.

Clarke touches all the bases of possible comparisons between blacks and whites, showing the good and the bad of both sides. The less likable qualities of the blacks are exposed for the world to see, while those of the whites are concealed by their wealth. They can get away with behaviour that the blacks cannot; they are protected, for they are aware of the rules of their own game, while the blacks stumble through life in Canada committing a multitude of mistakes they often don't know exist. But they learn, as Clarke must have learned, for he knows both sides. He reveals the physical underside of urban life in Canada, in all its awareness of being looked down upon (in this respect resembling Richler), and he compares it with similar explicit knowledge of the white upper-class community the blacks love and hate. Both sides—white and black—are alike in sharing human failings and possibilities. In *Storm of Fortune*, an ugly episode of a white man forcing his attentions on a black girl is followed immediately by a similar one with a black man. Clarke's fairness is obvious. He is understanding with various attributed stereotypical qualities of West Indians which attract the disapprobation of white Canada—their apparent laziness, love of loud music and colourful clothing, and their readiness to lie even to themselves in order to protect their desired images as prosperous arriviste Canadians. These are cultural affectations, and both blacks and whites balance each other in good and bad qualities.

In *The Meeting Point* much of the tension is created between Bernice and her wealthy Jewish employers, the Burrmanns. Mrs. Burrmann is represented as a rich person who happens to be white. Her insensitive treatment of Bernice, full of petty reminders of the mistress-maid relationship, is due to the protection of her wealth, and is not shown to be just a function of her colour. When she finally fires Bernice, she replaces her with a Polish refugee whom she treats even worse. Mrs. Burrmann, dissatisfied with her husband, vacations in Mexico where she hires Mexican lovers. Throughout Clarke's work, as in reality, the myths of the blacks' sexual superiority[26]—which he himself openly states are myths—operate almost as facts because people believe in them. Mr. Burrmann is impotent with his wife and his frustration drives him to practically rape Estelle and then carry on a secretive affair with her for some time before leaving her pregnant. Sam Burrmann's past is explored in more psychological detail than that of any other white character. His history of guilt is twofold: as a youth in the Spadina area of Toronto, Sam let a black acquaintance take the blame for a

26 Austin C. Clarke, *Storm of Fortune* (Boston: Little, Brown, 1973), pp. 157-58.

minor act of theft which he had committed, and this friend was sentenced to two years in prison when he was too afraid to speak up and save him. His first sexual experience was with a black woman who mocked him for his childish inadequacy, yet black women remained with him as an image of sexual enjoyment and fulfillment. He is attracted to Estelle for this reason. This was all that was necessary for the plot, but Clarke went deeper to make his point clearer. There is the suggestion that he deliberately places Jews in the racist positions because of their former minority position and their history as victims of racism, to show that no one group is ever free of such vices.[27] Groups are not inherently racist until they accumulate wealth, and wealth monopolized by anyone creates the atmosphere of protectionism which under certain circumstances gives rise to racism. Sam himself was poor and faced discrimination as a student at the University of Toronto; his sexual problems and wishes are only one aspect of his damaged ego. Clarke delves no further into the psychology of interracial sex. It is enough for him that this white couple has to seek satisfaction independently with non-white partners. Similarly Henry and Boysie pursue white women as images of white achievement. The blonde Brigitte is an ideal for both of them, for she represents a world of success which they can temporarily obtain because of her lowly position as a maid. Henry finally marries Agatha, a Jewish doctoral student who idolizes him for his negritude, despite her parents' objections. Henry's awareness of his lack of education and his financial dependence on her drives him desperately first to despairing poetry and eventually to an unexplained death.

Love alone cannot conquer perceived racial differences, as far as Clarke is concerned. Such differences matter little when both partners are equal materially. The blacks learn how to survive in Canada and buckle down to the hard work some seem to have come to avoid, and by such work gain a measure of independence and self-respect that elevates them above images and façades. Money is the key to success in Canada. They work to achieve that success, but when they gain it they risk losing something of their past in the process. Blacks can become whites when they become moneyed. In *Storm of Fortune*, in a scene quite reminiscent of the conclusion to Orwell's *Animal Farm*, Bernice recounts her spying on a "paint-in" in which the lone black guest was painted white, as the fashionable party-goers merged their differences in a hedonistic orgy that left Bernice shocked.[28] Clarke reduces both sides to their common denominator of lust and avarice and dishonesty. He does show that instead of slavishly imitating whites and

27 Clarke's wealthy white Canadian characters are almost all Jewish not, he admits, because in reality Canadian wealth is Jewish, but because blacks in Toronto believe so, and he wished to be faithful to his chosen narrative perspective. Personal interview with Austin C. Clarke, Oct. 3, 1981.
28 Clarke, *Storm of Fortune*, pp. 296-99.

renouncing one's Caribbean roots, blacks should establish themselves as independent workers in Canada with their backgrounds kept intact. In a short story, "Four Stations in His Circle," Clarke described a materially successful black immigrant who lives by himself, saving every penny to buy an imposing house in Rosedale, where his past in the shape of the people he has lied to and renounced to get ahead appears to haunt him to the point of madness. His empty life, symbolized by his superficially impressive residence which he can't afford to furnish, is the antithesis of Boysie's search for meaning beyond material success.[29]

There does seem to be a wealthy Jew versus poor black dichotomy in place in the trilogy. However, Clarke is too wise to accept the corollary which Dyson Carter, for example, followed blindly, that poor whites and poor blacks would get along better automatically because of their common troubles. In some cases this is so in Clarke's work, but usually such idealistic proletarian unity is accompanied by or even explained by sexual attraction. There is no transracial solidarity among the poor in Clarke's Toronto. He even includes a scene in which Henry is rebuffed while trying to rent an apartment in an area where "all the names were mostly European names. *Chuck* or *Chich* or *Gowski* or *Shev*, Godblindthemall!"[30] He appears to be making the point that despite their mutual immigrant status, European newcomers are as racist as established English-Canadians. Colour is important for various irrational reasons Clarke doesn't bother to explore; the cruel naked fact of its importance is his point. Racism is a psychological weapon which provides reassurance as much as actual defence, and Clarke shows how it is used. The German immigrant maid who earns an enormous salary working for a wealthy Jewish family in Toronto is discussed by Bernice and Dots in *Storm of Fortune*:

> Now, Mistress Gasstein, being a born Jew, wouldn't think of hiring a black woman like you or me. No. That ain' a high enough social position for her, in terms o' domestics and maids, since every blasted little white woman with a husband making more than five-thousand dollars a year wages, and with a house, want to and could hire a blasted person as a living-in slave. But that do not bring prestige. You see the sperspective I driving at? But when she could spend her riches on a German woman, who she know is a German, and therefore a Nazzi, well, she could brag to all her Forest Hill friends that she have *one o' them* working *under* her.[31]

What this describes is a form of racially motivated revenge. When Dots describes herself as "a living-in slave" she expresses the resentment at the

29 Austin C. Clarke, "Four Stations in His Circle," in *When he was free and young and he used to wear silks* (Toronto: Anansi, 1971), pp. 51-63.
30 Clarke, *Storm of Fortune*, p. 284.
31 Ibid., p. 109.

subservience blacks feel is imposed on them by whites who do it partly for their own psychological gratification. There is no difference between the way in which Mrs. Burrmann uses Bernice and the way Mrs. Gasstein uses her German maid. It is the exercise of wealth corrupted. Each time Bernice and Mrs. Burrmann conflict in *The Meeting Point*, instead of Bernice being punished, her salary is raised, confusing her. She doesn't see that she is being bought off, seduced into continuing subservience. Mrs. Burrmann realizes that with her wealth she can do anything and get away with it, though a price is paid, as the tells Mrs. Gasstein: "You don't really understand why everybody hates us Jews. Everybody hates people who are as wealthy as us."[32] Clarke makes it clear that possession of wealth is itself not incriminating. Her abuse of people because of the security of wealth is the main reason Mrs. Burrmann is hated. Agatha gives up her wealthy Jewish background to marry the have-not Henry for love, and Henry's friends think she is mad to surrender money, but they understand love because that is all they have ever had.

Within all this two-sided bantering about racial equality Clarke includes a condemnation of white Canadian society on several grounds. The police are presented as actively violent racists, whites are hypocritical about morality, and illegitimate children are uncared for. An illegitimate child himself, Clarke's strong feelings on this subject came out in his *Growing Up Stupid Under the Union Jack*, and were expressed in *Storm of Fortune* as an indictment against the cold, unfeeling behaviour of whites, as Bernice tells her sister about the terrible necessity for adoption agencies in Toronto: "They is Caffolick, Anglican, Jewish and Protestants. And *all* of them are full-up to the top with unwanted kids. That's what they call them in this country, *unwanted children*. Back home we calls them *outside-children*. Back home we does cherish children! never mind they born outside wedlock, but be-Christ, they born *inside* love!"[33] Clarke is not an admirer of Canadian society, for he has seen it from the bottom and knows its dirty secrets. He has an alternative: work like a Canadian but be free to live like a West Indian. He provides a local and partial solution based on a thorough explanation of the unpleasant facts that people would probably rather avoid, and he does so with fairness and controlled indignation. Clarke has much in common with Richler, both men rising above sides to present comprehensive views of the larger situation, firmly based on a belief in a common humanity regardless of race. The main difference is that Clarke works harder to defend his West Indians, perhaps because their fragmented culture is harder to vindicate before Anglo-Saxons than the more established Jewish tradition, and because their colour is a continual reminder of their origins and their differences.

32 Ibid., p. 230.
33 Ibid., p. 32.

The belief that race is ultimately unimportant in the face of human qualities that must be respected informs most of the work of these non-charter-group Canadian novelists, yet it co-exists in much of their fiction with strong feelings of ethnic pride reluctantly suppressed to resist ethno-centric fanaticism in favour of a multiculturally tolerant comprehensive Canadian nationality. These feelings developed into a compromise position, keeping a little ethnic identity back while giving in as much as necessary to English-Canadian demands. In the course of compromise the English-Canadian position shifted in literature, responding to the varie-gated protestations of ethnic pride, and being outflanked by the "ethnics'" appeal to the democratic vision of Canadian identity. The books discussed above represented pressure as much as surrender, and this paradox led towards a gradually negotiated compromise which raised the status of immigrants and gave them acceptance as Canadians. Their existence on paper confirmed their existence in history as much as in present reality.

Chapter Five

The Synthesis of
Multiculturalism, 1939-1980

Personally, one cannot care much for those who have renounced their own country. They may have had good reason, but they have broken the rules of the game, and ought to be penalized instead of adding to their score. Nor is it true, as men pretend, that a few meals and fine clothes obliterate all taint of alien instinct and reversion.

Letters to the Family, by Rudyard Kipling

I

Various pressures combined to induce a synthesis of the English-Canadian and immigrant views of race: both views were afflicted with regional insularity; both groups were hampered by ignorance of each other's true attributes and motives; and both groups and views operated at cross purposes with obvious negative results. The English-Canadians encouraged assimilation, by which they meant the dissolving of immigrant attributes into their own solution, but they also reserved total assimilation for reasons that were nothing less than prejudices. The immigrant groups, all possessing their own ethnocentric superiority complexes, lacked inter-group co-operation while pursuing (and being forced to pursue) charter-group ideals. Internationally the persecution of Jews in Europe forced the issue of anti-Semitism to a head in Canada, ultimately destroying (at least temporarily) the possibility of its literary expression within the country. Biological and sociological attitudes in Canada developed to the point where non-Anglo-Saxon cultures were seen as historically interesting and even independently valid, and the alleged purity of races was more univer-

95

sally denied. Relatively more tolerant attitudes began to penetrate the periodical press. Diamond Jenness, the noted anthropologist, in 1925 calmly discussed the eventual fate of the Eskimo in an article in *Queen's Quarterly*, in which he prophesied their interbreeding with whites to the point of disappearance, for everyone's mutual benefit rather than separate losses.[1] The *Canadian Forum* published in 1929 an article which stands out starkly amidst the general trend of anti-Asiatic diatribes in the periodicals of the inter-war period. In "The Oriental in British Columbia," A. S. Whitely called for reduced immigration from the Orient *because of* the discrimination they were receiving in Canada, put forward a plan of education to help those already in Canada adjust to local conditions and escape prejudice, and explained racism in class rather than biological or even cultural terms.[2] Furthermore, some prominent English-Canadians, such as Watson Kirkconnell and Robert England, both internationally minded men, continued to publish their support for aliens, albeit with certain qualifications. Also writing in *Queen's Quarterly* in 1929, England attacked the idea of a quota system for immigrants: "We have no Monroe doctrine and our immigration policy must be justified on other lines than racial or religious prejudice. The Sermon on the Mount is a more satisfactory guide than the Gospel of Hate whose only logical corollary is the trenches in one form or another."[3] More facts emerged to dispel the myths and falsehoods that ignorance had fostered. The uphill battle to gain recognition and respect for aliens in the West could be seen to be progressing in the academic press while it lagged behind in the more popular periodicals. In general, blatant racism was becoming more and more unfashionable. To be anti-anti-Semitic (as distinct from being pro-Semitic) became the mode. Gordon's statement that racism was unchristian was finally accepted well beyond the point he was able to reach himself.

The body of fiction dealing with racial issues during and after the Second World War may be divided into two categories. The immigrant writers (first, second, and even third generation) wrote from outside the safety of English-Canadian membership and exposed the terms of that membership as un-Canadian. The developing English-Canadian group looked at the problem from outside traditional English-Canadian definitions of society, and spoke to those English-Canadians who continued to discriminate against others for various reasons. The literature of the anglophone writers who looked out upon the problem from their still privileged position inside the crumbling garrison will be examined here. In particular, the attempts

1 Diamond Jenness, "Canada's Eskimo Problem," *Queen's Quarterly* 32, No. 4 (1925), 324.

2 A. S. Whitely, "The Oriental in British Columbia," *Canadian Forum* 9, No. 106 (1929), 342-44.

3 Robert England, "Continental Migration," *Queen's Quarterly* 36, No. 4 (1929), 728.

by Graham, Callaghan, Laurence, Bodsworth, and Mitchell to reach some
compromise between both positions and to deny racist tenets will be
discussed.

One early example of such work is Howard O'Hagan's *Tay John* (1939),
which is a non-Indian's investigation of the Albertan Indian legend of Tête
Jaune. O'Hagan's background in the mountains there provided him with a
unique geographical perspective and an allegiance to the people of the area
that supported a new attitude. O'Hagan's Indians, not only in *Tay John* but
also in his later works and notably in *Wilderness Men* (1958), are linked with
the exploring whites of the early century in remote areas, in that they share a
feeling for the land and the freedom the outdoors offered. *Tay John* is the
first Canadian work of fiction to move the reader inside an Indian tribe with
any degree of authenticity. It does so with sympathy and without condes-
cension. In detailing the unusual circumstances of Kumkleseem's birth,
O'Hagan delicately and without apology lets the Indians' explanation
stand. Their tolerance of the mad self-appointed missionary, Red Rorty, is
exemplary until it is abused by his rape of one of their women; his murder,
with its symbolic echoes of Christ's crucifixion, reminds us of the history of
inhumanity among whites. The Indians are a community of conformists,
just as the whites in the wilderness, despite their lonely eccentric ways, are
mostly at heart gregarious conformists. Two individuals stand above them
as individuals: Kumkleseem/Tay John, the yellow-headed half-breed; and
Ardith Aeriola, the Central European beauty who undertakes a mountain
vacation to escape scandal in the East. Tay John, the offspring of Red
Rorty's rape, left his Shuswap people when they venerated him to the point
of denying him a wife. Earning a meagre living guiding whites and
trapping, he haunts the fringes of white civilization, very much his own
man. His masculine independence—"machismo" might suit O'Hagan's
idea of him—fatally attracts Ardith, who runs off into the bush with him,
dying months later presumably in childbirth. She also operates on the edge
of society, her easy morality offending the white communities she visits,
and with her foreign ways she does not entirely belong to English-Canada.

In fact, English-Canada is symbolically kept at arm's length throughout
this novel. Events occur for which non-Indians have no explanation, and
which are left in suspension simply as beliefs of the Indians. The narrator,
Jack Denham, who takes over the story in Part Two (suggestively entitled
"Hearsay"), imposes a basically English-Canadian interpretation upon Tay
John's life, but one that definitely remains open to the heroic and the
mysterious. The combat between the bear and Tay John, which Jack
witnesses from across a river, is very significant. In the elemental struggles
of nature, the white man is an observer, not a participant. It is Jack's
awareness of Tay John belonging to the land that raises his narrative above
pedestrian mediocrity and the possibility of stereotyping, and which pro-

vides Tay John with unusual stature as a character. The point of view, and the difficulties Jack has articulating it against the accumulated myths about Indians and half-breeds, is important in that the effort to understand the Indian psychology is made, and the point that such an effort is difficult but worthwhile is confirmed.

Tay John is the first successful half-breed in the Canadian novel. Indeed it is his position halfway between two worlds that forces the qualities upon him that make him larger than other characters. The publication of *Tay John* in 1939, complete with its significant prefatory note conceding the author's indebtedness to Diamond Jenness, marked the demise of the old English-Canadian view towards Indians and half-breeds in serious litera-ture. The Indians began to come into their own, if only in print.

Gwethalyn Graham's *Earth and High Heaven* (1944) did much the same for Canadian Jews as O'Hagan had done for Canadian Indians, but Graham's novel was nothing less than a frontal assault on anti-Semitism. As such it is also a first in Canada, and seems to be something of a rarity anywhere in the world. A product of wartime, it impresses into fiction Graham's indignation about racism plus her naively optimistic solution. Set in 1942 in Montreal, the novel follows the romance between Marc Reiser, a second generation Jewish-Canadian, and Erica Drake, an English-Canadian heiress. Erica's father, a Montreal businessman, snubs Marc and refuses his permission for the couple to marry. Marc's parents too would be happier seeing their son married within their faith. In the end both pairs of parents give in and the novel ends on an optimistic note. Prejudice has been defeated, the lady won, and a bright future secured. It all seems too good to be true.

While anti-Semitism is the main target of this ambitiously reformist work, it extends beyond the religious to take in other aspects of discrimina-tion, and the entire phenomenon is doubtless best defined as racism. Graham attacked this in several ways. Primarily she exposed the conformist nature of popular prejudice. The Drakes are like geese as they follow public opinion, not realizing how their refusal to judge for themselves limits their attitudes. Graham suggests that such mentally lazy people find it much easier to live in a world of myths and stereotypes, where preconceptions will always turn out to be true because they cannot be recognized otherwise, and where change is minimal. In this sense the Drakes could fit right into one of Gordon's books. But Graham is trying to straddle the problem and present the inadequacies of both sides. Marc's family has its ethnocentric pride taken to a fault too. Graham permits a certain amount of this to be preserved, possibly to better balance the scales between the two sides in the eyes of English-Canadians (because this is first and foremost a *lecture* directed at them). Marc finds and maintains a certain pride in his Jewish heritage which need not conflict with his Canadian identity and which is based on facts most Christian Canadians ought to be able to understand. For example: "As a Canadian and a Jew, he had to admit that eleven million Canadians had so far failed to produce one individual as outstanding as uncounted living Jews, out of a total world population before Hitler of approximately sixteen million—let alone the innumerable Jewish scientists, philosophers and artists no longer living."[4] Pride in one's ancestry is permissible, but discrimination against others because of it is shown to be wrong.

Graham moved intelligently to break up stereotypes. Marc's father is a pragmatic lumbermill owner in Northern Ontario. His brother is an altruistic bush doctor, also in the North. Marc himself does not fit previous literary models. He seems an ordinary Canadian with some Jewish religious trappings. There are none of Gordon's "little Jews" here, and even Gibbon would have to admit that Marc's family is all "white." Graham divides up her Jewish characters deliberately to reveal their differences, denying that there is one Jewish point of view. Her differentiated characters possess so much individuality, and display so many of the best qualities that racist English-Canadians had apportioned only to themselves, that the common humanity of both sides becomes obvious. The connection with *Romeo and Juliet*, which Eli Mandel pointed out in his introduction to the 1969 New Canadian Library edition, perhaps operates on an archetypal level in the novel, requiring no elucidation to make itself felt. Neither side expresses the hatred of the Montagues and Capulets, but the effect—the interruption of young love—is the same. Graham's solution is that these ancient rivalries dissolve in democratic Canada and that intermarriage will eventually make them disappear entirely. Love is her answer.

The book is often noted as a landmark in Canadian literature for its positive rebuke of prejudice. It remains an important work because it was the first, but several qualifications can be attached to its praise, indicative of the rudimentary level of her attempt.

Graham's privileged background may have dictated her choice of setting and characters, which have little to do with most Canadians, then or now. The Drakes in their Westmount castle have little in common with the average Canadian who might be leaning towards anti-Semitism. Similarly the elder Reisers were wealthy immigrants, involved in an industry which Jews were popularly thought to avoid, and their son, David the doctor, has not only made good in a (then) reserved occupation but did so with no aim of self-aggrandizement. One might complain that Graham bent over backwards in order to explode Jewish stereotypes and in so doing removed important elements of credibility from her novel. Such criticism would hardly be fair because the stereotypes were false in the first place, albeit

4 Gwethalyn Graham, *Earth and High Heaven* (Garden City, New York: Sun Dial Press, 1945), p. 257.

credible by habituation. Also, it might be argued that because of the emotions these stereotypes had raised and the attitudes they had promoted in such extreme ways, they deserved and indeed required such severe reparations. One might more effectively complain that the Reisers have as little in common with the average Jewish immigrant, so well portrayed in Saul Bellow's *The Victim* or in Richler's St. Urbain Street scenes, for example, as the wealthy Drakes have in common with the average Protestant. Even though Marc and Erica do have more in common with the average Canadian reader, Graham's characterization of them, and especially of Erica, is wooden, leaving them more as spokespersons for their gospel of love than as realistic individuals.

Earth and High Heaven treats racism as the psychological failure to face the realities of other people. It is the desire to make life simpler and easier by imposing simple preconceptions upon it. Graham exposed this narrow mode of thought while insisting that although real cultural differences between people must be respected, the common humanity everyone shares is more important.

As a recorder of prejudice, Graham's indignation is very valuable. She pointed out what few people seemed to realize then: that there were, in Montreal, hotels and restaurants which did not admit Jews. Only Richler and Garner also expressed such practicalities of racial discrimination, the former with regard to resorts in the Laurentians, and the latter concerning parks and beaches in Toronto, in *Cabbagetown* (1950; complete edition, 1971).

Garner's perspective was almost the opposite of Graham's. Where she wrote of wealth and sophistication, he concentrated on the poor and the ignorant. His early espousal of socialism clearly influenced his choice of subject matter. His attitude on race was affected by his politics and is probably best summed up in *Cabbagetown* when a hobo introduces Ken to the laws of the hobo jungle and tells him:

> That's the trouble in this goddamn country, nobody sticks together. The Englishman hates the Frenchman, and the two of them hate the Jew, and the Jew hates everybody, and everybody hates the hunkies. The only guy that benefits is the capitalist. He loves to see us hating each other 'cause it stops us hating him.[5]

Sensible co-operation, not love, is Garner's solution. Politics on the most elementary level lies beneath *Cabbagetown*.

There can be no doubt that Garner thematically incorporated racism into his work in a very deliberate manner. *Storm Below* (1949), his first novel and one written out of his experiences on corvettes in the Second World War, included a subplot involving a Jewish officer's reaction to the anti-Semitism

5 Hugh Garner, *Cabbagetown* (Toronto: Ryerson Press, 1971), p. 161.

of his shipmates. This Lt. Harris is a Marc Reiser figure, a volunteer not so much *against Nazism* as *for Canada*, and this is very significant. Garner allows him recognition as an ordinary Canadian first and introduces his Jewishness secondly. He seems to be as capable as the other officers, and his Jewishness is not an issue until one obnoxious fellow-officer raises it in purely racist terms. This officer is clearly less attractive a character than most. After the initial confrontation between them, Harris's soul-searching reveals the injury racism does to its victims. The reader dissociates himself from the senseless drivel of Smith-Rawleigh and sympathizes with the sensitive Harris. In the end the ship's captain takes much the same attitude that Gordon had done in *The Major*, that Harris should not resign his commission but remain on the ship, proving that in the war in which all Canadians must participate, Jews can claim no special distinctions nor do they deserve any special discrimination. Acceptance comes from staying in the ring and asserting one's presence and rights. Retreat from prejudice can only encourage it and discourage its victims. This episode is a sub-theme which contributes to the novel's main theme, the co-operation of men of all classes and several ethnic backgrounds within a complex organization, a Canadian *Pequod*.

In Garner's second novel, *Cabbagetown*, the working-class perspective is even clearer. The story traces the maturing of two Toronto boys, Ken and Theodore, during the Depression. Ken runs away from his futureless existence in Toronto and learns the cynical philosophy of the down and out. A poor English-Canadian himself, his limited exposure to other groups of people is expanded as he travels and he eventually goes to fight in the Spanish Civil War with a Jewish comrade. His tolerance emerges from his growing sense of community and his school-of-hard-knocks education. Theodore is a far less likable character who avoids hard work and sacrifices principles to escape the prison that Cabbagetown is for its youth. He joins a fascist organization, the "National Canadian Youth," to make contacts with wealthier people and he develops all the trappings of a racist and an anti-Semite. Garner makes the point that Theodore is not really a committed fascist or racist or anything, but merely an unprincipled opportunist with no thought for anyone but himself. Theodore attends a rally of his new friends in a Toronto park to protest the presence of Jews there and on the beach, and he joins in the chasing of a frightened Jew into Lake Ontario where he throws stones at him. What Arendt called the banality of evil is evident here in the surprisingly simple way one ordinary Canadian boy could slip down to the level where he could join a pogrom and stone another human being. The contrast between Theodore and Ken is obvious. Theodore is not the villain so much as the victim of a society which by its nature fosters inhuman conduct. His racism is not the product of reason but simply a reflection of selfish protectionist instincts. Garner does not try to make

Jews into heroes. Lt. Harris was a Canadian like the rest of his characters, not a spectacular naval hero. In "The Stretcher Bearers," a short story in *The Yellow Sweater* (1952), a Jewish volunteer in the International Brigades in Spain is shown as neither braver nor more cowardly than his fellows. Garner was satisfied to include Jews in his philosophy of the working man. He did not find it necessary to include a Jewish version of Dr. Schweitzer, as Graham did, and as Buller did for blacks in *One Man Alone*. Graham's upper-class background illuminated her work with illusions of success, while Garner wrote of inevitable failures.

Garner's concern with racism was not limited to anti-Semitism. In *Storm Below* the one French-Canadian in the corvette's crew is the butt of constant ethnic humour. Garner takes the time to defend him as an intelligent and literate man whose education is unappreciated by the English crewmen because of his lack of the English language. His intelligence ironically is probably best expressed by his own good-humoured acceptance of the crew's teasing. In *The Yellow Sweater*, "Interlude in Black and White" is the story of a young man with venereal disease who is humiliated and rejected by an ignorant orderly at a hospital where he has gone for treatment. The man is married and is clearly involved in some matrimonial tragedy. He is also black and that seems to be why he is given such a hard time, but his colour otherwise is unimportant. The way Garner presents him, he could be any man, anywhere. It is his status as a person that makes this more than an episode in discrimination, and that seems to have been Garner's point. In yet another story, "One-Two-Three Little Indians," Garner wrote about the death of an Indian couple's child at a tourist camp in Northern Ontario. The parents had neither the money nor the transportation to take their sick infant to a doctor in a nearby town. Their tragedy is simply not recognized by passing whites who could easily have helped them. The Indians are invisible in Ralph Ellison's sense of the word in *Invisible Man*. The whites ignore the baby's illness, the parents' pleas for a ride into town, and the lonely father's attempt to hitch-hike into town with the child. Obviously the realities, the physical and emotional consequences of extensive racial discrimination, were appreciated by Garner and he did not hesitate to display the victims' plight in his fiction.

In *Silence on the Shore* (1962) Garner elaborated these ideas of racism which had permeated his earlier work. The setting of Mrs. Hill's boardinghouse is an excuse for the book's multicultural characterization, just as Ruth Wheeler's boardinghouse is for Jane Rule's *The Young in One Another's Arms* (1977), another, later novel that goes beyond racial stereotypes to explore sexual ones. *Silence on the Shore* deals with the problems of good and evil, disclaiming absolutes to prove that people vacillate weakly between the polarities. The ease by which a supposedly good person can lapse into bad behaviour is extended to racism. Derogatory racial comments and slurs are made carelessly without thought, just as Theodore had lapsed foolishly into fascist racism in *Cabbagetown*. Garner blamed the poor Anglo-Saxon-Celtic immigrants as being the source of most of the prejudice directed against "foreigners" such as Russian displaced persons, and he seems to have felt that their feelings were simple xenophobia.[6] He avoids extremes in his definitions as always, but despite its xenophobic roots it is pure racism that looms out of his novels. In fact, its ubiquitous presence in his work suggests that he felt the particular Canadian society which he portrays could not be realistically described without the inclusion of racist acts and their tragic consequences.

In *Silence on the Shore* Mrs. Hill reveals that she had been a German immigrant, but because of anti-German feeling during the war she married an Englishman for his name, explaining her accent thereafter by claiming to be Swiss.[7] Simply by bringing to the public notice the idea that prejudice was so powerful a force in Canada that people felt compelled to change their names, or that Jews could be stoned out of a public park in Toronto, Garner provided a valuable service to the cause of erasing racial distinctions. As a publicist he was energetic and skillful; as a thinker, aware of the economic rivalries that bred racism, he was a practical realist. The fact that he remained a realist and was not tempted to make his victims larger than life symbols, as Graham had done, surely makes his accumulated work more impressive.

In Garner's work in the 1950s, Indians, "aliens," and blacks appear as complete people and not just as role players. One wonders to what extent the scattered appearances of blacks in Garner's work are due to their portrayal in Morley Callaghan's *The Loved and the Lost* (1951). Another Montreal book, this one portrays Westmount English-Canadians and the blacks of the St. Antoine section of the city. (St. Antoine is to Callaghan's Montreal what St. Urbain Street is to Richler—a title for a ghetto.) This novel squarely confronts the issue of racial discrimination against blacks.

The plot centres upon Peggy Sanderson, a white woman who enjoys the company of blacks in St. Antoine. Her nightly visits to nightclubs there cause bitter scandal behind her back among the other whites who suspect that her motivations are ultimately sexual. Jim McAlpine, the otherwise tolerant and sensitive intellectual who pursues Peggy, cannot accept her interest in blacks at face value, even when he learns of her childhood experience with them. In a brief aside, Peggy tells of the point in her life when she was apprised of the difference a person's colour does make, and

6 Hugh Garner, *Silence on the Shore* (Toronto: Ryerson Press, 1968), p. 120.

7 Name changes to avoid racial discrimination, or to attract racial favouritism, can be found in Marlyn's *Under the Ribs of Death*, Salverson's *The Dark Weaver*, Wiseman's *The Sacrifice*, Laurence's *The Fire Dwellers*, Richler's *The Incomparable Atuk*, and Wiebe's *The Blue Mountains of China*.

how her father, a Methodist minister, forbade her to associate with her black friends, in part because of his concern over the negative reaction of his congregation. The hypocrisy of the church is directly attacked, as it is shown to be an instrument which confirms and enforces public opinion rather than conducting it along more positive lines. Peggy triumphed over this pious duplicity and followed her own feelings. Her attraction to blacks is partly sympathy for the prejudice they face and the economic circumstances they are shown to be trapped in, and partly for the enjoyment of their *joie de vivre* and music. There is no proof of her sexual involvement but it remains an open hypothesis which *should* remain open. In fact, so much of her true character is kept hypothetical by the author that her behaviour is open to various and contradictory interpretations, ranging from sublime but naive innocence to deliberately provocative flirtation. Callaghan is able to maintain a realistic tension between idealistic innocence and cynical promiscuity by not defining Peggy's stand according to the too rigid definitions of the society he is criticizing.

In my view, the main theme of the novel is Peggy's innocence versus everybody else's experience and disillusionment, and much depends on the reader's acceptance of her as innocent. Her behaviour is not neurotic or inexplicably irresponsible, but may seem so in social contexts which penalize unorthodox behaviour. Peggy is not herself too good to be true, but just too good for her society to allow to be true. She risks chaos and violence to achieve peace and integrity on her own terms.[8] She moves through the plot untouched by the scandal-mongers who are jealous of her escape from their group, of her attainment of a freedom they lack, until eventually her goodness leads to her destruction. Her innocence is what lifts *her* above racial prejudice, while society's loss of innocence is what limits *it* to racial prejudice. Callaghan's only attempt to explain racism psychologically is spoken by Peggy when she tells Jim of the berserk reaction of a young white man whose advances she had rejected, and who knew of her association with blacks: "When he felt himself rejected, the last remnant of his pride was rejected, and he couldn't stand it. If he couldn't retain his belief in his superiority over a few Negroes, then he would go wild with hate, and rape and destroy everything."[9] Ethnocentric pride employed individually to supply security and self-confidence seems to be Callaghan's rationale for racism.

Peggy is an ideal as well as an idealist. She operates outside the conventions of her society. Its power is shown in the excellent hockey scene where mob rule takes over. McAlpine recognizes the violence inherent in social

8 The link between Peggy's solution for finding peace and the violence it arouses in others is quite similar to the paradoxes between peace with integrity and violence with no integrity in Richler's *A Choice of Enemies* and Wiebe's *Peace Shall Destroy Many*.

9 Morley Callaghan, *The Loved and the Lost* (Toronto: Macmillan of Canada, 1951), p. 121.

groups to keep free-thinkers like Peggy in line. Throughout the book he tries to reclaim her for white society and himself by revealing this violence in others to her, despite being attracted to her innocence. He attempts to redecorate her mind with European symbols, by hanging Matisse prints in her apartment to attract her attention away from African sculpture and music. He tries to limit her culturally in order to limit her socially to her own colour. Peggy is too clever and too advanced in her idealism to be caught so easily.

The blind violence that Peggy's lifestyle rouses in the white men is also seen in the black woman, the wife of a musician Peggy knows. The woman's jealousy and her ignorance about Peggy's ways match the fury of the whites. Both sides take up arms against her in the final nightclub scene, even finding a temporary unity in their assault on her. Callaghan impartially writes about people first and colour second, as he explained in a later interview:

> Well, I wrote a book in which the Negroes of course are a belittled people, but my point that emerged out of the book and which was very disturbing to everybody and quite unsatisfactory, was that the Negroes of course, being men, had the nature of men, and white men had their nature, and it was the same human nature. You see, what people didn't understand was that I was really uniting black and white. They didn't understand that I was really writing a book completely destructive of class valuations.[10]

The class issue is *not* immediately apparent. The colour conflict perhaps attracted more attention because Canadian readers do not easily accept or recognize class distinctions and affiliations. Even so, the racial issue does seem more important, though class *is* tied to race. There are no wealthy blacks in this novel; in fact, the poverty of some of them (the women all seem to be washerwomen) is stressed, and connections are implied between their colour and their poverty. The poor of the book are blacks, the rich are English-Canadians, the French-Canadians and Jews are in the middle, and Peggy moves among them all as if class and race did not exist. In arguing that the book is about class rather than colour, Callaghan seems to be trying to say that he wrote a book about the poor of Montreal and they all turned out to be black. He tried to show that he had not fallen into the same trap that he was trying to expose, the trap that imposes colouration on characterization, that Garner skirted admirably in "Interlude in Black and White," mentioned above, and that Ernest Buckler would evade equally well in "Long, Long After School," mentioned below. By writing about class one can override differences of colour, and humanity as a whole becomes the

10 Morley Callaghan, "A Talk With Morley Callaghan," *Tamarack Review*, No. 7 (1958), pp. 24-25.

topic—which was what Callaghan wanted. He did not explore economic reasons for racism, although they are vaguely implicit, preferring instead to offer his psychological causes.

Alongside the black/white theme is a complicating secondary one. McAlpine meets a Jewish tavern owner named Wolgast, an immigrant from Poland, who is passionately proud of his enterprise. Like everyone else in Montreal, he knows Peggy. At one point she invites a black to drink with her in his tavern, and Wolgast is infuriated by this threat to his custom. Callaghan has already made it clear that the colour bar was a fact in Montreal, that blacks "couldn't live in the good hotels or go into the select bars and knew it. There was never any trouble."[11] Wolgast believes that Peggy brought the "jig" to his bar because she thought his Jewishness would inhibit him from complaining, that the Jew and the black were somehow connected as minorities. McAlpine tells Wolgast that Peggy chose his bar because she respected him and thought him an unprejudiced person. Concerned about his clientele's desertion if more blacks come, Wolgast reacts violently to protect his livelihood.

An ultimately pessimistic book, *The Loved and the Lost* presents Montreal society as a closed society, composed of groups secure in their differences, "knowing their places," uniting only to confirm and enforce conformity by extirpating innocents such as Peggy. Society wins in the end: Peggy is dead and McAlpine cannot find the ideal vision of a church she has shown him. The cold city has swallowed it up.

A long way from Gordon, Callaghan specifically criticized the Methodist church for its hypocrisy about race, as well as the Catholic church for its promotion of schismatic groupings of people. Peggy responds to an ideal church which only she can find. She is too good for a world which can institutionalize religion to the point where it can condone the differentiation of peoples for protection from each other. Where Graham concentrated on introducing and describing exemplary Jewish-Canadians to English-Canadians, Callaghan is content to leave blacks in the background as poor people and concentrate instead on the anti-racist figure of Peggy. Graham's couple (Marc and Erica) are anti-racist figures motivated by their own love for each other. Their personal romance entangles the didacticism in a confusing manner. The pairing up of all Jews with Anglo-Saxon Protestants is hardly a practical solution. Their love *does* make their parents' restrictions look out of place, however, and it *does* win out so that the novel ends optimistically. Peggy is above class, in effect abolishing its barriers by ignoring its existence. Peggy is also, and in the same way, above racism. She is the first true anti-racist figure in Canadian literature, and in her perfect purity she shows the extent to which society has accommodated itself to the unpleasant facts of racism. Her innocence could be reality for all, but it

11 Callaghan, *The Loved and the Lost*, p. 37.

obviously is not. Society and reality are made by people, and they have made it in such a way that innocence like Peggy's must either be corrupted or destroyed. As a perfect anti-racist figure, Peggy is doomed. For an anti-racist book, the lesson of her death seems very negative and gloomy.

Another anti-racist figure appeared in Ernest Buckler's short story, "Long, Long After School," published in the *Atlantic Advocate* in 1959.[12] Miss Tretheway was a school-teacher who protected her one black student, Wes Holman, from the teasing and discrimination of the other students. Wes was a good student and worked hard, but at the graduation dance none of the girls would dance with him. Upset, he punched a window, and when he required a blood transfusion at the hospital where his hand was treated, Miss Tretheway was the only volunteer. At her death Wes, then the school caretaker, honoured her memory.

This is a slightly awkward story, but it is about an awkward situation. Wes was a victim because of his colour, and his teacher was the only person who sympathized with him and who tried to help him overcome the prejudices of his peers. She herself was a homely, lonely old maid who nevertheless became beautiful for helping the other "outsider" in the community. Like Callaghan, Buckler stresses the inhumanity that an ordinary community is capable of and indeed takes for granted. The connection between being victimized for one's colour and for one's physical shortcomings is a generalization. Buckler presents racism as just such a commonplace tragedy. Acts of inhumanity are the norm, and Miss Tretheway's sensitivity and altruism are not only unusual but are probably the result of her own victimization. Her gesture as an anti-racist is practically forgotten by all but Wes, its significance lost on an insensitive society. Like Callaghan, Buckler attacks his society by exposing its cruelties. Like Callaghan's blacks, the Holmans are poor and Wes's future is limited; class restrictions seem to be arbitrarily imposed as punishment on the victims, a punishment that ignores their feelings as people because of their colour.

Callaghan has complained that the class element of *The Loved and the Lost* has been unappreciated. Certainly class analysis is quite evident in Dyson Carter's novel, *Fatherless Sons* (1955). Carter's Communist attitude led him to substitute economic rather than psychological biographies for his novel's characters. *Fatherless Sons* is a novel of industry and political action, and expresses an openly pacifist and Communist bias along with strong anti-American sentiments. Alongside the main theme of the organization of labour at Deep Rock (a thinly disguised Sudbury), the political education of the workers, pacifism, and racial prejudice are minor themes. The book is ostensibly on the side of the worker and the veteran. When the novel begins

---

12 Ernest Buckler, "Long, Long After School," *Atlantic Advocate* 50, No. 3 (1959), 42-44. This story is now available in *The Rebellion of Young David and Other Stories* (Toronto: McClelland and Stewart, 1975).

in 1945 an Ojibwa Indian, Johnny Hawke, is a bemedalled veteran and a close friend of the protagonist, Dave. Carter makes it clear that a uniform gives Hawke no protection from prejudice, as it was supposed to do for Heinrich Kellerman in Gordon's *The Major*. On his return to Deep Rock, at a banquet held in a hotel for the returned soldiers, Hawke is asked to leave because he is an Indian. The scene is manipulated by Carter so that Ottawa politicians are seen to be responsible, and to take full advantage of the fact that a native Canadian and war hero could not drink in a hotel without being discriminated against in a particularly insulting manner. The working people, Carter's collective hero, are above such prejudice, and Hawke is accepted by them—most noticeably by those of them who are of the political left—as a friend. Carter's view is that the common bond among people is severed unnaturally by politicians and capitalists the better to exploit the masses. His aim is to enlighten Canadian readers as to how they could take their own destiny into their hands by escalating labour agitation to bring about a truly classless and "raceless" society.

Fatherless Sons is too absurdly extremist to be credible. Although Carter writes well, he exaggerates his metaphors and his characters, and the result must be unpalatable to any reasonable mind. His simplistic logic makes it seem that his real evaluation of the intelligence of the working class must have been low. The novel is rooted in the Canadian situation insofar as most of it, including the episode of Hawke's abuse, is not unfamiliar or unrecognizable to Canadians, but it soon loses itself in bitter and violently exaggerated ranting. Carter alone took the leftist view of race, which had been toyed with by several writers including Garner, to the logical extreme of Communism, and he is the sole representative among Canadian novelists of the political "pie-in-the-sky" theory for the extermination of prejudice. There are hints of a similar idea of a Marxist supra-nationalist class consciousness in Earle Birney's *Down the Long Table*, published in the same year as *Fatherless Sons*. In this novel Birney drew upon reports of fascist anti-Semitic demonstrations in Toronto during the Depression and also included a newspaper clipping about the "Exclusion from Canada of unabsorbable Races" as background material.[13] These indicate his awareness of the problem but he did not develop it to the extent Carter did. The leftist political attitude of the time was otherwise untouched by English-Canadian writers. Herman Buller was the only other novelist to write from this perspective, in *One Man Alone* (1963), and in non-fiction it has surely reached a rhetorical peak in Davis and Zannis's *The Genocide Machine in Canada* (1973).

John Cornish's *Olga* (1959) is a light-hearted romance involving a second generation Ukrainian-Canadian woman, Olga Stepanyskaya, and a pure

13 Earle Birney, *Down the Long Table* (Toronto: McClelland and Stewart, 1975), p. 171.

English-Canadian, against a West Coast background of Doukhobors burning houses and sabotaging railway lines. The platonic love that develops between Olga and Donald is threatened, she feels, by the danger of his confusing her, a Russian Orthodox churchgoer, with the madcap antics of the Little Brothers—the Sons of Freedom. Cornish, like Graham, evidently believed that true love conquers all. Despite the many obstacles to their relationship, Donald asks Olga: "What crushes the barriers of religion and class and race? What laughs at locksmiths?"[14] It is sex or love which brings down all the barriers. While Donald reads Dostoevski to understand Olga, she reads Trollope to understand him. This literary trade-off, with its deliberate irony, reflects the merging of their cultural traditions. Neither side loses, and both individuals gain.

Similarly Luella Creighton's dismemberment of Mennonite life in Ontario in *High Bright Buggy Wheels* (1951) uses love as the instrument which removes (or even rescues) one girl from a life of old-fashioned European misery. Tillie Shantz gets a chance to learn about the world outside her parents' narrow Mennonite community, and uses it to escape from an engagement to the too-good Simon Goudie in order to marry instead an English-Canadian druggist and live a "normal" life. Creighton demonstrated the Mennonite lifestyle to be backward and shallow, and the people to be dull. There is little feeling shown for the religious beliefs of either side and too much emphasis on excitement and materialism. As Gordon had done, Creighton displayed a lack of sympathy for and an ignorance of her subject matter. Her aim seems to have been to open the way for the Mennonites, who she felt were pitifully miserable without knowing it, to enter fully into the English-Canadian way of life. She seems never to have thought that such a step might not be a great step forward for them. She is not dealing with racism per se, but her book shows how the type of arrogant self-satisfaction that afflicted Gordon's work could live on in the 1950s. *High Bright Buggy Wheels* also shows the persistent influence of the English-Canadian attempt to standardize all Canadians after their own likeness.

II

Religion plays little part in Fred Bodsworth's novels. *The Strange One* (1959), a book written about racism in Canada, intensifies the lessons of Graham and Cornish.[15] Bodsworth's ornithological expertise, which had

---

14 John Cornish, *Olga* (London: Andre Deutsch, 1959), p. 108.
15 The book is obviously an anti-racist lesson, but it was not written primarily as such. Bodsworth claims that, as a journalist, his first concern was for a book that would sell. Accordingly he began *The Strange One* with only birds as characters, along the lines of *The Last of the Curlews*, and included the racism motif later. Personal interview with Fred Bodsworth, Sept. 26, 1981.

informed *The Last of the Curlews* (1954), also contributed to *The Strange One*. Published in the United States as *The Mating Call*, the novel compares the mating urges of a pair of wild geese with those of a human couple. The book is composed of two parallel plots, one for the birds and one for the people. In the first one, a barnacle goose is windswept from the Hebrides to James Bay where, lacking another barnacle goose to pair with, it mates for life with a New World Canada goose, despite its physical dissimilarities and the strange habitat. Similarly a Scottish graduate student, Rory MacDonald, goes to James Bay to study geese and meets Kanina Beaverskin, a Cree woman with whom, despite their obvious physical dissimilarities, he mates, again for life.

When Rory meets Kanina on the Polar Bear Express bound for James Bay, she is returning to the North and the Indian way of life after losing her job as a teacher further south. Well-educated from childhood in southern schools and trained there as a teacher, Kanina had hoped to make a life for herself away from the primitive conditions of James Bay. However, whites objected to an Indian teaching their children and she was fired. Discouraged by this rejection she determined to turn her back on the white world and return to the Indian ways, of which she knew too little. Bodsworth plainly describes Canada as a society where racism against Indians flourishes. Even the Polar Bear Express is unofficially segregated, Indians and whites occupying separate cars. The man who introduces Rory to his job in the North flatly tells him: "We don't need Jim Crow laws in this country. The Indians know their place. We could teach them Southerners in the States something, you know. You have to handle inferior races firmly but quietly, that's the thing, quietly. . . . You have to have race discrimination."[16] His attitude does not seem too extreme within the contexts Bodsworth has erected, of Kanina's experiences and the segregation on the train. Bodsworth brings racism into his book as an established and well-entrenched force in the land. Kanina hopes to find a place for herself among her own people, but this proves difficult.

Bodsworth's attitude towards the Cree is very practical and seems based on firsthand knowledge of their way of life. Don Gutteridge, in discussing Bodsworth's later novel, *The Sparrow's Fall* (1967), wrote: "Bodsworth, being Canadian, seems instinctively to reject the noble savage myth, the Rousseauesque retreat to the territory."[17] Certainly Bodsworth presents the modern Indian way of life in very earthy terms, stressing the problems of living close to nature. Kanina's return to the traditional lifestyle shows what she has missed and what she has gained by being away. A sickly child, she would doubtless have died of tuberculosis if whites had not removed her

16 Fred Bodsworth, *The Strange One* (New York: Dodd, Mead, 1959), p. 84.

17 Don Gutteridge, "Surviving the Fittest: Margaret Atwood and The Sparrow's Fall," *Journal of Canadian Studies* 8, No. 3 (1973), 63.

from her people and cured her in the South, educating her at the same time. She returns to people who love and protect her. She has difficulty in explaining the circumstances of her dismissal as a teacher to people who have no concept of race discrimination: "The theory that some people were born inferior or somehow less deserving than others would be an idea so foreign to their thinking, so incompatible with their cooperative way of life, that their minds would probably fail to grasp it."[18] Kanina takes pride in the closeness of the Cree to nature, feeling that if that connection can be maintained it will provide the independence and self-reliance that in turn will give dignity to her people and herself. It is this search for identity that drives her to undertake the full responsibilities of a Cree woman and this brings out some of the less attractive aspects of Indian life. A constant theme in Bodsworth's work is the apparent cruelty of nature, which with its cycles of drought and floods, lean years and good years, indifferently weeds out the less capable forms of life. Civilization provides some protection against this, but the closer one gets to nature, the more vulnerable one is to her caprices. Kanina puts up with the dirt of the Indian camp, its stultifying intellectual half-life, and the heavy manual labour expected of women. Wintering in the bush with her family in an off-year for game and coming close to starvation convinces her that in simple terms of survival the white way is preferable. Marrying Rory and using him as an introduction into white society enables her to escape the fate of her people, who Bodsworth feels must either assimilate or die out because of the fatal interference by whites in their ecology.

Kanina defends her people before Rory in an attempt to justify her retreat from white civilization. By creating their dialogue about science and technology, Bodsworth is the only writer in Canadian literature to address the issue of whites promoting their acknowledged technical superiority over other peoples as evidence of their superior intelligence and ability, and even of their predestined position as the superior race. Kanina argues that "the luck of history gave you the wheel" while the Indians solved their transportation problems with the canoe, technologically a "blind alley."[19] The wheel was developed into the basis of modern technology, and the accident of its discovery coupled with the possible influence of environment is what gave Europeans their advantage. Rory is slowly convinced that "her basic thesis that the relative position of the world's races was largely a matter of accident was probably true."[20] Yet he vacillates over the question of

18 Bodsworth, *The Strange One*, p. 177. Bodsworth protected the Indians from the charge of ethnocentric pride raised to a fault which he assigned to whites. It makes the whites' attitude appear worse if the Indians are clearly superior to them by being free of racial prejudice, but as to whether or not they are, or why they should be, he admits he does not know. Personal interview with Fred Bodsworth, Sept. 26, 1981.

19 Bodsworth, *The Strange One*, p. 216.

20 Ibid., p. 217.

marrying an Indian. His mentor, a distinguished professor at the University of Toronto, calls the Indians "gooks" and warns him that his own ambition to become a professor could not be achieved with an Indian wife as a social handicap. Finally, however, in the spring when the mating urge is at its peak, Rory takes a lesson from the barnacle goose who has made the amazing journey a second time across the Atlantic to join its Canadian mate, and he returns to the North to claim Kanina despite the consequences. Bodsworth doesn't just talk airily about romantic love; for him it is sexual contacts that will break down the artificial barriers of race that have been created in ignorance.

This is a very practical and thoughtful book which directly confronts the problem of racism and, while questioning various justifications of it, actually turns to nature to show that miscegenation is neither unnatural nor wrong, but a part of the natural process of life. Race is proven invalid by the mere existence of miscegenation.

In his next book, *The Atonement of Ashley Morden* (1964), Bodsworth tackled the anti-war theme, but retained racism as a minor strain. An ex-RCAF bombardier, Morden becomes a scientist devoted to finding a cure for a tropical disease as his way of atoning for his self-inflicted war guilt. His work is criticized by a colleague at the University of Toronto because "the only persons who could possibly benefit were a bunch of niggers in Africa."[21] Morden nobly replies: "I refuse to consider any suggestion that the lives of Africans or Indians are somehow worth less than the lives of Canadians or Americans."[22] The point that racial categorization is unscientific and that humanity is a whole is reiterated in this book with reference to Hitler's absurd "Rassenkunde." Anyone who acts against one human being acts against all. Competition between groups need not be taken to the point of warfare and the extermination of one of the groups. Again turning to nature for his didacticism, Bodsworth uses the example of wolves fighting for territoriality and leadership, not to the death but just until one surrenders. This psychological check prevents race suicide at the expense of the territoriality instinct to prevent overcrowding. Humanity has lost this and instead has adopted racism as a philosophy of defence legitimizing conflicts that escalate into warfare and can result in genocide. Bodsworth idealistically presents war as being caused by an appreciation of racial differences that actually are not significant.

In his fourth and final novel, *The Sparrow's Fall*, Bodsworth wrote of the ordeal of an Indian couple during a bad winter in the North. A white missionary, an alien to them and not a man who lives off the land, has confused them with his preaching that the killing of God's animals is at

21 Fred Bodsworth, *The Atonement of Ashley Morden* (New York: Dodd, Mead, 1964), pp. 234, 247.
22 Ibid., p. 247.

times wrong. Jacob Atook in desperation learns to accept the harsh realities of nature and shoots a pregnant doe caribou to feed his own pregnant fiancee. Nature makes allowance for such killing, but later Jacob cannot murder Taka, his rival in love, when he has the chance. Taka is of the same species and human must not harm human. A successful look into the world of Indians and their environment, the world of subsistence life where philosophies are necessarily simple and practical, *The Sparrow's Fall* reinforces the theme of its predecessor, that humanity is one "race."

Margaret Laurence touches on the problems of race in some of her work without ever bringing it to the forefront as Bodsworth did. Her awareness of it is clear but her preoccupation with life as a whole has prevented a focusing of her attention upon it. A novel such as *The Strange One* is off balance in its depiction of reality because it emphasizes racism as an issue so that little else seems to matter. Laurence is a much more balanced writer who, by giving race a lesser role in some of her work, probably places it more accurately. Race does not exist in a vacuum and it is only one aspect of life. While the indignation against racism that such books as *The Strange One* and *Earth and High Heaven* may stir up may be quite effective in drawing attention to prejudice, one may argue that the incorporation of a theme in a novel should reflect its significance in reality.

Laurence's first impressions of Africa were gathered together years later in *The Prophet's Camel Bell* (1963). It shows a significant change in attitude. On first arriving in Africa she seems to have believed that she as a Canadian could approach Africans differently than French or British expatriates or colonials simply by being outside the bitter history of Africa's exploitation. This feeling gradually altered into an acceptance of the fact that as a white she too was considered responsible for Africa's ills. Her Canadianness still made a difference to her, but not to the Somalis. Her idea of treating all people the same fails when she is treated differently by them. Her initial idealism in this respect presumes the unlikely removal of real historical or psychological barriers intervening between blacks and whites in Africa. She expresses resentment of these barriers when she writes: "If only Europeans could work here without an axe to grind."[23] She fails to show how the axes can be laid aside, simply implying that true understanding could only come about by not having any axes in the first place. Her failure to work this out in any constructive sense, preferring to hint at mysteries and deep secrets, flaws her argument as well as her book.

Laurence explains black/white racism in Africa with reference to O. Mannoni's *Prospero and Caliban: A Study of the Psychology of Colonisation*, which views the imposition of so-called racial differences in a social system as a psychological activity to guarantee the superiority of one group.

23 Margaret Laurence, *The Prophet's Camel Bell* (Toronto: McClelland and Stewart, 1963), p. 229.

Mannoni contends that white administrators and colonials are attracted to superior roles because of inadequacies in themselves, and the inability to accept within their own society differences between people. It is much easier to deal with stereotypes, necessarily at a distance, than with real people with all their eccentricities. From this basis Laurence came to see imperialism as a psychological state of imposition, "but the empire we unknowingly sought was that of Prester John, a mythical kingdom and a private world."[24] Depending on Mannoni for such psychological insights, Laurence came to view racism in terms of individual psychology and hardly at all related to class or economic forces. It is a simplistic, one-sided interpretation of a complex issue, and one which can be seen in her later, Canadian work as well.

Her other African books display conflicts that are seen to be racial. *This Side Jordan* (1960) presents an extremely racist reaction by European expatriates in Ghana first to Africanization and later to independence. Their prejudice seems to increase with the danger to their privileged positions as little gods in Africa, and Mannoni's influence is clear here. Where personal interests can be made to agree with Africanization, racism can be controlled though not abolished, as Johnnie Kestoe's treacherous ploy proves. Laurence shows village life to be a natural and satisfactory way of life for Africans and puts the cause of most African troubles at the feet of the meddling whites. In *The Tomorrow-Tamer* (1963) she explicitly condemned European missionaries for bringing confusion to Africa in much the same way Bodsworth had done in *The Sparrow's Fall*. Matthew, a missionary's son, puts it bluntly in "The Drummer of All the World": "My father thought he was bringing Salvation to Africa. I do not any longer know what salvation is. I only know that one man cannot find it for another man, and one land cannot bring it to another."[25] Africans require an African God, not a white God, and independence is their birthright. In *This Side Jordan* Laurence made the economic excuses for racism clearer than elsewhere. The story entitled "The Rain Child," which traces the difficulties experienced by an African girl brought up in England who tries to integrate into Africa and ends up caught unhappily in the middle, is interesting for its fair-mindedness. Avoiding the questions of survival, health, and sanitation, which Bodsworth had faced directly, this story reiterates the shared humanity of all people yet insists on the rights of groups to follow their different

24 Ibid. Mannoni is quoted twice at the end of this book to explain her final evaluation of her own success in building relationships with Africans. His book is also cited in her short story, "The Poem and the Spear," in *Heart of a Stranger* (1976). This story is a deliberate readjustment of the previously one-sided view of the struggles of the Mad Mullah in Somaliland, fairly presenting the evidence of both sides. It has much in common with Wiebe's *The Temptations of Big Bear*.

25 Margaret Laurence, *The Tomorrow-Tamer* (Toronto: McClelland and Stewart, 1963), p. 18.

ways. Race and culture are divorced, the former being valueless and the latter essential but not qualitative. Race is insignificant and artificial, Laurence is saying; culture is real and inviolable.

The fictional world of Manawaka left Africa behind while setting up new tensions. Two "racial" conflicts exist in Manawaka. The tragedy of the Métis Tonnerres is traced piecemeal through *The Stone Angel* (1964), *The Fire Dwellers* (1969), *A Bird in the House* (1970), and *The Diviners* (1974). Ukrainians replace Métis in *A Jest of God* (1966). In it the town is represented as being evenly divided between Rachel's own Scots and the Ukrainians, whom her mother called "Galician or Bohunk." Although both groups were immigrant groups, arriving on the same terms and for the same reasons, "the Ukrainians knew how to be the better grain farmers, but the Scots knew how to be almighter than anyone but God."[26] The assertion of superiority seems ironic when Rachel envies the Ukrainians for what seems to her to be their freer, more fun-loving and open way of life, compared to her own guilt-ridden Calvinist upbringing. Her lover, Nick Kazlik, who is a Ukrainian success story in that he escaped from the farm and became a teacher in Winnipeg, attracts her because she sees these qualities in him that are not only outside her life but outside her community and philosophy.

The prejudice that invests this story is at times explicit but mild, appearing as an accepted part of Rachel's life. Rachel, a victim like Buckler's Miss Tretheway who feels unwanted and exploited, operates beyond the limits of prejudice and exorcises its effects. Her mother lives with it as a part of her whole mean attitude. It is far from being a major theme in the book, yet its presence and Rachel's reaction to it contribute to the development of her character and ultimately the plot. A book without race is a book without reality in a society that has not yet learned how to do without it. *A Jest of God* gains in this way because, without it being emphasized unduly, racism appears in its place, always ready to be used when necessary.

In her other Canadian novels Laurence matched Métis against Scots, ultimately merging their cultural identities in a symbolic trade-off at the end of *The Diviners*. The first appearance of the Tonnerre family is in *The Stone Angel* where, like the Ukrainians in *A Jest of God* two years later, the Métis live outside town and are able to behave in ways the more restrained Scottish-Canadians cannot. John, the son of Hagar, trades the plaid pin symbolizing his Scottish heritage to Lazarus Tonnerre for a knife, the exchange revealing their lack of interest in their own traditions as well as the new requirements of modern Canada where plaid and knives alike are unnecessary. Yet in *The Diviners* Morag recognizes in these symbols intrinsic traditional values which are emotionally or conceptually necessary.

26 Margaret Laurence, *A Jest of God* (New York: Alfred A. Knopf, 1966), p. 80.

Laurence's short story, "Crying of the Loons," which appeared in the *Atlantic Advocate* in 1966 and was included later in the collection *A Bird in the House* (1970) as "The Loons," elaborated further on the Tonnerres' story, focusing on the life and death of Piquette. The family tree is established. Jules Tonnerre (the first) was the founder of the Tonnerre shack and clan. His son, Lazarus (in effect brought back from the dead at Batoche) was a drunk too, a hanger-on at the edge of town and white civilization. Lazarus's children almost all die by the end of *The Diviners*, Piquette hellishly in the fire that destroys the shack, Valentine of disease in Vancouver where she has been working as a prostitute, Paul in mysterious circumstances while guiding whites in the North, and Jules (the second) of throat cancer in Toronto. Pique, the half-Scot half-Métis child of Morag and Jules, learns to take pride in her background and conquers her immature wildness by going off and helping the remaining Tonnerre brothers operate a hostel cum orphanage for Métis children in the bush. As a half-breed herself, Pique illegitimately combines traditions and goes her own way, independent, capable, and strong.

"Crying of the Loons" links the eerie call of the loons, who are on the brink of extinction, with the sullen outbursts of Piquette, a Métis child whose tuberculosis jeopardizes her life just as her relatives' lives are threatened and eventually taken by whites. Their habitat altered and put to other uses, the Métis are dying out, just fifty years after the Riel rebellion from which Jules (the first) had retreated to Manawaka. The care, both medical and emotional, which Dr. MacLeod gives Piquette prolongs her life. She escapes from Manawaka by marrying an English-Canadian in Winnipeg, but after several years her marriage fails and she returns to her father's shack where she dies when the stove catches fire. The Métis are doomed—they can exist only marginally with whites who refuse to make room for them. When Vanessa relates Piquette's story she tells of her last visit to the lake where the loons had been and her statement may be extended to refer to the Métis too: "I did not know what had happened to the birds. Perhaps they had gone away to some far place of belonging. Perhaps they had been unable to find such a place, and had simply died out, having ceased to care any longer whether they lived or not."[27] There is no real evidence of racial prejudice in this story that would account for the extinction of the Métis. It is an overall neglect, a crowding out of an unwanted people whose lifestyle was a nuisance. They have no place of belonging. There are no obvious villains, and there are no anti-racist figures. The victims are no worse nor better than the whites, in the author's view. They are all dying. When Stacey meets Valentine Tonnerre in *The Fire Dwellers* she would "like to go back in time, to explain that she never

---

27 Margaret Laurence, *A Bird in the House* (Toronto: McClelland and Stewart, 1970), p. 127.

meant the town's invisible stabbing, but this is not possible, and it was hers, too, so she cannot edge away from it."[28] It is a shared responsibility, applicable to all members of the victimizing group—which Laurence defines as English-Canadian with a strong dash of Scotch.

The Diviners brings the Tonnerres to the forefront. It is not a book about racism, as *The Strange One* was, but without racism it would not be the same book at all. It pulls together the threads of their family that had appeared in previous work. In particular the character of Jules, Morag's first lover, is built up to the point of a polarity in contrast with Brooke, her Anglo-Saxon husband with the imperial colonial background. Jules is outside Brooke's inhibitions and conventions—the restrictions which Laurence's heroines combat in each novel. He offers friendship and certain freedoms that do not exist for the Scots in Manawaka. Where Piquette tried to turn her back on her Métis past, Jules becomes a folk-singer, recreating the legends of his people in song, interpreting the injustices of it all to nightclub audiences who do not care. Lacking real freedom in larger social contexts, he is the personification of liberty within personal relationships. In turn his daughter, Pique, finds her own place because of his songs about the valley of the Tonnerres and Morag's stories about the Highlands of Scotland, and in the end can sing herself:

> Ah, my valley and my mountain, they're the same
> My living places, and they never will be tame
> When I think how I was born
> I can't help but being torn
> But the valley and the mountain hold my name.[29]

More and more up to *The Diviners* Laurence's work reveals her increasing preoccupations with her roots as a writer and as a person. In *The Diviners* Morag transcends her cultural garrison out of desperation and penetrates the ghetto of the Métis, the half-life of the half-breeds, the world in which ambition, hopes, and love remain transient possibilities, and where the only sane reaction to oppression is the defiant scorn of the hopeless. This is a world where racism rules—a world in Canada. Morag's ability to pass from one side to the other and back depends upon her perception and sensitivity, the quality one notices as remarkable in Laurence's other narrators, Rachel, Vanessa, and even Stacey and Hagar, and without which much of the value of these books would be missing. Laurence stresses the need to accept people as people regardless of race, and her novels indicate that victims who are made more aware by their own private pain are more likely to sense that of others and be above the cruel causes. Morag's husband, Brooke, is the closest to a racist figure in her Canadian work, and it is one part of his whole

28 Margaret Laurence, *The Fire Dwellers* (Toronto: McClelland and Stewart, 1969), p. 264.
29 Margaret Laurence, *The Diviners* (Toronto: Bantam Books, 1974), p. 467.

personality. He personifies WASP restraints and she moves away from him to the (at first) apparently less-restrained world of Jules, in which she does not belong either.

In *Sawbones Memorial* (1974) Sinclair Ross dealt with racial discrimination against Ukrainians on the prairies. His dissection of the little town of Upward, Saskatchewan, reminiscent of Wilder's *Our Town*, shows that in the forty-five year time span reviewed, conditions of life have improved while human nature has not. In the almost all Anglo-Saxon town, one Ukrainian family resides, looked down upon by everybody except Dr. Hunter. His sensitivity to the Ukrainians' situation is in part because he himself has been disappointed in love. He is the victim of an unhappy marriage to a frigid woman. His position in the town plus the mores of the community preclude divorce, so he ends up finding relief secretively in the Ukrainian woman's bed. Nick, whose situation as the illegitimate son of Anna and the doctor is explained at the end of the novel, is brought up as the Ukrainians' own child, and no one suspects the doctor's paternity. As much as he can, and while pretending a more publicly defensible interest in another, English-Canadian boy, the doctor helps Nick through school to become a doctor himself. Then Dr. Hunter insists on Nick's return to his community where he suffered so much as a child from the teasing of his schoolmates. On his return he proves to be a fine man with a distinguished war record, and a capable doctor. Nick has done better than anyone else in the town, but some people still see him as a "hunky" and think little of him. The irony of the situation is that they do not know that Nick is the son of the man they respect the most, and while his career proves their racist judgements to be false, the foolishness of their absolute categories and racial values is also exposed. Dr. Hunter has successfully confronted the racism of his small community and forced its members to change their attitudes, for with his retirement and his recommendation of Nick as his successor, the townspeople must depend on the "hunky" for medical treatment. Much like the close relationship which develops between the German Mrs. Hill and the Jewish Dr. Kohl in Garner's *Silence on the Shore*, Nick's very presence as a doctor will go a long way towards healing the racial rupture in the town. Noteworthy too is Dr. Hunter's insistence that Nick return to his home town to practise at least for a while, in order to exorcise his resentment over his treatment as a child. Nick would have preferred to begin elsewhere, but Ross makes it clear that running away from discrimination solves nothing and may encourage it. Dr. Hunter himself is one of the strongest anti-racist figures in Canadian literature. He is cynical without being bitter, knowledgeable yet discreet, active but not too bold, and over the years he carries out his own successful campaign to defeat prejudice.

W. O. Mitchell's *The Vanishing Point* (1973) is another attempt by an already established writer to discuss Canadian racism in fiction. An awkward novel which seriously sets out to raise most of the issues concerning Canadian Indians, it was originally written for *Maclean's* as "The Alien." Like most of the works mentioned above, it accepts racism as a given in Canada, at least with regard to Indians, but it deals with it more on an institutional than a personal level.

The vanishing point is where Mitchell sees history leading the Indians. He concentrates on a band of Stoney Indians and their agent/schoolteacher, Carlyle Sinclair, from whose point of view the story is mainly told. Sinclair came to the reserve looking for peace after the death of his wife. The Indians who at first irritate and exasperate him finally provide the peace he has been searching for, in their own way. Much of the story is taken up by Sinclair's search for a teenage girl he has taught and pressured into nursing school in the city, who ran away from the school, drifted around the city for a while, and then returned pregnant for a reunion with him. Like Bodsworth's *The Strange One*, *The Vanishing Point* gives the impression of several associated arguments being combined towards one logical goal. Mitchell's arguments are far more obvious than Bodsworth's, turning the novel into a debating forum not unlike Gordon's *The Major*.

Mitchell tries for an overall view of modern Indian life subdivided into several compartments. The fatal attraction to alcoholic drink is linked with the general apathy of the Reserve's population and the limited possibilities open to them within their officially circumscribed territory. Their apparent listless indifference to their own conditions and their provoking (and apparently lazy) refusal to undertake self-help projects for their own benefit is explained by this restrictive apathy. Christianity is shown to be a worthless force in their lives. Rev. Dingle, the missionary teacher who preceded Sinclair, is shown to be a fool, totally removed from the realities of the Indians or the world at large. Yet Ezra Poundmaker, his helper, has adapted Christianity to the Indian situation and supplies a good deal of entertainment in a way which yet indicates the Indians' real need of some effective beliefs. The Rev. Heally Richards, a flashy American faith healer who passes through, attracts their attention briefly, but his failure to resurrect a dying geriatric turns them back to the reserve and their dancing. Their susceptibility to disease—especially tuberculosis—is discussed. The difference in value judgements, particularly in the area of sexuality, is explored by an episode in which a young woman, Martha Bear, elopes with or is kidnapped by Wilfred Tail-feather, as well as by the prostitution and unwed motherhood of Sinclair's special protegée, Victoria Rider. The links with George Ryga's *The Ecstasy of Rita Joe* (1967) are obvious.

The Department of Indian Affairs (whether this is meant to be a real provincial or federal body, or a fictional amalgam, is unclear) is severely attacked in the person of Ian Fyfe, Regional Director. He is responsible for the Fyfe Minimal Subsistence Cooky, an almost inedible oatmeal concoction which the Indians can barely stomach, and the idea of which, in its blunt necessity, is almost inhuman. This cooky made Fyfe's career a success, but defined the Indians as inmates in reserves, fed just enough to keep them alive. However, Fyfe has a larger role than this. It was he who first warned Sinclair against becoming involved emotionally with his charges—as if any human relationship could be purged of emotions and as if these people, being Indians, were somehow not human. Fyfe's hobby is raising orchids, and here eugenics emerges again as he explains to Sinclair his attempts to breed perfect flowers. He has certain standards in mind that he tries to meet, and eccentric failures or accidents are culled mercilessly. The comical dénouement when a bee is discovered in a bloom reserved for cross-pollination with another purebreed known as "General Eisenhower" under-scores Fyfe's strict sense of values. An eccentric mixed-race offshoot such as Victoria Rider would be a "miss" in Fyfe's eyes, incapable of development. By including the episode of Fyfe's hobby, with its concomitant lesson to be applied to Indians, Mitchell raises an important point. Sinclair recognizes and comes to appreciate that such a philosophy, whether applied to orchids or to people, is dangerously in error. The world is full of accidents. People themselves are accidents and not the products of systematic breeding, and the application of value judgements on the grounds of physical differences is misleading, whether done for the purpose of aesthetics or just simplification of categorization. Fyfe is no neighbourhood crank or neo-Nazi. He is the Regional Director of the Department of Indian Affairs and only Sinclair seems to see his unsuitability. Fyfe would like to further seclude the Indians from contact with whites, which he sees as inevitably injurious. He would like them to be isolated for their own good.[30]

Finally, the problem of young Indians being sent out into the world to be educated, carrying the heavy burden of being representatives of their people, their successes or failures reflecting not just their own individual merits but those of entire tribes and "races," is explored with Victoria Rider. When Sinclair finds her, and tries to persuade her to return to school, he tells her:

> "You are the whole thing! You have been the whole thing for a long time! Do you understand that? Not just for me—for all of them."
> "Please, Mr. Sinclair—don't load me up like that."[31]

It is a burden no one should have to bear, and Sinclair eventually realizes how great it is and releases her. He himself plays the part of a well-meaning

---

30 The polarization of the two solutions to the problems of native groups in Canada— assimilation or isolation—is well illustrated by Mitchell. Isolation depends upon racial discrimination for group identification, yet assimilation threatens culturally small groups. The idealistic compromise of multiculturalism is the logical conclusion, explicit or implicit, in most of the works discussed in this chapter.

31 W. O. Mitchell, *The Vanishing Point* (Toronto: Macmillan of Canada, 1973), p. 365.

liberal with enough idealism to try to change things for the Indians, but it is precisely his idealism that causes much of his trouble. The book ends with the Indians retreating from the city to their Paradise Valley Reserve and their dancing tent, where he and Victoria come together for the Prairie Chicken Dance and he begins to accept their way of life at last. The ending is inexplicably optimistic. Beulah Creek, which had dried up, comes to life again, Archie Nicotine's truck is repaired after years of idleness, and Sinclair and Victoria presumably will live happily ever after. However, there is no real basis for any optimism. Nothing has really changed. Christianity has failed the Indians who have also lost touch with their own religion. The urban white world has only hurt them and will do so again. Education and even modern medicine (especially the mobile tuberculosis x-ray unit) frightens them. Isolation offers a bleak future, but not as bleak as that of the city. Answers have not been provided to substantiate the final optimism.

Mitchell devoted a good deal of the novel to providing a background for Sinclair, just as Clarke did for Sam Burrmann in *The Meeting Point*. Sinclair too is a victim, having lost his mother at an early age and having been cared for by a strict and unloving aunt. The loss of his wife in childbirth and the feeling that he might never find love again before he arrived in Paradise Valley place Sinclair in a position to truly sympathize with other victims. It is institutionalized victimization he deals with, racism raised to the level of officialdom with the aim of concealing the Indian question. Mitchell concentrated on the liberal re-alignment of racism, perpetrated by do-gooders such as Fyfe, instead of the blatant prejudice one finds expressed in Callaghan's *The Loved and the Lost* and Bodsworth's *The Strange One*. The Indian reaction to whites is well expressed, with Archie Nicotine as their main representative giving Sinclair a hard time about the evils and frivolities of the white people's world. The novel allows the Indians the right to do as they wish on their own reserve, but otherwise recounts only tales of the tragedies of Indians trying to relate to the outside world. The optimism generated by their return to their own ways on the reserve is undermined by the obvious fact that they are virtually prisoners there, rejects of white Canada and victims in perpetuity.

The 1970s saw a resurgence of interest in Indians and the Métis, with the Riel rebellion acquiring a national epic status. The half-breeds could be safely memorialized at a distance. James McNamee's *them damned Canadians hanged Louis Riel!* (1971), an example of historical fiction, is a brief background to Riel's execution from a thoroughly Western point of view. McNamee sides with the West, inclusive of whites, Indians, and Métis, against the Eastern Orangemen who crushed the rebellion, and shows how the promises to the "no-fight" Indians, the ones who were bribed into staying out of the fighting, were abandoned after peace was attained.

McNamee castigates the "tame" Indians for not having enough fight to stand up for themselves. The shameful episode of the Blood Indians lining up for charity from the whites is an impressive one.[32] But by 1971 this was the standard way of depicting native people. Self-criticism on the part of white authors had escalated to self-flagellation as history was raked over for new examples of white barbarism.

None of the writers mentioned in this chapter discussed the theory of racism in any detail. In most of these books, fictional acts of racism have been incorporated into other acts of inhumanity, insensitivity, or intolerance, and in works of fiction which attempt to make statements about the human condition it must be expected that race will appear in its place as one aspect of life. In Michael Sheldon's *The Unmelting Pot* (1965), for example, ethnicity seems important to the immigrant characters, but is shown by the author to be subservient to the larger effects of North American materialism. Dogmatic discussion of race in depth, in most of these novels, would remove the work somewhat from the realm of fiction. Fiction provides the dialectical contexts that are needed to appreciate a single factor such as racism. Yet the novels discussed in this chapter approach the topic from a different direction than works by Gibbon and Gordon. The careful indignation in the work of Graham and Bodsworth, for example, is quite different from the angry protests of Salverson against the prejudice directed against Icelanders, or even the deliberate and quietly dignified defence of Russo-Germans that Grove offered. For them, racism was something that needed to be exposed as an immediate evil.

32 James McNamee, *them damned Canadians hanged Louis Riel!* (Toronto: Macmillan of Canada, 1971), p. 68.

Chapter Six

Klein and Wiebe

[W]e are beginning to realize that the value of any ethnic culture in a
nation such as ours can never depend upon its power to isolate people
from one another, that Canadian Consciousness can be a good deal
more than, to use MacLennan's own phrase, "race-memories lonely in
great spaces."

"The Body-Odour of Race," by Ronald Sutherland

I

During the twentieth century a number of writers have explored the theme
of racism in the Canadian context from varying points of view. They may be
divided into three main categories. The early English-Canadian attitude
was one of defensive protectionism, demanding the assimilation of aliens to
essentially British social patterns but simultaneously exploiting them on a
racial basis. A milder version of the aggressive xenophobic arrogance that
had preceded it, it was strongly expressed in the romances of Gordon,
Gibbon, and Stead, and is found scattered throughout the work of Leacock
and McClung. It lasted until World War Two, being increasingly countered by an immigrant or second generation non-charter-group viewpoint
which attempted to repudiate racial stereotypes (in each case) and, almost
paradoxically, to make associations between English-Canadian society and
their own unique ethnic attributes in order to minimize the differences that
simultaneously were promoted. Wishing to avoid outright discrimination
because of their obvious differences, yet still trying to retain some of these
differences as their cultural heritage as well as making cultural connections
with Anglo-Saxons, Grove and Salverson best exemplify this point of view.

123

On the whole, it was a fragmented view, as writers frequently supported their own groups alone, which they compared with English-Canadian society and occasionally contrasted with other alien groups. First appearing in the 1920s, this viewpoint is still current, being maintained by established citizens and more recent arrivals who perceive persistent discrimination. The third category is the modern liberal one, often put forward by well-meaning English-Canadians in an effort to synthesize their position (which itself is basically unchanged) and one non-charter-group position. Thus Mitchell and Bodsworth concern themselves with Indians, Graham with Jews, and Callaghan with blacks, each in one novel. In many ways this third view is morally an improvement over the original English-Canadian view, for it offers more understanding for and tolerance of alternative positions, and it includes the exposure of racism per se.

The inculcation of nationalism has been a goal of much of Canadian literature, various groups seeking to impose their definitions upon the whole, such definitions occasionally embodying racial qualifications. In the synthesized view, these definitions are compromised, their various qualifications cancelling each other out before the goal of national unity. The self-congratulatory Anglo-Saxon rhapsodies that mar Gordon's work have given way to the pious self-flagellation that distinguishes that of Wiebe. Religion emerges as an ideal uniting force rather than the divisive force it often seems to be in earlier Canadian literature.[1] Yet still the capacity of religion to be the nucleus for groups that may attain ethnic or even racial definition, in the popular mind, contrasts with its potential for abolishing group definitions altogether.

A. M. Klein's novel, *The Second Scroll* (1951), is perhaps the best example of a novel that moves in these two directions simultaneously, a paradox that surely reflects his own struggle to maintain a cultural heritage divorced from racial definition. Certainly his poetry before 1951 reveals his concern with racism in Canada and Europe. Acutely aware of the links between European fascists and French-Canadian demagogues such as Adrien Arcand and Mayor Houde of Montreal, Klein condemned them in *The Rocking Chair* (1948) for their sinister exploitation of discredited and senseless racist political theory:

> *Et, pour vrai dire*, what more political
> is there to say after you have said:
> *À bas les maudits Juifs!*[2]

---

1 Even Northrop Frye has admitted that "while religion is ideally a uniting force in society, it is more likely in practice to be a divisive one." "Conclusion" to the revised *Literary History of Canada*, ed. Carl F. Klinck (Toronto: University of Toronto Press, 1976), 3:328.

2 A. M. Klein, *The Rocking Chair* (Toronto: Ryerson Press, 1948), pp. 15-16, 46.

A victim by conscious proxy, Klien thought in cosmopolitan terms (which exceeded small-group introversions, although he admitted their practical existence) to unite humanity in a holistic ideal of peace and harmony. *The Second Scroll*, is a powerful statement of this ideal, and is far more effective than the occasional echo of it one finds in his poetry before 1951.

That *The Second Scroll* operates from a Jewish religious and cultural basis is obvious. Klein seems to move from his own Jewish basis (for although Jews are dispersed geographically he discusses them in the sense of a group with more unity than divisions) through Canadian and English literary traditions to the level of the world as a whole. Like Richler and Kreisel, Klein expands the scope of the Canadian imagination, extending its formerly ingrown concerns to those of Everyman. Grove too showed something of this international awareness, but it was undercut by his Nordic superiority complex. Klein ignores such restrictions, delighting in all colours and groups as his narrator's odyssey around the Mediterranean touches the various cultural foundations of Western civilization. The narrator delights in the colourful display of humanity he observes. He describes the Casablanca market scene with an anthropomorphic metaphor which reflects this unbiased delight:

> this was cornucopia and these people an arc of the rainbow of race. I lingered in the markets and souks, my eyes luxuriating upon each opulent still life displayed on barrow or heaped up behind the windows of the cool marble-slabbed arcades—the golden oranges of Tetuan, pyramided; navelled the pomegranates of Marrakech; Meknes quince; the sun sweet inside their little globes, and upon their skins the mist of unforgotten dawns, the royal grapes of Rabat. . . . And dominating—whether in the cool smooth round or, sliced, as crimson little scimitars adorning the Negro smile—were watermelons, miniature Africas, jungle-green without, and within peopled by pygmy blacks set sweetly in their world of flesh.[3]

The metaphor implies the renunciation of the introverted mentality that Jewishness can display simply by virtue of being a (relatively) small group: Klein focuses instead on its truly religious core which is available to anyone, regardless of group affiliation. For Klein, Jewishness is neither a nationality nor a race, nor is it any form of closed shop. Being Jewish could be seen to be a benefit for Klein as a writer, liberating him from the conventional perspective (in Canada, at least) to recognize in the multi-faceted face of world Jewry his share in the multifaceted world of humanity.

The Jewish religion is shown to be one of tolerance and its aims are identified with the primary goals of other religions. While Klein offers Judaism as a solution to the world's selfish habit of subdividing itself into

3 A. M. Klein, *The Second Scroll* (Toronto: McClelland and Stewart, 1969), p. 58.

competing groups, specifically with regard to Canada, he nevertheless opposes narrow assimilationist forces and tendencies which threaten the cultural identities of minority groups. The apparent paradox could be explained by his belief that Jews, admittedly a small group in Canada, must resist assimilation into a Canadian cultural whole that is worth less than Judaism is. The popular sense of race becomes subordinate to culture, specifically religious culture, for religion is presented as *the* common denominator of humanity. If Judaism was purely a religion, this attitude would be fairly straightforward, but Klein's support of Zionism, a nationalist and possibly even self-consciously racial outgrowth of Judaism, confirms the paradox in his own work, a paradox that seems to be a pragmatic acceptance of social realities. The anchoring of Klein's Jewish identification in the people and land of Israel weighs down the religious idealism that is supposed to free humanity from national definitions.[4] Klein's appeal is a Jewish appeal, in the same sense that Rudy Wiebe's is a Mennonite appeal. Both authors deliberately set out to avoid small-group politics by discussing international potentials for humanity to fulfil, but each remained the product of his respective group. It is hardly too much to claim that Klein wrote to persuade the world to convert to Judaism just as Wiebe wrote to convert the world to Mennonitism. Both originally attempted to destroy small-group mentalities by attracting all other groups, like moths to the light of their own groups, thus eliminating groups in the name of God. The paradox of preaching a racial unity while defending a cultural categorization, avoiding the connections that are too often made between them, is one that involves all authors to the extent that literature is usually the product of a group. Klein emerges then as a combatant instead of the referee he thought he was, because of his vested interests; Wiebe escapes this charge by repudiating land and its political consequences and stressing spiritual wealth instead.

II

While the distinction between a Jewish "race" and the Jewish religion is often blurred in the popular imagination, no such difficulty applies to Mennonites, although there is almost the same (and equally invalid) justification for it in that there is the same sense of a chosen people beleaguered by the world and made homeless for their beliefs. Rudy Wiebe might be thought to have less of a background of victimization than Klein or Richler, but even a superficial study of the persecution that many Mennonites (including Wiebe's parents) experienced in Russia in the 1920s and 30s contradicts this. Wiebe shared with Klein the idea that religion is not a

---

4 See Tom Marshall's unconvincing attempt to resolve this paradox in *A. M. Klein* (Toronto: Ryerson Press, 1970), p. xv.

racial quality, and, moreover, both their philosophies presume that their religions should be outward looking enough to embrace all humanity, and not introverted to define and protect small groups as groups. Both see religion as one essential force for good in the world, capable of uniting instead of dividing humanity. They show religion to be racially unlimited. There is in many religions a sectarian influence that can grow to the extent of racial restrictions if not opposed by this more tolerant view. The accumulation of sectarian identity is an ongoing controversy in Judaism as well as Mennonitism,[5] and is a major theme in Wiebe's *Peace Shall Destroy Many* (1962). Wiebe shows the potential for a small-group mentality to accumulate through conventions and traditions via religious commonality to the point where the group becoomes more important than the religious principles, and therefore no better than secular groups organized for less altruistic reasons. Both Klein and Wiebe separately see their religions as the best paths for humanity to follow to find peace and spiritual fulfillment. Practical considerations, chiefly economic jealousy by other, less fortunate or less organized groups, cause problems that the groups' religious bases may exacerbate instead of solve.

Wiebe's Mennonite upbringing invests his writings with a dogmatically conscious theological importance. Nowhere is this more obvious than in the short story, "The Vietnam Call of Samuel U. Reimer," which forms part of the loose novel, *The Blue Mountains of China* (1970). In other novels too, Wiebe's vision of a society informed and guided by Mennonite principles towards common humanist ideals is obvious. It shows up in *Peace Shall Destroy Many*, in which a Mennonite community is revealed as corrupted by its own attempts to remain a closed shop. It appears in his second book, *First and Vital Candle* (1966), in disguise, not obviously Mennonite but clearly Christian. It appears also in *The Scorched-Wood People* (1977) where Riel's dream of a religious organization in the West is closely related to Wiebe's own purpose. In each case religion is presented as a bond between all people, above petty institutional conflicts. More obviously a pacifist then Klein, Wiebe writes powerfully of the violent tensions inherent in contemporary life, offering an all-embracing religion as a means of transcending conflicts to achieve peace. As one of several bases for human groupings, racism is one of several divisive factors he condemns in his attempt to show the way to a unified world. It is from this foundation that any analysis of race in his work must begin.

Peace Shall Destroy Many was written by Wiebe as a project for his M.A. in creative writing at the University of Alberta. It examines the situation of

---

5 Wiebe has acknowledged in 1964 that persistent persecution has driven the Mennonites into an appreciation of an ethnic identity "at the expense of Christian doctrine." Rudy Wiebe, "For the Mennonite Churches: A Last Chance," in *A Voice in the Land*, ed. W. J. Keith (Edmonton: NeWest Press, 1981), p. 26.

Mennonites in Canada in 1944. In some ways it is a descriptive work introducing Mennonites to Canadians who probably did not understand them very well (although Wapiti is not a typical Mennonite community). But chiefly it struggles with the same themes that troubled the Mennonite community at large during the war, as Wiebe attempts to direct church opinion towards his own sense of Mennonite orthodoxy. He attacks the increasingly isolated lifestyle of the Mennonites in Canada during the war, arguing that if their religion was to have any meaning *in* the world then it must be presented *to* the world. Retreat is an abnegation of responsibility. Wiebe's fundamentalism struck hard at first at the introversion of Mennonites in a war-torn world that desperately required spiritual examples and direction, and later at the Mennonite surrender to secular attractions which corrupted and diluted their strength as a religious force. He attacks Mennonites for having become a group; like Klein he requires that religious vision and strength be shared with everyone.

Peace Shall Destroy Many focuses on the Mennonite community of Wapiti in 1944, a community that is in hiding from the world which encroaches more and more upon the people's lives as the training planes fly overhead and conscription forces the conscientious objection issue to a head. The community is beleaguered: "There was no longer enough bush between themselves and the world."[6] Once the beliefs and sociology of Mennonites have been reconstructed, a dichotomy is presented, with Thom Wiens as the adolescent seeker of truth caught in confusion between the authoritarian leadership of Deacon Block and the less strict and more tolerant position of Brother Dueck. Block's name indicates his hard nature, his dedication to his own group solidified into a contempt for all outside the group. Brother Dueck represents Wiebe's own position, preaching the "brotherhood of man" which is part of the original Anabaptist position. Yet this "brotherhood" is not to be achieved so much by communal efforts as by the attainment of dignity by individuals, or, as Hildegaard Tiessen put it in an article about Wiebe's concept of peace: "In his fiction Wiebe attempts to demonstrate that the man who would seriously wish to express that principle of brotherhood, and so live at peace with his neighbour, must first find peace within his own soul."[7] The torture of moving beyond one's upbringing, especially in a community so closely knit and so filled with spiritual traps, is obvious in the troubled minds of both Thom and Dueck. Dueck leaves the community when he is drafted into the army, and his farewell speech accuses those left behind of betraying the concept of "brotherhood" they pretend to live by: "As a Christian I must *do* something about the

6 Rudy Wiebe, *Peace Shall Destroy Many* (Toronto: McClelland and Stewart, 1962), p. 17. The symbol is repeated on pp. 63, 71, and 164.
7 Hildegaard E. Tiessen, "A Mighty Inner River: 'Peace' in the Fiction of Rudy Wiebe," *Journal of Canadian Fiction* 2, No. 4 (1973), 71.

misery in the world, even though there are aspects about the Medical Corps none of us like. I find I cannot—lose myself behind bush and pretend the misery is not there."[8] Pacifism is maintained as a necessary value but one that is hard to reconcile with the equally immediate necessity of combatting evil in the world.[9]

An obvious racial conflict is developed between the Mennonites and the local Métis whom they employ as part-time labour. Thom becomes aware of them as human beings not by contact with them, for in spite of his "summer's work with the breed children every Sunday afternoon, he suddenly knew that he had not yet seen them as quite human."[10] Just as suddenly he is confronted with an illicit (according to Mennonite custom) relationship between Herman Paetkau, a Mennonite, and Madeleine Moosomin, a Métis woman. This liaison is doubly illicit for being outside their endogamous custom, and Herman is effectively ostracized by all of them except Thom, but *not* by the Métis.[11] Interracial sex is a threatening idea to most of the Mennonites, an opening in their ranks to the opposition. Dueck and Thom come to see it as an opportunity to expand their ranks, not just as Mennonites but as Christians within a "brotherhood." However, for Thom the awareness of the Métis as human beings, with souls and minds as much in need of spiritual assistance as his own, comes when Madeleine tells him of her great-great-grandfather, Big Bear, and he is made aware that the Métis have a history too. He learns that Canada has a pre-Mennonite history, and that the Métis have a right to be there, perhaps even more so than he does. A local sense of religious determinism cannot survive multiple displacement without conflicting with other group-histories somewhere. Canada requires new systems; the importation en bloc of old systems from Europe cannot satisfy the new land.

Deacon Block's hard-hearted nature and devotion to the material prosperity of his farm—prosperity that ironically is increased in wartime by

8 Wiebe, *Peace Shall Destroy Many*, p. 63.

9 Klein seemed to see Germany as the national representative of evil on Earth, not racially but more by accident and by the failure of goodness. In Europe, the Mennonites were often thought to be German, although most were of Swiss or Dutch extraction and had resided in Russia for two centuries. They seem to have kept to themselves, above national distinctions, preferring to be just Mennonites instead, but Wiebe points out that in so doing they created and perpetuated an equivalent group identity with the same inevitably negative results. Like Klein he wishes to return to fundamentals and turn his religion outward-looking again in order positively to influence a world in chaos. Peace, as Dueck comes to define it, cannot be an unchanging escapist situation such as the Mennonites' avoidance of the world. That type of peace is built upon selfish hypocrisy and so possesses the potential to destroy those who participate in it—hence the book's title. Evil should not be seen as an innate national quality or prerogative.

10 Wiebe, *Peace Shall Destroy Many*, p. 110.

11 Because he is supposed to have been married outside the Mennonite church, Herman is still not accepted by them.

military purchases which offset his pacifism—drives his daughter, Elizabeth, to Louis Moosomin. Her death inflames Block to drive the Métis out of the area, increasing the insularity of the community, even though he realizes Elizabeth's trouble was not caused by outside influences but largely by forces in himself he could not control. Yet characteristically he reacts by buying up the Métis land and forcing them away. Block, the old-style Mennonite leader, is out of place in Canada and out of time with his own religion, a man caught between theory and practice, crushed inwardly by the self-knowledge that he does wrong but *must* do wrong. The failure of the Mennonites to live with the rest of Canada is shown further by their single concession to the obligatory conversion of others—the sending of a missionary couple to India instead of facing up to their responsibilities among the Métis in their midst. Wiebe promotes the same sort of religious complex that Gordon did, but he refuses the racial consequences that Gordon stumbled over, and by showing Block's dilemma and failure to be the result of group consciousness intensified, Wiebe proves his own understanding of the problem. Instead of associating his own religion with his own "race," Wiebe throws it wide open for the benefit of the unity of all humanity, deliberately denying the validity of racial distinctions before God. This message—that such a peace would certainly destroy the many who have invested in divisiveness and sectarian hatred—is a religious version of the more political theme of Richler's *Son of a Smaller Hero*.

Wiebe's second novel, *First and Vital Candle*, is set largely in Northern Ontario in an Ojibwa settlement, but it travels widely, as Wiebe's writing tends to do, and includes chapters set in the Arctic and Winnipeg. It is similar to Mitchell's *The Vanishing Point* and Bodsworth's *The Strange One* in that all three novels enter into Indian communities and explore in depth the effects of the whites' intervention in their lives. While Mitchell and Bodsworth are contemptuous of white religious interference, Wiebe makes religion the most serious theme in his novel, and the ultimate salvation for both whites and Indians. All other themes, including the pacifist and anti-materialist motifs, are subservient to and derived from this primary theme. Yet Wiebe does not have Christianity imposed upon the Ojibwa with all the incongruous results recorded in Mitchell's work or the near-fatal results in Bodsworth's. He recognizes the same values in Ojibwa culture as he prizes in his own, and in recognizing the shared ideals promotes a supra-racial unity.

The Satanic figure of Sigurd Bjornesen struggles for the Indians with the innocent protagonist and the selfless missionary couple so aptly named "the Bishops." Bjornesen and Abe are rival factors, competing for the Indians' furs. Bjornesen wins their custom with his monopoly of yeast used for homebrew liquor, which Wiebe condemns as the main reason for the crime and the fighting which keep them unhappy. Their traditional values are dying out and being replaced by an unsatisfying, purely material, artificial, and imported pseudo-culture. Abe is caught in the middle at first, but slowly is swayed to an awareness of religion in his life. After the defeat of Bjornesen optimistic hopes take precedence over the implications of the ending, which is shadowed by a death that paradoxically is meant to reinforce Abe's new strength. This optimism is supported by the volunteering of a bright young Indian girl to go "outside" to study so that she can return and teach her people.[12]

The Indian band is exploited and abused by the various whites who deal with it. The Indians themselves are presented as passive victims. The racism in the book is not that of a myriad of relatively minor incidents but the tragedy of a whole group of people being pushed towards their own vanishing point by another group. The Indians are not ill-treated *because* they are Indians, but as a different group they are certainly not well-treated. Wiebe's optimistic ending requires faith, taken virtually to the point of fatalism. God is in control and whatever happens is so desired by him. This is the only way for Abe and the reader to deal with the unsettling death of Sally. Practically, Sally's death inspires Violet Crane to try to become an intermediary for the good of her people, but this is not pursued in the book. Abe's idea that the trading companies remove themselves from the area, leaving their businesses for the Indians to operate as a co-op fur trade venture assisted by Bishop, the disinterested and dedicated missionary, is an idealistic vision. Wiebe stresses the necessity for the removal of material interests which corrupt people, in favour of the introduction of more moral principles, best personified by Bishop. As Abe explains it to Bjornesen: "Maybe I'm just sick of us bloodsucking these poor buggers dry for a few lousy bucks. . . . Neither of us'd be here if they weren't worth skinning. Only him. He's here because they're human beings."[13] The imposition of the fringe elements of the material white culture on a formerly independent non-white culture is the problem, as Wiebe sees it. He seems to be advocating the isolation of the Indians. In this his one book about the contemporary Indian situation, his thoughts seem contradictory and not worked through to consistent ends. There is not even the earthy practicalities of how to survive in a bleak marginal environment, which Bodsworth raised so capably in *The Strange One*.

The movement of Abe from aimless private indignation towards illumination and maturity resembles the struggles of other characters in Wiebe's

12 Violet Crane's "call" and her concomitant disciplining of her own physical desires which hitherto had precluded it contrasts with Victoria Rider's failure in a similar situation in *The Vanishing Point* and Kanina Beaverskin's defeat by racism in *The Strange One*. Compared to the cynical realism of Bodsworth and Mitchell, Wiebe's optimism seems short-sighted and inconclusive.

13 Rudy Wiebe, *First and Vital Candle* (Toronto: McClelland and Stewart, 1966), p. 331.

novels to achieve dignity. Dignity consists of self-awareness and self-discipline, founded upon faith. It is Wiebe's term to describe the religiously competent person. Dignity can be withheld from one group by another simply by denying them freedom and the necessities of survival. Dignity defines the full person, and is available to everyone.

What is probably Wiebe's best book, *The Blue Mountains of China* (1970), returned to the theme of Mennonite survival in the twentieth century. In this disjointed novel, land is an illusion of security eagerly sought for by the Mennonites dispersed from Russia to Canada and Paraguay. They seek liberation from various atheistic and insufficiently religious regimes (including that in Canada)[14] by creating their own little communities insulated, like Wapiti behind a thinning wall of bush in *Peace Shall Destroy Many*, from the rest of the world. Land and insularity become ends in themselves, demanding ultimately unchristian behaviour in their defence, as Deacon Block discovers in the latter book. Wiebe shows that the liberation they should be seeking is spiritual and personal, and unrelated to place.

The book moves around the world in its settings, but the story basically moves from the Molotschna Mennonite settlement in Russia in the 1920s to Paraguay and Canada in the 1960s. It involves people of many "races," deliberately to test the Mennonites' reactions to them. Some of the uncompromising Mennonites soften their intolerant stance over the years and come to appreciate others as human beings too. Their original contentment with their prosperous life in the Ukraine is shattered by the war and a revolution which brands them as kulaks; the Bolsheviks criticize their capitalism in political terms quite similar to the religious criticism which Wiebe directs at them. In the Ukraine the Mennonites had become more than a religious group, attaining considerable status and wealth as successful farmers. Their prosperity increased their introversion, making them a closed group capable of acts of inhumanity towards outsiders, and this introversion is their weak point—the beginning of the hypocrisy that corrodes their lives and their religion from within.

Wiebe takes the view that the Mennonites are wrong to wander the world seeking land, a search which he negatively associates with Zionism. As John Reimer tells Jacob Friesen: "You know the trouble with Mennonites? They've always wanted to be Jews. To have land God had given them for their very own, to which they were called; so even if someone chased them away, they could work forever to get it back."[15] John's own landless

14 This book is a condemnation of a Canada too secular and corrupt for a truly religious person to live in. The only possible response for a devout Christian to such a situation, according to Wiebe, is preaching by example and evangelical mission work, *not* self-exile to South America.

15 Rudy Wiebe, *The Blue Mountains of China* (Toronto: McClelland and Stewart, 1970), p. 227.

condition and his cross-bearing odyssey across Alberta represent one man's protest against materialism and the return to spiritual values that Wiebe is advocating.

As in *Peace Shall Destroy Many*, the superiority complex of the Mennonites is shown to be unchristian. If one has more of anything, whether material wealth or theological wealth, one is obliged to share it with those who need it. Anyone who turns away, inwards, and refuses to share impoverishes himself. The Mennonites, if their religion is to have any meaning in the world and if the peace they so earnestly claim to desire is to be achieved on earth, must interact with other people as human beings, to raise the level of religious consciousness for all concerned. Small-group consciousness leads to evil actions, and is a form of racism. Racism is then seen as irreligious and anti-social.

The historical novel, *The Temptations of Big Bear* (1973), picks up the pieces of history that were dropped in *Peace Shall Destroy Many* to trace the clash between whites and Indians in the West in a far more historically authentic way than Gordon managed to do with his *Corporal Cameron* and *The Patrol of the Sun Dance Trail*, and with far greater understanding for the motives and emotions of both sides. In fact, only Frederick Niven's *Mine Inheritance* (1940) and *The Flying Years* (1942) approach the fairness that Wiebe brought to Indians in his fiction.

The secular crux of *The Temptations of Big Bear* is the theft of the land that Wiebe places as the unavoidable foundation-stone of white expansion in the Canadian West, an unpleasant fact that racism helped to smoothe over and conceal in the past, but which Wiebe feels must be faced up to now.

Wiebe presents Indians and whites in this novel on equal terms at this historical distance. In fact, if anything he bends over backwards to show the Indians in a better light than the whites, a didactic exaggeration that mirrors his sympathy for the Indians and shows his strong desire to highlight the racial conflict.[16] The whites are contemptuous of the Indians in such a way that the reader turns their contempt back on them. They are aggressively lying to gain land. Their speech alone is dishonest, vulgar, and bluntly awkward, compared to the direct statements of the Indians, expressed with dignity and accompanied by natural metaphors. The whites are completely out of place, their flags and band preposterously incongruous beside the Indians who fit in so naturally with their environment. The Indians, and especially Big Bear, have the true dignity of an independent

16 Wiebe once considered changing the title to "Red and White" (the title of a short story by Nellie McClung in *All We Like Sheep* [1926] referred to above in note 38 for Chapter 2). Such a title would have given the racial confrontation far more prominence. (The suggestion is found in a letter to John Newlove at McClelland and Stewart, dated January 4, 1973. A copy of this letter is in the Wiebe papers at the University of Calgary. I am indebted for this information to Professor W. J. Keith.)

nation, while the whites bring with them only the assumed dignity which uniforms and military trappings convey. A clear bias in favour of the "reds" is apparent, and perhaps made necessary by the one-sided view of history which to a large extent still prevails. The winners not only won the land but the right to tell how it was won. Wiebe presents the Indians not just as individuals in old photographs but as members of a complete society with a spiritual awareness just as developed (if not more so) as that of Europeans. Certainly Big Bear as a philosopher is far wiser than any of the pragmatic military Europeans he faces, and when he complains that he has never been able to speak to a white man of equal importance, he is actually complaining about the inferior position in which he has been placed.[17] Big Bear, as the spokesman for the Indians, is as far as Wiebe is concerned equal to Sir John A. MacDonald and Louis Riel for all three were involved in constructing confederations for much the same reasons. Big Bear tries to encourage diplomacy, but is out-maneuvered by the chicanery, deceit, and force of the whites who are not diplomats but thieves.

Big Bear is not just a politician. Within the complicated Indian society Wiebe reconstructs he is also a religious and philosophical leader, a seer who personifies the collective dignity of his people. Wiebe's own religious sympathy for the Indians' beliefs emerges in contrast with the irreligious whites whose official duplicity belies their theological institutions. Big Bear wrestles with the theoretical implications of the coming of the whites. He decides and maintains that whites are different from Indians, but feels that this is a cultural difference based largely on their sedentary habits and their untrustworthy ways. He wonders at an early stage if whites are really people (the Indians always refer to themselves as "Persons" or "The People"). He questions the idea that a common humanity embraces both whites and Indians in the face of the implied inhumanity of the whites, and he wonders if it is possible that whites, not being people, are actually outside God's scheme and therefore evil. This temptation to denounce others as evil and sub-human is defeated, as he concludes:

> The Spirit must have sent these whites to us so we must find the way He wants us to live with them. We see we cannot fight them. Fighting is good in raids, and makes men, but we know it cannot be His way for us to do nothing but kill. One only becomes more manly by killing other men and I don't think American soldiers are men: they have deliberately killed too many women and children.[18]

The sense of the unity of humanity informs his decision in the end. A lack of that sense forces the whites on their course of dispossession. The conflict is

17 Rudy Wiebe, *The Temptations of Big Bear* (Toronto: McClelland and Stewart, 1973), p. 197.
18 Ibid., p. 105.

reduced by Wiebe to basic economic terms; the Europeans' thrust is understood by the Indians in the traditional terms of an "alien" group trespassing to live, and not just for temporary greed as on a "raid." The Indians are not unwilling to share what seems to be a material surplus of wealth, but do not expect to lose everything. The Indians put the whites to shame, as Big Bear realizes, and he hopes that the whites may be forced to recognize their own duplicity when it is so clearly contrasted with the straightforward honesty of "The People."

Big Bear's fatalistic acceptance of events as God's will leads to death that faith alone can justify. Wiebe seems to be suggesting that deaths are God-given and therefore purposeful. The fatalism behind such acceptance contradicts the optimistic pragmatism of Big Bear: the book derives much of its interest from the tension between the two groups and the extent to which Big Bear can defend his interests and convince the whites of the extreme nature of their demands—demands that ostensibly arrange for a sharing of the land but which everyone tacitly knows means the end of the Indians' way of life and probably their very existence as a people. A paradox of active effort versus passive acceptance undercuts this novel's religious teleology. However, the principles of universal brotherhood and peace combined with the literary redistribution of historical "verities" and the more-than-fair characterization of non-white personalities and their society, make up for this flaw in terms of the book's efficiency as an anti-racist work (which, of course, is not *all* that it is). But once again Wiebe suggests, as he did in *First and Vital Candle*, that the only way for Indians and whites to live together is to live apart. This at least is Dewdney's interpretation of Big Bear's position.[19]

The Scorched-Wood People (1977) takes the sympathetic approach to the historical underdog even further.[20] Focusing on the Métis rebellions of 1869-70 and 1885, it is told from the Métis point of view. Again Wiebe starts with the premise that the whites had no right to take over the prairies, and he blames them and their colonialist expansion for the troubles that developed when the Métis reacted so violently to being dispossessed.

Again, as in *The Temptations of Big Bear*, Wiebe disinters an extinct society, performing an autopsy to determine the cause of death. The crime is re-enacted and the victims are given a chance to tell it their way. The Métis are presented as a people living at peace with their neighbours and able to get along with the Scottish settlers, the various English half-breeds,

19 Ibid., p. 114.
20 Wiebe does habitually write of the underdog, or of victims. Anne Montagnes commented on this in the *Globe and Mail*: "It is among Wiebe's missions to seek unification of the country by promoting understanding of the minorities and these so-called losers, and he does this partly because he, a Mennonite whose mother tongue is not English, identifies with them." A. Montagnes, "Of Many Books," *Globe and Mail*, August 8, 1981, p. E14.

and the few Americans who wandered through their territory. However, Upper Canadian farmers arriving to fence off open land could not be tolerated. The land itself is thought of differently by both sides, the whites visualizing deeds to fenced plots while the Métis need open areas for their buffalo hunts.

Wiebe portrays Riel and the rebellions in religious terms.[21] He sees Riel as a religious leader, inspired by God to try to prevent the catastrophe that overwhelmed a less active Big Bear in his previous work. Riel is shown as mixing his fatalism with intemperate fanaticism, yet Wiebe presents in positive terms Riel's concept of the rebellion as a supra-ethnic crusade for the rights of everyone—Indians, Scotch, Americans, Métis—who inhabited the West and who were being pressured by incoming Easterners to change their way of life. The rebellion, with its unsuccessful attempts to unite the peoples of the land regardless of ethnicity, appealed to Wiebe's own sense of the unity of humanity. Riel's vision of a raceless utopia is destroyed by the political machinations (on every level) of white Canada. Riel at one point argues with Gabriel Dumont that diplomacy is superior to violence: "We must trust them . . . show we trust their word. . . . That's the only way different peoples can live together."[22] Behind Riel is Wiebe speaking. Proffering the hand of friendship in hopes of peace is Wiebe's solution to racism, yet in both *The Temptations of Big Bear* and *The Scorched-Wood People* that overture fails because of the greed of the whites. The "villains" win in both books, and the "heroes" are exterminated as symbolic martyrs for following the very lesson the book preaches. Wiebe demands a great deal of faith from his readers, disproving by example the way *not* to get along with one's fellow man.

The sell-out of native land rights to whites for temporary bribes of food is re-enacted in Wiebe's play, *Far as the Eye Can See* (1977), but with more of a belligerently defensive mood. One of the ghostly characters is Crowfoot, and his sell-out is linked with a similar act of surrender by Anton Kalicz, a man whose farm was expropriated by an industrial firm called Calgary Power. All the significant characters in this play except Premier Lougheed and Crowfoot have "foreign" names, providing a definite sense of a non-Anglo-Saxon community in the West. The immigrant, Anton, thought he had escaped the insecurity of land ownership in Poland by settling in Canada, but he discovers that even in Canada one must be prepared to fight for one's land against the greed of corporate interests that can even put you in a position where fighting them seems wrong. This play is not prose fiction, but does show the development of Wiebe's pacifist beliefs to the

---

21 Wiebe's interpretation of the events and the participants is supported by Thomas Flanagan in *Louis 'David' Riel: 'Prophet of the New World'* (Toronto: University of Toronto Press, 1979).

22 Rudy Wiebe, *The Scorched-Wood People* (Toronto: McClelland and Stewart, 1977), p. 109.

point where active defence is recognized to be a sad necessity where greedy thieves institutionalize and even "nationalize" their thefts.

Wiebe concentrates on the religious effects and causes of racism. When one group defines itself as religiously good and an opposing group as evil, then irreconcilable troubles exist which only the exposure of such antipathies as basically irreligious might alter. Wiebe's emphasis on trust, which the quotation ascribed to Riel above exemplifies, is naively an answer to expectations of evil. Evil is everywhere, causing hatred between the smug Mennonites as well as in the outside world. Evil does not belong to any one group, but must be fought by individuals each on a personal odyssey for dignity. Both Klein and Wiebe employ individual characters seeking religious bases which have the potential to make superfluous all collectivities that have become competitive and hostile. In the same sense that Klein and Wiebe each reduce their own religious backgrounds to the common denominators of the world's religions (as each sees it) and that both open their groups up to all comers (Wiebe much more obviously than Klein), they produce more positive answers to racism than most of their predecessors. They believe that humanity can achieve the religious consciousness that recognizes all other people as individuals; such a condition might therefore cause group mentalities to lose their appeal.

Chapter Seven

Conclusion

It may be that, like myself, some child of immigrants longs to justify
her race as something more than a hewer of wood; dreams in the
starlight of the lonely prairie of some fair burnt offering to lay upon the
altar of her New Country, out of the love of a small, passionate heart.

How to do it, in a strange new language? How to do it, in the face of
poverty and isolation, and the cold indifference of an alien people?
How to hold fast to a purpose that no one counts as precious as a
new-turned furrow, a pelt of furs, or a load of grain.

Confessions of an Immigrant's Daughter, by Laura Salverson

While Canada has been remarkably free of the ugliest forms and consequences of racism that have caused so much tragedy elsewhere in the world,
its appearance as a theme in so much of Canadian literature suggests its
effects have been and remain present to a significant degree. Racism has
always been present as an undercurrent in Canadian fiction,[1] whether as a
mild form of xenophobia, or in one of the more fanatical forms of group-
hatred such as anti-Semitism. Racism as a popular term has expanded
beyond its relatively simple if contestable biological implications to include
religious, linguistic, and cultural attributes. It has come to mean an
extreme form of group awareness which deliberately encourages antipathies
towards other groups, often with some form of economic competition as a
stimulus. Our concept of nationality rests uneasily upon ethnic, regional,
and religious struggles for control and survival. A surfeit of natural re-

---

1 Of course, racism is the theme of many non-fiction works as well, two recent examples
being Maria Campbell's *Halfbreed* (1973) and Anthony Apakark Thrasher's *The Three Lives
of Thrasher* (1976).

sources has kept these conflicts from escalating to European proportions, but on a smaller scale and in a less violent manner harmful hostilities persist.

The history of Europeans in Canada unrolled from East to West over a century of tentative expansion and consolidation, a movement which saw various battles fought at various times between various groups who thought of themselves as races different from each other, for what amounted in their minds to racial dominance, but which can be better defined as political control. Politics has always used racism when convenient. The earliest movements of people from Ontario and Quebec to the prairies saw a struggle for dominance between English and French that was not settled until Riel's defeat at Batoche and which saw the victory of the English charter group soon develop into a defensive campaign against the overwhelming numbers of non-charter-group immigrants as the twentieth century progressed. Settlement was in part accomplished by ethnic groups as groups, creating a patchwork of cultural dissimilarity. Regionalism, as an explanatory basis for Canadian history and as a determinant of the literature that the history produced, is very closely linked with ethnicity.

In a Centennial year speech, J. M. S. Careless, the historian, emphasized this link while arguing that, unlike the American model of a nation melted together, Canada is and must be accepted as a collection of regional identities not necessarily committed to one common definition of nationalism. Careless insisted that one factor contributing to the necessity of orienting historiography along regional lines is the persistence of the ethnic mosaic: "Each region has virtually a distinctive ethnic composition of its own, according to the proportion and variety of immigrants it has received, with consequent effects on its political as well as cultural responses."[2]

What Careless views as regions are such because of the cultural differences of their populations, and not just their intrinsic geographic properties. The importance of ethnicity remains obvious in Canada, even as new ethnic groups evolve: the competition between these mostly cultural territories, as they swell and compete commercially, cannot be ignored. The attempts in every way—militarily, politically, economically, and in literature—by English-Canadians to dominate Canada and make it one homogeneous state modelled after Britain, are perhaps the most significant internal events in its history. At least until World War Two many English-Canadians viewed these attempts as a racial struggle. They acted as if they were a race superior to others, even at times, paradoxically, superior to the British model they referred to for their superiority. They attempted to enforce their own cultural attributes upon "aliens" using racism as one justification. Literature that condoned or assisted this was racist. Writers

2 J. M. S. Careless, "Limited Identities in Canada," *Canadian Historical Review* 50, No. 1 (1969), 8.

who could not see above the confines of their own groupings, regardless of which side they were on, encouraged racism by celebrating the act of grouping. Literature as such has been more a series of acts of war than of peace.

Wiebe and Klein are the first Canadian authors to rise significantly above not only regional ethnic conclaves within Canada but also provincial and national territoriality to take in the entire world. Their destruction of artifical boundaries leads to a true internationalism, which is the only viable response to racism that Canadians have produced. It is neither an isolated nor an original response, but one that depends on ancient theology and, in Canada, which has developed through the cultural vicissitudes attendant upon mass immigration. Racism in Canada can no longer be thought of as the internal problem it never was. It is part of the conflicts of groups prevalent throughout the world, less violent perhaps but certainly not less substantial. It is a problem that must be assaulted on all fronts simultaneously and internationally, and Klein and Wiebe have apprised Canadians of their larger responsibilities in this regard, responsibilities that have still to be acted upon.

Canadian attitudes to racism, as expressed in literature, have shifted in various ways: stereotypes have been used less and less by writers increasingly conscious that members of other groups have as much psychological validity and individuality as they do, and that to treat people as stereotypes is a misrepresentation of reality; the twin faiths of religion and Marxism have been appealed to by various writers seeking ethical principles to prevent discrimination rather than to justify it; similarly, codes of morality have been invoked to attack arguments of cultural and racial dominance; and rationalism has been appealed to by didacticism that confronted the problem clearly and directly.

The level of stereotyping that appeared in the work of Charles Gordon has not survived him. It has indeed been publicly exposed and discredited to the point where it cannot be used without attracting negative criticism.[3] Its denial of authenticity and originality to literary characters has been appreciated in works of the past, and one hopes that we are not blind to it in the present. Modern authors have replaced stereotyping often by "bending over blackwards" to confer fully human personalities upon characters of other groups (whether or not they respect or even recognize the validity of such groups). The trend towards the exposé of one's own group stereotypes

3 This is probably as much because of the influence of recent American television shows, such as "All in the Family," which have made racism and bigotry out to be stupid, as because of the work of interested authors. Northrop Frye has noted this: "Eskimos, blacks, Indians, perhaps even Wasps, cannot go on being comic-strip stereotypes after they have been fully exposed on television." "Conclusion" to the revised *Literary History of Canada*, ed. Carl F. Klinck (Toronto: University of Toronto Press, 1976), 3:328.

and leadership idols, which both Richler and Wiebe have been accused of by their respective "groups," and which leads outwards beyond group demarcations, is almost the opposite of stereotypical characterization. One must not confuse the realities of accepted situations and occupations with the stereotypical delineation of character which facilitates both the writing and the reading by limiting change and challenge. The black women in Callaghan's *The Loved and the Lost* as well as the one black woman (the mother of Wes) in Buckler's "Long, Long After School," and the mother in Clarke's *Amongst Thistles and Thorns* are washerwomen in these works because such characters would probably have been washerwomen in actuality, and the resultant possible stereotype of black women as washerwomen for whites must be and is ameliorated and denied by their human resistance to their sociological circumstances. Typing them as washerwomen forever, doomed to fulfil a social role rather than live wholly human lives, is the now unforgivable crime in literature, whether race is involved or not. Even in *The Gay Crusader* Gordon did not speak of Jews as people, for his distrust of them as a group was always present and precluded his acceptance of them totally as Canadians and as individuals. By consistently using the short-cut, "the Jew," he refused to consider individuality, but spoke instead of the "always Jew"—the stereotyped Jew who could not escape the abstract imprisonment Gordon imposed on the group and which itself encouraged the persistence of that group in literature.

Richler directly attacked the use of stereotypes in several books, notably in *The Incomparable Atuk*, which is largely a satire of the myths which stereotypes support so fragilely. However, a surprising product of the literary reaction against stereotypes is the production of new ones. In many of the anti-racist works discussed above, there are easily identifiable racist figures opposing the anti-racist characters. In *The Loved and the Lost*, Peggy is contrasted with Walter Malone; Garner's *Storm Below* pits the understanding Captain against the obnoxious Smith-Rawleigh; Bodsworth's *The Strange One* sees Rory fighting the racism of his academic mentor. In some of Laurence's work as well as in that of Ross, Grove, Wiebe, and, to include a dramatist, Ryga, it was not enough to have simply a racist character; associations were added that made that character an unlikable person in other respects if not an out-and-out villain. An obvious danger in combatting stereotypes is that they will only be turned inside out and operate just as well under new colours.

Sexual stereotyping is a byproduct of this reversal of stereotypes. In a number of anti-racist books, authors have played up the sexuality of another group at the expense of their own. In *The Temptations of Big Bear*, Wiebe presents the Indians as sexually better adjusted than the whites, and closer to elemental nature. In Alan Fry's light novel, *The Revenge of Annie Charlie* (1973), this same idea is taken even further as a group of Indian women contrast their way of life with the frigid, disciplined customs of whites. Similarly, in Harold Horwood's *White Eskimo* (1973) the Eskimo are shown to be sexually more natural and freer of psychological anxieties than whites. In Mitchell's *The Vanishing Point* Sinclair turns to an Indian for sexual comfort, as did Rory in Bodsworth's *The Strange One*. Sinclair Ross and Margaret Laurence both portray English-Canadian protagonists repudiating their own group for Ukrainian-Canadian lovers, and in *The Diviners* Morag forsakes her husband for a Métis lover. Richler pokes fun at the curiosity his Jewish male characters express about "shiksa" girls, and he explores mixed marriages with a great deal of lusty humour. There are even suggestions in Grove's work that he envied Jews a sensuality he denied his own group. More than just a yearning for greener grass, and more than the self-inflicted abnegation to make up for past negative treatment, this ubiquitous practice may indicate Freudian tensions based upon deep-rooted and enduring racial jealousies as well as personal anxieties. Indeed sex can even be seen as an interracial weapon, as Henry realizes in Clarke's *The Meeting Point*.

Religion seems to have done more to promote racism than to combat it, according to those writers who have expressed an opinion about it. Callaghan's ideal church in *The Loved and the Lost* is covered symbolically from view by the *white* snow of uncaring Montreal. Bodsworth and Mitchell presented religion (at least in its institutional form) as more show than action. The confusion between Rev. Richards's faith-healing performance and a circus in *The Vanishing Point* is surely deliberate. Religion has often been presented as another form of group definition, and thus as a limiting factor. Yet it is clear that for Klein and Wiebe, and to a somewhat qualified extent for Gordon, religion (in each case) offered a promise of peace for all. The problem of how positively to use religion in this sense is to learn how to open what is essentially a closed and inward-looking structure in practice, thus avoiding discrimination against "outsiders." Neither Klein nor Wiebe seem to have fully achieved this, though they have progressed further towards it than any other Canadian novelists to date, with the possible exception of Audrey Thomas.

The record of Marxism is remarkably similar to that of Christianity as far as the theme of race is concerned, and it may not be as incongruous as it first seems to compare the treatment of the two ideologies. Both offer panaceas requiring faith, and both are generally viewed as mutually exclusive. Both idealistically view humanity as a whole but in practical terms have tended towards rigid and even institutional categorization. While religions have historically had ethnic or national foundations, Marxism reacts with race in a different manner, viewing capitalism as the origin of social flaws. Thus capitalists *must* be racists and working-class people *must* be anti-racist. Such simplistic logic seems removed from the complexities of reality and contributes to stereotypes in the negative sense referred to above, best exemplified by Dyson Carter's *Fatherless Sons* in which the capitalists are politically stereotyped to unreasonable extents. Garner and Buller employ more understanding and practical views of socialism which allow for the idiosyncrasies of human personality.

A direct appeal to rationality has not been a popular anti-racism device in Canadian literature. Early English-Canadian writers understandably saw nothing wrong with actively defending what they saw as their own race, and only the increasingly felt presence of a culturally diverse immigrant population constantly enlarging the possibilities of tolerance altered that defence from being aggressively discriminatory. The Holocaust, which in Canada was felt to make racism inconsistent with Allied war aims, drained the last elements of logic from anti-Semitic racism, and led to the post-war reversal of values in theory if not in practice. Rather than preaching, which only Gordon reverted to at times, authors have preferred to allegorize anti-racist preachments, as Graham did in *Earth and High Heaven* and Bodsworth in *The Strange One*. By presenting Jews as people first, and by industriously repudiating stereotypes, Graham's anti-racist message is implicitly delivered, absorbed rather than considered intellectually. Plot competes with dogma, the literary values of the novel depending on a relative evaluation of the success of the mixture. Anti-racist characters act as good examples, while racists are defeated, implying a Manichean originality to the characters, who become representatives if not new stereotypes. Fortunately there is little of this in Canadian literature, for after Gordon the authors who dealt with race usually did so in the context of other concerns to portray society as a whole and racism in its place. Best of all, over-simplification was left behind as Garner, for one, avoided absolute judgements, portraying humanity in merging shades of grey.

A related solution frequently found in anti-racism novels has been the promotion of education, one character idealistically becoming a teacher to enlighten others (the minority, or majority, or both). Often this character's decision is made at the end of a novel, leaving such an optimistic solution up in the air, as in *First and Vital Candle* and *Mountain Shadows*. Lysenko's *Westerly Wild* demonstrates such a teacher in action in a multi-ethnic school, but the unwillingness of other writers to follow through with an idealistic solution, investigating the practicalities of its application, undercuts it somewhat.

The most common approach to racism in Canadian literature by anti-racism writers has been the appeal to the morality and sensitivity of readers, often in the semi-allegorical form mentioned above. This has almost always involved the presentation of obvious victims in the plot. Frequently the narrator is a victim, which provides an insider's point of view.

Victimization has been exploited by a number of writers to attract the sympathy of readers for people affected by racial discrimination. For an author to leave his or her own group and enter into another to expose and describe their sufferings is never easy. A. M. Klein's attempt to poeticize French-Canadian habitant life remains questionable. Graham's depiction of Jewish family life in *Earth and High Heaven* ignores almost completely its religious basis, just as Gordon's treatment of the Stern family in *The Gay Crusader* did. Both use third-person detached observation to bring out their points. These novels give the impression of being the products of research rather than empathy and personal experience. Even Wiebe's *First and Vital Candle* can be criticized for this weakness. In each case the "outside" narrator remains outside.

Novels that have been told from inside a group foreign to the author have achieved more success in terms both of reality and interest. These authors fulfil their interpreter's role more effectively by breathing life into personalities which would otherwise remain as wooden and half-formed as Graham's Jewish characters. Bodsworth's *The Sparrow's Fall* and *The Strange One* both achieve this inside view with remarkable success, similar to that of Yves Theriault's *Agaguk* (1958). Life is presented from new and often startling viewpoints. Racism becomes of immediate concern, unavoidable and overpowering.

Marlyn, Lysenko, and Clarke may be thought to have had little choice in their narrative angle of attack, being members of "New Canadian" groups writing about the effects of that membership, but clearly their novels are the better for pulling English-Canadians into their worlds and showing people to be all much alike even if their cultures differ.

Closeness to the victimized group, whether contrived or natural, appears to have been an important aim among anti-racism writers. In fact, most of the writers, whether they wrote to encourage or discourage racism, tried to exploit readers' sympathies for a victimized group. Hilda Howard did this quite dramatically in *The Writing on the Wall*; ignoring the factual victimization of Asiatics in British Columbia, she invented a hypothetical future situation which portrayed the whites as being barbarously victimized by Asiatics, and she channelled the resultant indignation towards practical forms of legislated discrimination. In more modern times novels have moved from general groups to specific individuals, the novelists trying to create sympathy for one or two characters—Kanina in *The Strange One*, Sinclair in *The Vanishing Point*, Jules in *The Diviners*—in order to tap the readers' sensitivity to unjust circumstances and cruel behaviour by allowing the one victim, who is obviously more aware of the human consequences of the situation, gradually to lead the reader into a rising sense of indignation. The more we learn of Sinclair's tragic background, in Mitchell's novel, the more we become sensitized to his frustrations in trying to help the Indian band he supervises. Mitchell did not overreach himself by attempting to show Victoria's feelings through her own mind; Sinclair is a necessary interpreter, cleansed of possible aloofness by his own experiences which have made him more sensitive to the problems of others. The orphan Morag is in a very similar situation in *The Diviners*; she is a reject of the town who finds some consolation with other rejects of white civilization, including Jules, her Métis lover. Victims flock together, appealing to the sympathy of readers and drawing them into some degree of identification with first the victim closest to the reader's own group, and then the "other" victim group itself. The victim is the medium by which familiarity is retained yet contact with another group is achieved, on a vital level which enables the recognition of common humanity to be made. The victim by virtue of being a victim transcends normal group conventions in search of affinities with other victims. If an entire group is so identified, then, while racism may be considered to be happening, on a rational level the reader is encouraged to see the problem as a social injustice and to be more aware of the crippling cruelties involved for individual victims.[4]

Not all writing is easily identifiable as racist or anti-racist (categories which can be misleading and, indeed, not very useful). Certain books and stories have been written with the aim of highlighting racial conflicts. Wiebe's *The Temptations of Big Bear* is one example of a novel which clearly presents a racial confrontation and its necessary background. A book such as Callaghan's *The Strange Fugitive* (1928), in which the omniscient narrator seems intimately attached to the protagonist's mind, even to the extent of using his language, creates a potential problem. Is the consistent use of pejorative ethnic slurs part of the author's delineation of character or an unconscious duplication (and publication) of conventional and popular racism? It is clear from this distance where Callaghan's sympathies lie, but one wonders if it was clear in 1928. The racist musings produced by Timothy Wellfleet's libido in Hugh MacLennan's *Voices in Time* (1980) can be categorized stereotypically, but are just sufficiently indistinct in context that various interpretations and excuses could be found for them—and such vagueness must be considered a fault. Racism will appear in any work of fiction that is true to life as a whole. It is the author's responsibility to clearly define his or her own position, and this seems largely to have been accomplished by identifying racism with villainous, stupid, or unpleasant characters, a device, as noted above, which works against itself by creating its own stereotypes.

Anti-racist writing must not confuse the evils of racial discrimination with the eclectic delight of a multicultural world, which A. M. Klein

4 Margaret Atwood's discussion of the immigrant as victim in *Survival* (1972) ignores this function of the stressing of victimization in the plot.

delineated so rhapsodically in *The Second Scroll*. Confusion between cultural and supposedly racial attributes has resulted in many groups trying to impose their version of order and culture on other groups, often with disastrous consequences. Modern Canadian writers seem to be moving outwards from small-group definition, accepting the responsibility to ease the friction between self-seeking groups. The ubiquitous problem of racism may never be wholly defeated, but in helping to discredit it and its supporters Canadian authors fulfil a valuable role. Remove those works which have channelled and still direct public opinion in anti-racist directions and Canada would probably be a much more violent society than it is.

Canadian writers have clearly tried to deal with racism and have obviously felt by and large that their intervention was and is not only necessary but also closely linked with all other aspects of human interaction. Racism remains, and one may question how literature can continue to undercut it. Any expression of group definition can lead to discrimination, especially when it is based upon physical rather than cultural differences. Therefore a work that refuses to delineate character in any way indicative of ethnicity, merging its cast instead into an undifferentiated mass, might be expected to contribute to the eradication of racist thought by eliminating its semi-factual foundations in the same way that Ashley Montagu argues that the outlawing of the term "race" would rule out the existence of the concept.[5] This argument is sometimes raised by minority groups in North America who protest the publication of the "racial" nature of their members who may be mentioned in the press in unfavourable lights. Yet in literature such censorship would destroy much of the effect of most writers' intentions. *It is not differences that need to be abolished but discrimination because of differences.* To this end an increasing number of writers have been and still are protecting the possibilities of cultural variety and contrariety while dogmatically insisting that discrimination which results from any form of psychological "centricity," be it ethnic, religious, or racial, is negative and harmful. Racism will probably never disappear, but it can be controlled, and in Canada literature has made a contribution towards controlling it.

5 Ashley Montagu, *Man's Most Dangerous Myth* (New York: World Publishing Company, 1964), pp. 130-31. Montagu traces this idea back to Julian Huxley. The character of Wes Holman in Buckler's story, "Long, Long After School" (see note 12, Chapter 5), is probably the best example in Canadian literature of characterization minus racial attributes, although Garner's "Interlude in Black and White" comes close. A reader might well be excused for not recognizing that Wes is black, and the story is told without reference to this fact until it is finally included to twist the conclusion. Yet while it should be irrelevant to the story, it does raise the narrative from being about simple childish games (cruel as they can be), retrospectively endowing the whole story with a thematic significance that has priority.

Selected Bibliography

Primary Sources

Bodsworth, Fred. *The Atonement of Ashley Morden*. New York: Dodd, Mead, 1964.

_____ . *The Sparrow's Fall*. New York: Dodd, Mead, 1967.

_____ . *The Strange One*. New York: Dodd, Mead, 1959.

Buckler, Ernest. "Long, Long After School." *Atlantic Advocate* 50, No. 3 (1959), 42-44.

Buller, Herman. *Days of Rage*. Toronto: October Publications, 1974.

_____ . *One Man Alone*. Toronto: Canada National Book Club, 1963.

Callaghan, Morley. *The Loved and the Lost*. Toronto: Macmillan of Canada, 1951.

_____ . *Strange Fugitive*. New York: Charles Scribner's Sons, 1928.

Carter, Dyson. *Fatherless Sons*. Toronto: Progress Books, 1955.

Clarke, Austin C. *Amongst Thistles and Thorns*. Toronto: McClelland and Stewart, 1965.

_____ . *The Bigger Light*. Toronto: Little, Brown, 1975.

_____ . *Growing Up Stupid under the Union Jack*. Toronto: McClelland and Stewart, 1980.

_____ . *The Meeting Point*. Toronto: Macmillan of Canada, 1967.

_____ . *The Prime Minister*. Markham, Ont.: Paperjacks, 1978.

_____ . *Storm of Fortune*. Boston: Little, Brown, 1973.

_____ . *When he was free and young and he used to wear silks*. Toronto: Anansi, 1971.

Cornish, John. *Olga*. London: André Deutsch, 1959.

Creighton, Luella. *High Bright Buggy Wheels*. Toronto: McClelland and Stewart, 1951.

Eggleston, Magdelana. *Mountain Shadows*. London: Heinemann, 1955.

Fry, Alan. *The Revenge of Annie Charlie*. Markham, Ont.: Paperjacks, 1973.

Garner, Hugh. *Cabbagetown*. Richmond Hill, Ont.: Simon and Schuster, 1971.

_____ . "Interlude in Black and White." In *The Yellow Sweater*. Toronto: Collins, 1952.

_____ . *Silence on the Shore*. Toronto: Ryerson Press, 1968.

_____ . *Storm Below*. Toronto: Collins, 1949.

_____ . *The Yellow Sweater*. Toronto: Collins, 1952.

Gibbon, John Murray. *The Conquering Hero*. Toronto: S. B. Gundy, 1920.

Gordon, Charles W. (pseud. "Ralph Connor"). *Black Rock*. New York: A. L. Burt, 1919.

————. *Corporal Cameron*. Toronto: Westminster, 1912.

————. *The Foreigner*. Toronto: Westminster, 1909.

————. *The Gaspards of Pine Croft*. New York: George H. Doran, 1923.

————. *The Gay Crusader*. Toronto: McClelland and Stewart, 1936.

————. *The Major*. Toronto: McClelland, Goodchild & Stewart, 1917.

————. *The Patrol of the Sun Dance Trail*. New York: George H. Doran, 1914.

————. *The Pilot at Swan Creek*. London: Hodder & Stoughton, 1905.

————. *The Sky Pilot*. Toronto: Westminster, 1902.

————. *The Sky Pilot in No Man's Land*. New York: George H. Doran, 1919.

————. *To Him That Hath*. London: Hodder & Stoughton, 1921.

————. *Treading the Winepress*. New York: George H. Doran, 1925.

Graham, Gwethalyn. *Earth and High Heaven*. Garden City, N.Y.: Sun Dial Press, 1945.

Grove, Frederick P. *A Search for America*. Ottawa: Graphic Publishers, 1927.

————. *Fruits of the Earth*. Toronto: J. M. Dent and Sons, 1933.

————. The Grove Collection. University of Manitoba.

————. *In Search of Myself*. Toronto: McClelland and Stewart, 1974.

————. *Settlers of the Marsh*. Toronto: McClelland and Stewart, 1966.

————. *Tales From the Margin*. Ed. D. Pacey. Toronto: McGraw-Hill Ryerson, 1971.

————. *The Yoke of Life*. Toronto: Macmillan of Canada, 1930.

Herbert, Xavier. *Poor Fellow My Country*. London: Pan Books, 1975.

Howard, Hilda G. ((pseud. "Hilda Glynn-Ward"). *The Writing on the Wall*. Vancouver: Vancouver Sun, 1921; rpt. University of Toronto Press, 1974.

Jarvis, W. H. P. *The Letters of a Remittance Man to His Mother*. London: John Murray, 1907.

Kiriak, Illia. *Sons of the Soil*. Trans. M. Luchkovich. Toronto: Ryerson Press, 1959.

Klein, A. M. *The Second Scroll*. Toronto: McClelland and Stewart, 1959.

Kogawa, Joy. *Obasan*. Markham, Ont.: Penguin Books Canada, 1984.

Kreisel, Henry. *The Betrayal*. Toronto: McClelland and Stewart, 1971.

————. *The Rich Man*. Toronto: McClelland and Stewart, 1948.

Laurence, Margaret. *A Bird in the House*. Toronto: McClelland and Stewart, 1970.

————. *The Diviners*. Toronto: Bantam Books, 1974.

————. *The Fire Dwellers*. Toronto: McClelland and Stewart, 1969.

————. *A Jest of God*. New York: Alfred A. Knopf, 1966.

————. *The Stone Angel*. Toronto: McClelland and Stewart, 1964.

————. *The Tomorrow-Tamer*. Toronto: McClelland and Stewart, 1970.

Lysenko, Vera. *Westerly Wild*. Toronto: Ryerson Press, 1956.

————. *Yellow Boots*. Toronto: Ryerson Press, 1954.

Marlyn, John. *Under the Ribs of Death*. Toronto: McClelland and Stewart, 1964.

McClung, Nellie L. *All We Like Sheep*. Toronto: Thomas Allen, 1926.

————. *Painted Fires*. Toronto: Thomas Allen, 1925.

McCourt, Edward. *Home Is the Stranger*. Toronto: Macmillan of Canada, 1950.

McNamee, James. *them damned Canadians hanged Louis Riel!* Toronto: Macmillan of Canada, 1971.

Mitchell, W. O. *The Vanishing Point.* Toronto: Macmillan of Canada, 1973.

Mphahlele, Ezekiel. *The Wanderers.* London: Macmillan, 1972.

O'Hagan, Howard. *Tay John.* Toronto: McClelland and Stewart, 1974.

Richler, Mordecai. *The Acrobats.* London: Sphere Books, 1970.

_____ . *The Apprenticeship of Duddy Kravitz.* Harmondsworth: Penguin Books, 1971.

_____ . *A Choice of Enemies.* Toronto: McClelland and Stewart, 1977.

_____ . *The Incomparable Atuk.* Toronto: McClelland and Stewart, 1971.

_____ . *Joshua Then and Now.* Toronto: McClelland and Stewart, 1980.

_____ . *St. Urbain's Horseman.* Toronto: Bantam Books, 1972.

_____ . *Son of a Smaller Hero.* Toronto: McClelland and Stewart, 1969.

Ross, Sinclair. *Sawbones Memorial.* Toronto: McClelland and Stewart, 1978.

Rule, Jane. *The Young in One Another's Arms.* Garden City, N.Y.: Doubleday, 1977.

Salverson, Laura G. *The Dark Weaver.* Toronto: Ryerson Press, 1937.

_____ . *The Dove of El-Djezaire.* Toronto: Ryerson Press, 1933.

_____ . *The Viking Heart.* Toronto: McClelland and Stewart, 1929.

_____ . *When Sparrows Fall.* Toronto: Ryerson Press, 1925.

Sheldon, Michael. *The Unmelting Pot.* London: Hutchinson, 1965.

Spivak, John. *Georgia Nigger.* New York: Brewer, Warren & Putnam, 1932.

Stead, Robert J. C. *The Cow Puncher.* Toronto: Musson, 1918.

_____ . *Dennison Grant.* Toronto: Musson, 1920.

_____ . *The Empire Builders and other poems.* Toronto: William Briggs, 1910.

_____ . *The Homesteaders.* Toronto: University of Toronto Press, 1973.

_____ . *Neighbours.* Toronto: Hodder & Stoughton, 1922.

Wiebe, Rudy. *The Blue Mountains of China.* Toronto: McClelland and Stewart, 1970.

_____ . *First and Vital Candle.* Toronto: McClelland and Stewart, 1966.

_____ . *Peace Shall Destroy Many.* Toronto: McClelland and Stewart, 1962.

_____ . *The Scorched-Wood People.* Toronto: McClelland and Stewart, 1977.

_____ . *The Temptations of Big Bear.* Toronto: McClelland and Stewart, 1973.

_____ . *Where is the Voice Coming From?* Toronto: McClelland and Stewart, 1974.

Wilson, Ethel. *Swamp Angel.* London: Macmillan, 1955.

Wiseman, Adele. *The Sacrifice.* Toronto: Macmillan of Canada, 1956.

Secondary Material

Abella, Irving and Harold Troper. *None is Too Many.* Toronto: Lester & Orpen Dennys, 1983.

Adachi, Ken. *The Enemy that Never Was.* Toronto: McClelland and Stewart, 1976.

An Observer. "The Ku Klux Klan in Saskatchewan." *Queen's Quarterly* 35, No. 5 (1928), 592-602.

Arendt, Hannah. "Race Thinking Before Racism." *Review of Politics* 6, No. 1 (1944), 36-73.

Arnold, Matthew. *On the Study of Celtic Literature*. 1867.

Atwood, Margaret. *Survival*. Toronto: Anansi, 1972.

Berelson, Bernard and Patricia Salter. "Majority and Minority Americans: An Analysis of Magazine Fiction." *Public Opinion Quarterly* 10, No. 2 (1946), 168-90.

Birney, Earl. *Down the Long Table*. Toronto: McClelland and Stewart, 1975.

Bitton, Janet. "The Canadian 'Ethnic' Novel: The Protagonists' Search for Self-Definition." Unpublished M.A. thesis, University of Montreal, 1971.

Bodsworth, Fred. *The Last of the Curlews*. Toronto: McClelland and Stewart, 1963.

Boudreau, Joseph A. "Western Canada's 'Enemy Aliens' in World War One." *Alberta Historical Review* 12, No. 1 (1964), 1-9.

Braroe, Neils. *Indian and White*. Stanford, Calif.: Stanford University Press, 1975.

Brown, Lennox. "A Crisis: Black Culture in Canada." *Black Images* 1, No. 1 (1972), 4-8.

Brown, W. O. "Rationalization of Race Prejudice." *International Journal of Ethics* 63, No. 3 (1933), 294-306.

Buitenhuis, Peter. "Writers at War: Propaganda and Fiction in The Great War." *University of Toronto Quarterly* 45, No. 4 (1976), 277-94.

Buller, Herman. *Quebec in Revolt*. Toronto: Centennial Press, 1965.

Callaghan, Morley. "A Talk with Morley Callaghan." *Tamarack Review* 7 (1958), 3-29.

Cameron, Donald. *Conversations With Canadian Novelists—2*. Toronto: Macmillan of Canada, 1973.

Campbell, Maria. *Halfbreed*. Toronto: McClelland and Stewart, 1973.

Careless, J. M. S. "Limited Identities in Canada." *Canadian Historical Review* 50, No. 1 (1969), 1-10.

Carter, Dyson. *Future of Freedom*. Gravenhurst, Ont.: Northern Book House, n.d.

Case, Frederick Ivor. *Racism and National Consciousness*. Toronto: Plowshare Press, 1977.

Chamberlin, J. E. *The Harrowing of Eden*. Toronto: Fitzhenry & Whiteside, 1975.

Chapman, Terry L. "Early Eugenics Movement in Western Canada." *Alberta History* 25, No. 4 (1977), 9-17.

Chicanot, Eugene. "English Townsmen on Canadian Farms." *Willison's Monthly* 3, No. 10 (1928), 383-86.

_____ . "The Foreign Immigrant in Western Canada." *Willison's Monthly* 4, No. 1 (1928), 32-34.

_____ . "Learning From New Canadians." *Willison's Monthly* 4, No. 3 (1928), 104-5.

_____ . "Maintaining the British Element in Canadian Farm Population." *Willison's Monthly* 3, No. 5 (1927), 182-84.

_____ . *Rhymes of the Miner*. Gardenvale: Federal Publications, 1937.

Clark, J. P. *America, Their America*. London: Heinemann, 1970.

Clarke, Austin C. "A Black Man Talks About Race Prejudice in White Canada." *Maclean's* 76, No. 8 (1963), 18, 55-58.

Cocking, Clive. "How did the Canadian Mounties develop their unfortunate habit of deporting people they don't happen to like?" *Saturday Night* 85, No. 6 (1970), 28-30.

Comas, Juan. "'Scientific' Racism Again?" *Current Anthropology* 2, No. 3 (1961), 303-40.

Creelman, George C. "State Aid for Immigration." *Willison's Monthly* 1, No. 8 (1926), 306-7.

Curtin, Philip D. "The Origins of the 'White Man's Burden.'" *The Listener* 66, No. 1695 (1961), 412-15.

Davis, Robert and Mark Zannis. *The Genocide Machine in Canada*. Montreal: Black Rose Books, 1973.

Disraeli, Benjamin. *Coningsby*. Boston: L. C. Page, 1904.

Edwards, Frederick. "Fascism in Canada." *Maclean's* 51, No. 8 (1938), 10, 66-68; No. 9 (1938), 15, 30.

England, Robert. *The Central European Immigrant in Canada*. Toronto: Macmillan of Canada, 1929.

_____ . "The Emergent West." *Queen's Quarterly* 41, No. 3 (1934), 405-13.

Favreau, Guy. "Articles of Creed Respecting Immigration." *Studies and Documents on Immigration and Integration in Canada* 8 (Sept. 1965), 35-43.

_____ . "The Values of Immigration." *Studies and Documents on Immigration and Integration in Canada* 8 (Sept. 1965), 4-9.

Fine, Charles. "Canadians and American Ethnic Viewpoints: A Study in Contrast." *Social Worker* 28, No. 2 (1960), 25-33.

Fischer, Gretl K. *In Search of Jerusalem*. Montreal: McGill-Queen's University Press, 1975.

Flanagan, Thomas. *Louis "David" Riel: "Prophet of the New World."* Toronto: University of Toronto Press, 1979.

Frank, M. I. R. "Jews." *Canadian Forum* 15, No. 176 (1935), 229-30.

Frye, Northrop. "Conclusion" to the revised *Literary History of Canada*. Ed. Carl F. Klinck. Toronto: University of Toronto Press, 1976, 3:318-32.

Gibbon, John Murray. "The Foreign Born." *Queen's Quarterly* 27, No. 4 (1920), 331-51.

_____ . *The New Canadian Loyalists*. Toronto: Macmillan of Canada, 1941.

Gobineau, A. *Gobineau: Selected Political Writings*. Ed. M. Biddis. London: Jonathan Cape, 1970.

Gordon, Charles W. *The Doctor*. Toronto: Westminster, 1906.

_____ . *Glengarry School Days*. Toronto: Westminster, 1902.

_____ . *Postscript to Adventure*. New York: Farrar & Rinehart, 1938.

_____ . *The Prospector*. Toronto: Westminster, 1904.

_____ . *The Runner*. New York: A. L. Burt, 1929.

Grant, Madison. *The Passing of the Great Race*. New York: Charles Scribner's Sons, 1916.

Grove, Frederick P. "Assimilation." *Maclean's* (Sept. 1, 1929), pp. 7, 74-75, 78-79.

_____ . "Canadians Old and New." *Maclean's* (March 15, 1928), pp. 3, 55-56.

_____ . *It Needs to Be Said*. Toronto: Macmillan of Canada, 1929.

_____ . *The Master of the Mill*. Toronto: McClelland and Stewart, 1961.

Grunstein, Michael. "Beyond the Ghetto and the Garrison: Jewish Canadian Boundaries." *Mosaic* (Spring, 1981), pp. 121-24.

Gutteridge, Don. "Surviving the Fittest: Margaret Atwood and The Sparrow's Fall." *Journal of Canadian Studies* 8, No. 3 (1973), 63.

Hamilton, L. "Foreigners in the Canadian West." *Dalhousie Review* 17 (1938), 448-60.

Hart, C. W. M. "The Race Myth." *University of Toronto Quarterly* 11, No. 2 (1942), 180-88.

Henson, Tom M. "The Ku Klux Klan in Western Canada." *Alberta History* 25, No. 4 (1977), 1-8.

Higham, John. *Strangers in the Land*. New York: Atheneum, 1966.

Horwood, Harold. *White Eskimo*. Toronto: Paperjacks, 1973.

Hough, Emerson. *The Sowing*. Winnipeg: Vanderhoof-Gunn, 1909.

Howard, Mary. "This Work of Canadianizing. When Are We Going to Do It?" *Christian Guardian* 91, No. 3 (1920), 12.

Hughes, David and Evelyn Kallen. *The Anatomy of Racism: Canadian Dimensions*. Montreal: Harvest House, 1976.

Jenkins, Charles C. "The Mennonites' Trek." *Maclean's* 35, No. 4 (1922), 23-24, 36-37.

Jenness, Diamond. "Canada's Eskimo Problem." *Queen's Quarterly* 32, No. 4 (1925), 317-29.

Kalbach, W. *The Impact of Immigration on Canada's Population*. Ottawa: Dominion Bureau of Statistics, 1970.

Keith, Russell. "Black Journalism: A Rich Canadian Heritage." *Black Images* 1, No. 1 (1972), 10-11.

Keith, W. J., ed. *A Voice in the Land*. Edmonton: NeWest Press, 1981.

Kipling, Rudyard. *Letters to the Family*. Toronto: Macmillan of Canada, 1908.

Kirkconnell, Watson. *Canadians All*. Ottawa: Director of Public Information, 1941.

_____ . "Icelandic-Canadian Poetry." *Dalhousie Review* 14, No. 3 (1934), 331-44.

_____ . *Our Communists and the New Canadians*. Toronto: Southam Press, n.d.

_____ . *Twilight of Liberty*. London: Oxford University Press, 1941.

_____ . "Western Immigration." *Canadian Forum* 8, No. 94 (1928), 706-7.

Klein, A. M. *The Rocking Chair*. Toronto: Ryerson Press, 1948.

Kmeta, Ivan A. "Literature and the Melting Pot." *Canadian Author* 15, No. 3 (1938), 12.

Kostash, Myrna. *All of Baba's Children*. Edmonton: Hurtig, 1977.

Laurence, Margaret. *Heart of a Stranger*. Toronto: McClelland and Stewart, 1976.

_____ . *The Prophet's Camel Bell*. Toronto: McClelland and Stewart, 1963.

_____ . *This Side Jordan*. Toronto: McClelland and Stewart, 1960.

Leacock, Stephen. *Canada the Foundation of Its Future*. Montreal: Gazette Printing, 1941.

_____ . "Does Canada Want Population?" *Maclean's* 35, No. 22 (1922), 20, 50-52.

_____ . *Economic Prosperity in the British Empire*. Toronto: Macmillan of Canada, 1930.

_____ . *Further Foolishness: Sketches and Satires on the Follies of the Day*. Toronto: McClelland and Stewart, 1968.

—————— . *The Hohenzollerns in America, with the Bolsheviks in Berlin, and Other Impossibilities*. Toronto: S. B. Gundy, 1919.

Lindsay, J. A. "National Characteristics." *Dalhousie Review* 9, No. 2 (1929), 181-87.

Luchkovich, Michael. "Racial Integration and Canadian Literature." *Canadian Author and Bookman* 36, No. 2 (1960), 14-16.

Lysenko, Vera. *Men in Sheepskin Coats*. Toronto: Ryerson Press, 1947.

MacBride, E. W. "The Various Races of Man." *McGill University Magazine* 5, No. 2 (1906), 294-319.

MacInnis, Angus and Howard Green. "Should We Send the Japs Back?" *Maclean's* 56, No. 23 (1943), 12, 34, 35, 37, 38.

MacLennan, Hugh. *Voices in Time*. Markham, Ont.: Penguin Books, 1980.

MacLulich, T. D. "Last Year's Indians." *Essays on Canadian Writing* 1, No. 1 (1974), 47-50.

Macphail, Andrew. "The Immigrant." *University Magazine* 19, No. 2 (1920), 133-62.

Magrath, Charles A. *Canada's Growth and Some Problems Affecting It*. Ottawa: Mortimer Press, 1910.

—————— . "Organization for Immigration." *Willison's Monthly* 1, No. 2 (1925), 52-55.

—————— . "A Sane Scheme of Colonization." In *Empire Club of Canada: Addresses Delivered to the Members During the Year 1928*. Toronto: Hunter-Rose, 1929, pp. 83-94.

Mannoni, O. *Prospero and Caliban*. Trans. P. Powesland. New York: Frederick A. Praeger, 1964.

Marshall, Ted, ed. *A. M. Klein*. Toronto: Ryerson Press, 1970.

McDougall, D. "Immigration into Canada, 1851-1920." *Canadian Journal of Economics and Political Science* 27, No. 2 (1961), 162-75.

McGoun, Archibald. "Race or Allegiance." *University Magazine* 12, No. 3 (1913), 421-39.

McKenzie, Ruth. "Life in a New Land." *Canadian Literature* 7 (1961), 24-33.

Monkman, Leslie. *A Native Heritage*. Toronto: University of Toronto Press, 1981.

—————— . "Richardson's Indians." *Canadian Literature* 81 (1979), 86-94.

Montagnes, Anne. "Of Many Books." *Globe and Mail*, August 8, 1981, p. E14.

Montagu, Ashley. *Man's Most Dangerous Myth*. New York: World Publishing, 1964.

Moodie, Susannah. *Roughing it in the Bush*. Intro. by Carl F. Klinck. Toronto: McClelland and Stewart, 1962.

Moss, John. *Patterns of Isolation*. Toronto: McClelland and Stewart, 1974.

Mphahlele, Ezekiel. *The Wanderers*. London: Macmillan, 1972.

Muddiman, Bernard. "The Immigrant Element in Canadian Literature." *Queen's Quarterly* 20, No. 4 (1913), 404-15.

Mukherjee, Bharati. "An Invisible Woman." *Saturday Night* 96, No. 3 (1981), 36-40.

Nash, Manning. "Race and the Ideology of Race." *Current Anthropology* 3, No. 3 (1962), 285-88.

Nelson, John. "Shall We Bar the Yellow Race?" *Maclean's* 35, No. 10 (1922), 13-14, 50.

Niven, Frederick. *Mine Inheritance*. London: Collins, 1940.

—————— . *The Flying Years*. Toronto: McClelland and Stewart, 1975.

Nordegg, Martin. *The Possibilities of Canada are Truly Great*. Ed. T. D. Regehr. Toronto: Macmillan of Canada, 1971.

O'Hagan, Howard. *Wilderness Men*. Vancouver: Talon Books, 1978.

Palmer, Howard. *Patterns of Prejudice*. Toronto: McClelland and Stewart, 1982.

—————— , ed. *Immigration and the Rise of Multiculturalism*. Toronto: Copp-Clark, 1975.

Palmer, Tamara J. "Ethnic Character and Social Themes in Novels About Prairie Canada and the Period from 1900 to 1940." Unpublished M.A. thesis, York University, 1972.

Paton, Alan. *Cry the Beloved Country*. New York: Charles Scribner's Sons, 1948.

—————— . *Too Late the Phalarope*. Markham, Ont.: Penguin Books, 1979.

Pike, W. H. "Slavic Stock and the New Canadianism." *Christian Guardian* 90, No. 49 (1919), 10-11.

—————— . "The Slav: An Asset or a Liability?" *Christian Guardian* 90, No. 50 (1919), 19-20.

—————— . "The Slav a New Canadian?" *Christian Guardian* 90, No. 51 (1919), 11-12.

Porter, John. *The Vertical Mosaic*. Toronto: University of Toronto Press, 1970.

Potrebenko, Helen. *No Streets of Gold*. Vancouver: New Star Books, 1977.

Report to the Minister of Justice of the Special Committee on Hate Propaganda in Canada. Ottawa: Queen's Printer, 1966.

Richardson, John. *Wacousta*. Toronto: McClelland and Stewart, 1967.

Richler, Mordecai. *Notes on an Endangered Species*. New York: Alfred A. Knopf, 1974.

—————— . *Shovelling Trouble*. Toronto: McClelland and Stewart, 1972.

—————— . *The Street*. London: Wiedenfeld and Nicolson, 1972.

Ryga, George. *The Ecstasy of Rita Joe*. Vancouver: Talon Books, 1970.

Salverson, Laura G. *Confessions of an Immigrant's Daughter*. London: Faber & Faber, 1939.

—————— . *Immortal Rock*. Toronto: Ryerson Press, 1954.

—————— . *Lord of the Silver Dragon*. Toronto: McClelland and Stewart, 1927.

Samkange, Stanlake. *On Trial for My Country*. London: Heinemann, 1971.

Selvon, Sam. *The Lonely Londoners*. Longmans, 1984.

—————— . *Moses Ascending*. London: Davis-Poynter, 1975.

Sessing, Trevor. "How They Kept Canada Almost Lily White." *Saturday Night* 85, No. 9 (1970), 30-32.

Shirinian, Lorne. "West Indians in Toronto." *Journal of Canadian Fiction* 2, No. 4 (1973), 96-97.

Siegfried, André. *The Race Question in Canada*. Ed. Frank H. Underhill. Toronto: McClelland and Stewart, 1966.

Sifton, Clifford. "The Immigrants Canada Wants." *Maclean's* 35, No. 7 (1922), 16, 32-34.

Sissons, C. B. "What Can We Do with the Doukhobors?" *Canadian Forum* 4, No. 46 (1924), 298-300.

Smith, Gary and Carl F. Grindstaff. "Race and Sport in Canada." *The Black i* 1, No. 1 (1972), 70-89.

Smith, W. G. *A Study in Canadian Immigration*. Toronto: Ryerson Press, 1920.

Soulsby, E. J. "Why Britons Stay at Home." *Canadian Forum* 8, No. 95 (1928), 743-44.

Stobie, Margaret R. *Frederick Philip Grove*. New York: Twayne Publishers, 1973.

Sutherland, Ronald. "The Body-Odour of Race." *Canadian Literature* 37 (1968), 46-67.

Swyripa, Frances. *Ukrainian Canadians*. Edmonton: University of Alberta Press, 1978.

Theriault, Yves. *Agaguk*. Toronto: McGraw-Hill Ryerson, 1967.

Thrasher, Anthony Apakark. *Thrasher*. Toronto: Griffin House, 1976.

Tiessen, Hildegaard E. "A Mighty Inner River: 'Peace' in the Fiction of Rudy Wiebe." *Journal of Canadian Fiction* 2, No. 4 (1973), 71-76.

Toomer, Jean. *Cane*. New York: Harper & Row, 1969.

Tremblay, René. "The Contribution of Immigrants to the Canadian Economy." *Studies and Documents on Immigration and Integration in Canada* 8 (1964), 33-39.

Tuttle, William M., Jr. *Race Riot*. New York: Atheneum, 1970.

Uris, Leon. *Exodus*. Garden City, N.Y.: Doubleday, 1958.

Vallee, Frank, Mildred Schwartz, and Frank Darknell. "Ethnic Assimilation and Differentiation in Canada." *Canadian Journal of Economics and Political Science* 23, No. 4 (1957), 540-49.

Vallières, Pierre. *White Niggers of America*. Toronto: McClelland and Stewart, 1971.

Van der Post, Laurens. *In a Province*. London: Hogarth Press, 1934.

Van Loon, Richard and Michael Whittington. *The Canadian Political System*. Toronto: McGraw-Hill of Canada, 1971.

Ward, W. Peter. *White Canada Forever*. Montreal: McGill-Queen's University Press, 1978.

White, John S. "Taine on Race and Genius." *Social Research* 10, No. 1 (1943), 76-79.

Whitely, A. S. "The Oriental in British Columbia." *Canadian Forum* 9, No. 106 (1929), 342-44.

Whitton, Charlotte. "The Immigration Problem for Canada." *Queen's Quarterly* 31, No. 4 (1924), 388-420.

Wiebe, Rudy and Theatre Passe Muraille. *Far As the Eye Can See*. Edmonton: NeWest Press, 1977.

Winks, Robin W. *The Blacks in Canada*. Montreal: McGill-Queen's University Press, 1971.

Woodcock, George and Ivan Avakumovic. *The Doukhobors*. Toronto: McClelland and Stewart, 1977.

Woodsworth, James S. "Nation Building." *University Magazine* 16, No. 1 (1917), 85-99.

————. *Strangers Within Our Gates*. Toronto: Frederick Clark Stephenson, 1909.

Younge, Eva R. "Population Movements and the Assimilation of Alien Groups in Canada." *Canadian Journal of Economics and Political Science* 10, No. 3 (1944), 372-80.

Index